The Original Code in the Bible

The Original Code in the Bible

Using Science and Mathematics to Reveal God's Fingerprints

Del Washburn

MADISON BOOKS
Lanham • New York • Oxford

Copyright © 1998 by Madison Books

Published by Madison Books
4720 Boston Way
Lanham, Maryland 20706

12 Hid's Copse Road
Cumnor Hill, Oxford OX2 9JJ, England

Distributed by National Book Network

Library of Congress Cataloging-in-Publication Data

Washburn, Del.
   The original code in the Bible : using science and mathematics to
reveal God's fingerprints / Del Washburn.
      p.   cm.
   Includes bibliographical references.
   ISBN 1-56833-115-0 (hardcover : alk. paper)
   1. Bible—Miscellanea.   2. Numbers in the Bible.   3. Ciphers in
the Bible.   I. Title.
BS534.W363   1998
220.6'8—dc21   98-24243
                                                          CIP

Contents

A Brief
Introduction

I began my journey with theomatics as a very young man in 1975. Over the past twenty-three years, I have devoted literally thousands of hours to research investigating this most amazing and miraculous subject.

Theomatics was first published in 1978. It has presently sold close to ninety thousand copies in hard cover and trade editions. It was written in conjunction with Jerry Lucas (Hall of Fame basketball player and world renowned memory expert) and was one of the top Christian best-sellers in the United States. *Theomatics* has continued to sell steadily over the years with very little promotion. There were initial appearances on the *700 Club* with Pat Robertson, *PTL Network,* on Christian TV across Canada, but for the most part *Theomatics* has been a grassroots publication. Of the several thousand letters I received from readers, about a third have come from people who read the book because a friend enthusiastically told them about it or lent them a copy. In 1994, *Theomatics II* was published—replacing the original edition.

The voluminous amount of research, findings, and data in my files and computer could easily create a single volume the size of an entire set of encyclopedias. And that is precisely why this was not an easy book to write—not because there is nothing to say, but because there is so much! It is difficult to know *what* to say or *where* to stop. You will see why shortly.

My previous book, *Theomatics II*, is 663 pages long in small type, and it had to be severely edited to lower the original number to that figure. I have also written a 300-page scientific work called *Theomatics and the Scientific Method.* It provides serious and compelling evidence—a complete scientific testing and analysis by computer. It is available for review by mathematical scientists, scholars, and anyone out there who is skeptical. Other findings have been put together as independent studies. One more major book is partially complete.

So why write another book?

A number of months ago, my publisher in Washington, D.C., contacted me with the idea of publishing a very different book on this subject. Theomatics needed to be condensed into a volume that was more practical and appealing to the general reader. It had to be a book tailored to our quick-paced, "just give me the bottom line," fast-food society—sort of a "McTheomatics" version that people could read while sitting on airplanes or in waiting rooms. Yet it would provoke and challenge them in ways that few, if any, books ever have.

While theomatics may be a profoundly deep and technical subject, this book has been written so that the ordinary reader need not work too hard to put it all together. But even the most astute individual, the mathematical theorist and physicist from MIT, will have their intellects stretched to the limit. No matter who you are, this is the place to start. There is no limit to how far you can go with this subject.

So that is what gave rise to this volume. My publisher likes to call it the "theomatics lite" version. It will be less filling, but will still taste great without all the calories.

1   Does God Really Exist?

And If So, Did He Write the Bible?

The book you are holding in your hand and now reading, is totally unique and different. It is unlike anything else in the entire collective sphere of man's knowledge. It also may be unlike anything else in the entire universe.

Although the words have been written by the author, who is a mortal and earthly man, the content of this book—what it is all about—is not of any human origin whatsoever.

God has written his entire word mathematically. Incorporated within the original text of the Bible is a hidden numerical structure and code of such awesome proportions, that there are no words in human language to describe it. I call this phenomenon "theomatics," and it means the "numbers or the mathematics of God."

History's #1 Question May Finally Have an Answer

The message of this book should be of universal interest to every man, woman, and child who lives and breathes. There is probably no question in history that has elicited more interest, concern, frustration, and anxiety than the question of whether or not God exists. From ancient Greece to modern times, philosophers have wrestled with the question "Why all things?" Did all the species evolve on their own by pure chance [evolution]? Or was there a universal Creator?

If there is a God, how can we know for sure? Most people find the idea untenable and the answer too debilitating. So in typical fashion they place it somewhere on the back burner of their minds and try to go on with life. But somehow the question is always simmering. It can never be gotten rid of.

If there is a God, then am I accountable in some way? Are my actions and sins being evaluated? Will this "God Being" someday judge me, condemn me, forgive me? If I die tonight, am I good enough to go to heaven—if there is such a place. And if heaven exists, does hell?

The Bible is a book that addresses these questions and answers them in very specific terms. Therefore, the answer to the question of whether God exists may be answered by another very specific question: *Who wrote the Bible?*

God Cannot Fit Inside a Test Tube

Before we proceed too far in our discussion, it is important to point out that it is scientifically impossible to prove the existence of God. The Bible tells us that God is a Spirit (John 4:24); He cannot be placed in a test tube and analyzed in a laboratory. The knowledge and acceptance of God will always be an issue of faith. The Bible clearly teaches that it is only through faith in Jesus Christ that anyone will ever have any hope of knowing about God (John 1:18). For Jesus is not only human like the rest of us; He is also Divine and, quite literally, God manifested in the clothes of human flesh (John 1:1,14). Before His supernatural birth took place in Bethlehem, the Bible tells us that *Jesus Himself,* as Jehovah, created all that exists in the entire universe (Col. 1:15-17).

God's Fingerprints Will Confirm His Existence

Even though the existence of God cannot be proven in a laboratory, what you are going to be reading about here—*can* be scientifically proven in a controlled testing environment. This will lead us to only one possible and inescapable conclusion. *Some sort of supernatural intelligence and mastermind composed and directed the entire process in which the Bible was written.*

The Bible is a book that is composed of sixty-six individual books. (Thirty-nine of these books are in the Old Testament; twenty-seven of them are in the New Testament.) It was written over a period of sixteen hundred years by at least forty different men. Yet there is a mathematical pattern throughout the Bible that defies explanation.

If God did not place this code in the Bible, then the only possible way it could have gotten there is for all forty writers to have concocted it in a secret conspiracy lasting over one thousand six-hundred years. There is absolutely no historical evidence that any such conspiracy ever existed—in fact, such an idea is ludicrous. No Bible writers ever employed such methods. If they had, history would be rife with writers and scribes who kept mathematical worksheets along with their texts.

Therefore, people who have denied, joked at, and laughed about the Bible may think of it differently after confronting the facts contained in this book. After you thoroughly examine this evidence, I believe that you will come to the same conclusion that myself and numerous others have come to:

Theomatics scientifically proves that a mind far beyond human capabilities and understanding planned, constructed, and formed every word in the Bible—as it was written in its original languages.

Therefore God must indeed exist! What other possibility is there?

No Other Work of Literature Contains This Phenomenon

Theomatics helps prove that the Bible is unlike any other work of literature ever written during the history of mankind. In fact, theomatics was planned by God—from eternity—before this world was even created.

In order to make this possible, God created two "heavenly" languages—Hebrew and Greek—and placed them unknowingly into human culture, and finally into the vocabulary of the Bible. (Note: The Old Testament was originally written in ancient Hebrew and the New Testament in Greek.) As we will soon see, both of these languages had to have been supernaturally engineered and each word precisely fit into the text, in order for this code in the Bible to work.

Every event that took place in the Bible, every story, every person, every truth, down to the minutest detail, was planned and preordained by God. Theomatics has lain dormant in the Bible for thousands of years. Yet its secret has just been discovered.

Others Had an Inkling

Even though the magnitude of this discovery is just starting to unveil itself, over the centuries many men have speculated, believed, and taught that some sort of hidden and supernatural phenomenon existed underneath the original Hebrew and Greek text of the Bible—based on the numerical values for the letters in the alphabets of these languages. They believed that a cipher, or key, that would unlock a deeper symbolic and spiritual meaning behind the literal words of the text, was placed there by a supernatural act of God, unbeknown to the men who actually penned the text.

Contemporary Bible scholars, and most all modern evangelical scholars, have either lampooned this idea or completely ignored the subject. As a general whole, modern biblical scholarship *does not even recognize the possibility* that such a phenomenon as theomatics could even exist. This subject lies completely outside the realm of conventional knowledge.

Torah Codes, ELS, and the Bible Code

Just recently, some supposedly amazing discoveries have been made along this line. Even you may have casually heard something about this. It has been on television, in newspapers and magazines, and all over the Internet. A national best-selling book called *The Bible Code,* by Michael Drosnin, has recently sold over half a million copies. *Oprah Winfrey* did a program on the subject, as did numerous other talk-shows.

A number of researchers in Israel and around the world have claimed to discover "secret" hidden codes in the text of the Hebrew Old Testament. These "codes," according to some proponents, reveal past historical events and even future world events. By skipping so many letters in sequence and creating words, detailed descriptions of events have supposedly been discovered, such as the assassinations of Israeli Prime Minister Yitzhak Rabin, and Egyptian President Anwar Sadat; the French Revolution, and even Adolf Hitler and the Holocaust. Some scholars claim to have found the names of modern-day Jewish rabbis embedded in the codes. Even Timothy McVeigh and the Oklahoma City bombing have been found in the text.

These discoveries have been referred to as "Torah codes," "Bible codes," and "ELS" (Equidistant Letter Sequences). Some of these claims are backed up by statistical "evidence" that has created a great deal of excitement in the scientific community. World-class mathematicians from some of the highest-caliber universities, the Pentagon, and elsewhere, have become involved in the investigation,

Theomatics Is Completely Different

It should be clearly pointed out that theomatics has no connection or relationship whatsoever to any of the above. It is a million light-years away and totally different. There is not even the slightest similarity.

The ELS evidence is mostly confined to the Torah, or first five books of the Old Testament (Genesis, Exodus, Leviticus, Numbers, Deuteronomy). Theomatics saturates the entire Bible—from cover to cover.

NOTE: While by no means a qualified expert, this author has some doubts about these recent claims. However, it is entirely possible that God may have embedded "something" in the Bible based upon ELS. The Bible codes have been rejected by many evangelical leaders and theologians as having "no credibility." Unfortunately, most of this criticism will be based not on hard science but on theological bias. In the back of this book, I will provide a general analysis of ELS and the Bible code.

After my own investigation into the massive research effort currently going on with the Bible codes, it is my firm belief that theomatics is a much more provable phenomenon. The statistical evidence is more compelling, and the data is much easier for the scientist and average person to understand and verify. While many scientists and experts are struggling with the validity of the Bible Codes, theomatics will provide a mathematically open and shut case.

Historically, Theomatics is the Original Bible Code

Whatever evidence there may or may not be for the Bible codes, one thing is certain. The *foundational basis* of theomatics—what you are going to be read about in this book—formulates an entirely *different* kind of a code.

This basis upon which theomatics is founded is without question the original code in the Bible. It has been well known and documented for thousands of years—even since the time before Christ. Unlike the "Bible codes," theomatics is not some Johnny come lately idea. Tens of thousands of scholars over the centuries have been very well aware of this code. It is no secret. (We will talk about it in chapter 3.) While many people have poked and prodded along the fringes of it, amazingly, no one has ever been able to more fully understand or decipher this code— until theomatics came along.

For some strange reason, I am apparently the only person who has performed the necessary research, and discovered the operational principles that will begin to unlock this original code that God *supernaturally* and *sovereignly* placed in the text of the *entire* Bible. For me personally, this fact has been excruciatingly humbling (see discussion in chapter 24 of *Theomatics II*). Over the past twenty years I have traveled a very lonely road—yet one that has been extremely glorious. It has been a fantastic ride. You will see why shortly.

Pyramids and Bridges Do Indeed Exist

What is most significant about all of the assertive claims of theomatics, is that the existence of theomatics can be scientifically proven in the laboratory—beyond any reasonable doubt. Its existence is mathematical fact.

No one debates whether or not the Great Pyramid exists, and no one debates whether or not the Golden Gate Bridge exists. The fact that these two objects exist is irrefutable beyond any reasonable doubt.

The reason for this is because the Great Pyramid and the Golden Gate Bridge can *scientifically* be proven to exist. (1) They can be seen, (2) they can be defined, (3) they can be measured, and (4) they are always there. In other words, people from all over the world can see, climb, walk over, photograph, touch, feel, and measure and test the validity of the fact that these objects are indeed real.

The same procedures and principles can be applied to the theomatics hypothesis. The scientific tests that validate theomatics are both repeatable and predictable. What you are about to see demonstrated is every bit as provable and verifiable as the fact that the Great Pyramid and the Golden Gate Bridge exist. *That is the intellectual level of proof and absolute certainty that theomatics will provide.* There is not a mathematical scientist on the face of the earth who will disagree with the logic or method of proof that theomatics uses to substantiate its claims.

Bring on the Debunkers

Are there people out there who—at the outset—will not take any of this too seriously? You bet. Will the skeptics and heresy hunters try to debunk theomatics? Perhaps. But they will refuse to do so on a level playing field using the unbending guidelines of the scientific method.

Why? Plain and simple: they will want to *control* the environment and play by their own rules.

Many will simply give the subject a "once over" glance, and then boldly declare that the whole thing is preposterous. They will open their mouths and state their opinions with impunity—all the while *refusing* to analyze and test the data in a thorough, comprehensive, and unbiased manner. This will be especially true when they discover that theomatics has no fatal flaws in either its logic or scientific testing procedures and is therefore impossible to debunk.

To date some very popular Christian fundamentalists and "watchdog" organizations have accused theomatics of being just that—evil and occultic. Insinuating that theomatics allies itself with such things as kabbalic mysticism, gnosticism, numerology, and divination (and possibly even the devil himself).

Still other skeptics call theomatics "a laughable ruse of arbitrary and selective calculations, circular rhetoric, and absolute poppycock." (This approach is generally used by schoolyard bullies when they can't think of anything intelligent to say.) Experts in the science of logic also refer to this approach as "deflection"—ignoring the positive evidence, data, and crucial arguments, instead creating a smoke screen out of noncritical issues.

However, if any skeptics, be they religious or otherwise, would simply apply the scientific method to my research, they would be amazed at just how provable the phenomenon really is. Theomatics stands up spectacularly and profoundly under the death rays of the scientific method and lives to tell about it!

It is my firm belief that it will be virtually impossible for someone to spend serious time investigating and analyzing this subject and not walk away thoroughly convinced. The evidence is not marginal. *It is absolutely overwhelming!* To deny theomatics will be equal to an outright denial of the pure mathematical assumptions and axioms upon which all of this is going to be based and validated.

For Many, This Will Be a Difficult Pill to Swallow

We live in a society where it seems as though everything can be questioned, analyzed, debated, and then easily discarded. Few people feel comfortable with the idea of absolutes—especially when it comes to the subject of religion. With so much sensationalism in the media, all sorts of stuff floating around out there, many people do not seem to know what to believe anymore. For that reason, even before examining the factual and objective evidence, numerous individual reactions to theomatics will be skepticism, apathy, and outright denial. The very idea that something this significant and paramount could be absolutely determinate—that God wrote the Bible—will automatically provoke a very subjective and cynical reaction, especially in the secular academic world.

Also, many theologians and evangelical Bible scholars will have a very difficult time with theomatics. It has often been stated that religious tradition and established ways of thinking do not die easily. Those who have formulated their ideas of how Christians are supposed to understand God and interpret the Bible—and carved these beliefs into granite—will find many of their premises and presuppositions cleanly leveled by the implications of this discovery. Theomatics is going to introduce a whole new element into the equation.

The Benefits Far Outweigh the Liabilities

So far, 95 percent of the reactions to theomatics have been very positive. *Criticism can only come from those who either don't understand or want to believe.* The discovery that is about to be shown in this book is the most exciting, blessed, and glorious thing imaginable. For Christian people everywhere, it will quite literally be the call for dancing in the streets. Your heart should be blessed and touched beyond words. Theomatics is a VIP reservation from the very Creator of the universe, inviting us to enter His castle and throne room, eat with Him at His table, and listen to His secrets. What could be more blessed and wonderful than that?

This Is a Frontier Subject

As you read this book, please keep in mind that we are dealing here with a frontier subject. Just like Columbus, we are going to be untying the rope from the dock and sailing out into the blue yonder to explore new worlds of objective and eternal truth. With theomatics, it has been discovered that the known world we presently live in is not all that exists.

We are not going to be content in saying that the only valid Christianity is historical Christianity. History has its place, and there is nothing wrong with it. But if the world has another side to it, one that can be proven to exist and is *really* out there—and if God has given us the means to get there—then we intend to raise the sails.

We are determined to leave behind us, back in the dust, all the old ways of thinking that limit either God or His ability.

> But as it is written, Eye hath not seen, nor ear heard, neither have entered into the heart of man, the things which God hath prepared for them that love him. (1 Cor. 2:9)

We must always bear in mind, that it is only by God's grace and sovereign will that we will ever be allowed to see and know anything about Him.

Why Is All This So Important?

To summarize this first chapter, the subject before us holds profound implications. These implications are incalculable, as they relate to our understanding of God, the Bible, and the very meaning of our existence.

Theomatics, as it is true, will *automatically* accomplish two things.

- It will provide conclusive scientific proof that the Bible is neither a man-made nor man-discovered book, but is solely of Divine origin—a direct communication from the very Creator of the universe.
- As the operating principles of this "hidden" mathematical structure are more fully revealed and understood, they will provide us with an objective basis for understanding the true and exact meaning of Scripture—*the original meanings that God had in mind when He wrote the Bible.*

Stop and think about it for a minute. As far as man's history on this earth is concerned, if the above statements are true, nothing could be more significant than the discovery of a deliberate, inherent, and embedded code in the text of the Bible.

What could be more significant than absolute scientific proof that God wrote the Bible? And then, *in the manner and only to the extent that God intended it,* being able to understand the system and code—the underlying numerical symbolism that will ultimately tell us the exact and precise meaning of what God is saying?

What could be more awesome than being able to actually climb inside the mind of God and understand how the Creator of the universe thinks?

The Purpose of This Book

My purpose in writing this book is to share what I have discovered with the world. My prayer is that all readers will be open-minded and fair in their assessment—that they will look at this subject objectively and scientifically, and allow the facts and message to speak directly to their hearts.

If you have always wondered about God and the Bible, you need wonder no more. Your life can take a turn for the better. Here at last is the absolute proof and certainty we have all been waiting for. *Why the Creator has waited so long to reveal it is a mystery that even I struggle with on a daily basis.* Every morning when I get up, I must pinch myself and remind myself that all of this has really happened. No, it wasn't just a dream. God really did do it!

Yes, there is indeed a personal God out there who cares and loves each one of us. For the Bible teaches us that we did not come into existence by chance; He created us. If we will accept Him and come to Him *on His terms*, the Bible assures us that we have nothing to fear and everything to live and hope for. Understanding the truth of theomatics will solidify all of this in the most unusual and objective way. It may be the best thing that has ever happened to you. It certainly has been for me.

2 A High-tech Wilderness

Chips and Windows and Nothing to Eat

At this point you are no doubt anxious to learn more. The formal presentation of theomatics begins in the next chapter. This chapter is not directly a part of the theomatics presentation. But it will lay some important groundwork. (If you can't sit still, you are welcome to jump ahead, but please come back. You won't want to miss the following.)

The World Pre-1900 vs. Post-1900

Fifty years ago, two days before Christmas, a group of three men devised a bizarre and crude-looking little gizmo: it looked like a paper clip jammed into a hunk of crystal. At first, the inventors did not fully realize what they were holding in their hands. However, a few years later Walter Brattain, John Bardeen, and William Schockley would win the Nobel Prize for their work.[1]

Since that time, the humble little transistor has virtually changed the world. Perhaps no single discovery—since the wheel and electricity itself—has had such an impact. Today, transistors are microscopic in size and powerful enough to shake the world's economy. One tiny Pentium computer chip contains over three million transistors embedded in its circuits (one hundred transistors can be wrapped around a single human hair).

A few years ago, Cray supercomputers, owned by a handful of universities and the world's largest corporations, cost millions of dollars and filled an entire building. Today, a personal computer selling for less than $2,500—with a new 400 MHZ Pentium II chip—is as powerful as the world's biggest and fastest supercomputer of a few years ago (processing one billion instructions per second.)

The transistor and its offspring, the integrated circuit and microprocessor, will ultimately influence the life of every living person—reaching even the most primitive peoples in jungles of the poorest Third World nations. Eventually the entire world will be "on-line." Anyone who fights the trend and refuses to use technology will be left in the dust.

The Last One Hundred Years

Just this year, I attended the graveside service of my aunt, who died at almost 101 years of age. She was born in 1896. As I reflected back on her life, I thought of all the changes that had occurred. Gertrude was born the year after Guglielmo Marconi broadcast the world's first radio signal. When she was seven years old, the Wright brothers made their first flight. When she was a teenager, Henry Ford built his first Model T.

We all know that in the past century, knowledge has exploded exponentially—compared to the last six thousand years man has been on earth. We have gone from the horse and buggy to walking on the moon, and beyond, in just one tick of the clock.

Now Comes the Information Superhighway

Only a handful of years ago, when a few young upstarts in California and Seattle began fooling around in their garages with parts from a Radio Shack store and writing a simple program called MS-DOS, few people had any idea of a device called the "personal computer."

Now as we look back, we are not far from the original vision of Bill Gates, who foresaw "a computer in every home and sitting on every desk."

As the year 2000 approaches and this vision *has* indeed become a reality, what effect are these changes having upon us as a society—socially and spiritually? How is this going to affect family life, bonds, and relationships? How is it going to affect our children's lives and future generations? How is this going to affect the Christian Church in the next millennium?

No one will question the fact that great benefits are coming from the new technology (even this book would hardly be possible without the computer). Every aspect of our lives is now computerized: mail, phones, banking, television, video—all communications, transactions, and entertainment. Soon, millions of people will be able to look at a screen in their car, a small device in a pocket, or a cellular phone and know within a few feet—via satellite—exactly where they are anywhere on earth. Potentially, there will not be another human being on the planet outside the reach of any other human being—instantly! Just about everything we want or need to know will be immediately accessible. The entire world is now coming together and speaking "one language." *This is the information age.*

The Tower of Babel

In chapter 11 of the Book of Genesis, right after Noah's flood, there is a remarkable story.

1 *Now the whole earth had one language and one speech.*

2 And it came to pass, as they journeyed from the east, that they found a plain in the land of Shinar, and they dwelt there.

3 Then they said to one another, "Come, let us make bricks and bake them thoroughly..."

4 And they said, *"Come, let us build ourselves a city, and a tower whose top is in the heavens; let us make a name for ourselves*, lest we be scattered abroad over the face of the whole earth."

5 But the LORD came down to see the city and the tower which the sons of men had built.

6 And the LORD said, *"Indeed the people are one, and they all have one language, and this is what they begin to do; NOW NOTHING THAT THEY PROPOSE TO DO WILL BE IMPOSSIBLE FOR THEM.*

7 "Come, let Us go down and there confuse their language, that they may not understand one another's speech."

8 So the LORD scattered them abroad from there over the face of all the earth, and they ceased building the city.

9 Therefore its name is called Babel, because there the LORD confused the language of all the earth.

It is very interesting to note that in Hebrew the word *Babel* is identical to the word for *Babylon*. It could have been translated, "the tower of Babylon." In the last chapters of the Book of Revelation, God describes the entire world system—when it reaches its zenith of evil and wickedness—as "Babylon the Great, mother of harlots and abominations of the earth."

The New and Modern "Tower of Babel"

I believe that the Internet (and the information superhighway that is coming), points to the rebirth and resurgence—the coming together again—of the tower of Babel.

Man is not going to let anything stand in his way. He is going to build a tower that reaches into the heavens. This is talking about much more than just rockets and space exploration. It is articulating what Lucifer and Satan said in Isaiah, "I shall ascend. I shall be like the most high." (Isa. 14:12) It is talking about the words that the serpent spoke to Eve in the garden of Eden "Ye shall be like God, knowers." (Gen. 3:5)

Man no longer needs God; he now is his own god. Technology is his god. As one reads magazines and surfs the Web, there is a spirit of arrogance in the air. People have the attitude that "all things are possible through technology." When every person can communicate, and every interest out there can come together instantly in spirit and in thought, we have "finally arrived." We are self-sufficient. We do not need to depend on a higher power—God, as our source—for we ourselves *are* the higher power.

A Utopia or a Cesspool?

However, not all is well in cyber-Shangri-la. Today on the Internet, one has instant access to it all—everything from ladies' missionary prayer groups to hard-core pornography. The Internet is saturated with over 70,000 hard-core pornographic web sites (that's *seventy* thousand!), promoting every deviant behavior and perversion imaginable. I have received unsolicited e-mails advertising live sex with nude women (and men), and all of it is available at the touch of a few keys. Hardly a voice is raised in protest as people just look the other way. As a society, we are currently in a "state of denial" about a lot of things.

Every satanic cult or religion is on-line, as are all the groups that promote white supremacy and racial hatred. There are sites on the Internet that will tell you how to build a pipe bomb or even a nuclear device (if you can find the plutonium). The FBI has hundreds of cyber-cops scouring the Web.

But there is a darker and even more sinister side to this advancement. Right now the information superhighway is only in its infancy; everything that relates to all aspects of our lives will be plugged into it. Yet all the elements that will compose it are in existence and *already* at work—shaping people's minds and the way they think. When it all comes together the tower of Babel will truly start to go up.

When so many minds get together in unison, anything can happen. We're not talking just about crime and things that are illegal. *We are talking about a materialistic "new age" secular-humanistic philosophy that has no knowledge of God, nor does it recognize any accountability to a Creator Being. It will stop at nothing and seeks only its own glory.*

A High-tech Wilderness

Intellectually, people are today more brilliant and capable than ever before. Society is at the point of greatest advancement. However, when it comes to spiritual perception—knowing and understanding God and walking with Him on an intimate basis—mankind is at its lowest point. *For the most part, we do not have any idea why this world exists or why we were even born.* Like a herd of animals, we move with the pack as we wander through life.

We are living in a high-tech wilderness. We have all the physical and technological advancements but are starving spiritually. As my brother-in-law recently said, "Never before in history has it been so easy for people to communicate with people, and never so difficult for people to communicate with God."

We know very little about the mind of our Creator. We know virtually nothing about how God thinks. We don't even know why He created us or why we exist.

For many Christians, church every Sunday has become simply a religious exercise and routine. It makes their consciences feel better and peps up the emotions, but even the effect of that wears off eventually.

The Social Results Have Been Devastating

When it comes to the issue of spiritual advancement, we are currently in a state of regression.

Let's go back in time to the early part of this century. Compared to today, people lived simple and uncomplicated lives. Sure, the growing and the sewing was harder, but lives and time revolved around family, children, church and community. Reading was the only form of intellectual entertainment available. In America, the Bible was in nearly every home.

In the 1950s and 1960s, lives were still different. A young family could easily make it with just one income, and fewer women found it necessary to work. Homes were much smaller and had single-car garages. The radio and black-and-white television were the available forms of entertainment. Games were Ping-Pong and volleyball. The family sat together around the table at meals.

Today's family is a different social animal altogether. Recently on the news it was pointed out that fewer women are cooking at home. A whole industry of precooked meals has opened up thousands of outlets across the country—food is bought and eaten "on the run." Families do not do projects together. Dad, mom, and the teenagers lead their own lifestyle and have their own circle of friends. Both parents work. It is almost impossible for a young family to buy a home on a single income.

The family unit has deteriorated. Men and women spend more intimate time with others at work than they do with their own spouses. Divorce is rampant, and many people just "live together." More and more children are being raised by a single parent. Just last year, for the first time in history, there were more single than married people in America.

These so called "great advancements" in our society, have had devastating social and spiritual effects. Television and technology have mesmerized our minds and thoughts to the point that nothing impresses us anymore. People are numb. Even Christian television has fallen into the trap of one-upmanship, as people flock to the program or event that has the most "signs and wonders." Economically and technologically, we have become successful and efficient. Yet in that process, we have also become detached from the simple pleasures and treasures of life.

This Babylonian spirit is going to be the Great Enemy that will blind people (Christians in particular) from seeing the significance and importance of theomatics.

In the next chapter, we will look at the most awesome thing imaginable—perhaps even the single most significant discovery of all time. Yet there is a formidable adversary out there that will do everything in its power to prevent people from seeing the truth and understanding the significance of what God has done.

The name of this adversary is "Information Overload."

The Crisis of "Information Overload"

Walk down the street and look into people's eyes. So many seem hollow, vacant, detached. People are running through life like so many rats through a maze. Why? When there is too much to do and too much to think about, caring, sharing, and intimacy get pushed into oblivion. As humans we become more like machines—so many worker bees in a hive. Other people and relationships are a dime a dozen. People come into and out of our lives as if moving through a revolving door. Stress, particularly in the workplace, is a huge problem. Why is all this happening? The answer, I believe, is "information overload."

- Hook up to cable television or satellite TV. At least forty to fifty channels are immediately available. Some networks now have over three hundred channels! There are channels with every type of programming imaginable. The average adult (and child) spends hours per day in front of the tube.

- Go into one of thousands of video rental shops and look at how many movie titles are available.

- Go into a music or record store and look at how many thousands of CDs are available, (everywhere you look young people are walking around with headphones on.) Christian music is an industry in itself.

- Go into a computer software store and look at how much software is available for business and entertainment on your home computer.

- Go into a video gaming center and look at how much Nintendo is there. The game industry is now a multibillion-dollar industry, and the games kids play are becoming more advanced (and violent), taking young people into the realm of virtual reality (as well as the occult).

- Log onto the Internet and get lost in cyberspace for the rest of your natural life (right now there are an estimated four-hundred million pages on the entire web.)

- Get addicted to sports television and watch ballgames twenty hours a week.

- Go into any bookstore or library and see how many books there are to study and read. Look at how many "Christian" books are available (mostly on Christian psychology and how to overcome stress).

- Join a social club or even a church. A person can pack his or her schedule with social events and "meetings" to the point where precious little time is left.
- If you have children, it takes all you've got to keep up with the activities kids are involved with in this day and age.
- If you are involved in a specific hobby or special interest, it can consume your entire life.
- Add to all the above the time devoted to working at your job and making a living. People today are struggling to survive with the high cost of living. Today everybody is in a survival mode.

Is it any wonder that people have so little time left for an intimate relationship with God?

Life is like a glass of water, which can only contain so much. The questions is, What are you filling your life up with? If you are not filling it up with God but with everything else, there will be "no room in the inn" of our hearts.

God Cannot Possibly Compete with Steven Spielberg

Our minds and brains are overloaded with more information than we can possibly digest. There are so many fascinating and titillating things out there! There are so many voices barking at the carnival. Nothing seems to impress people anymore. Nothing stands out.

This is especially true for the young people of our day. How can reading and meditating on the Book of Psalms or Proverbs possibly compete with the excitement of a Steven Spielberg movie? God is not the "ultimate ride" anymore. In order for God to be attractive, Christian leaders feel that they must use gimmicks (like Christian rock bands) in order to draw the crowds and then slip the gospel under the table!

When something comes along that is special, unique, real, from God—like theomatics—many people do not notice because it gets lost in the heap. It's just one more "sensational" thing out there.

All that Matters Are the Things which Are Eternal

As you read this book, you should keep in mind the following.

Theomatics is not of this world. Its origin is extraterrestrial and heavenly. Everything else is simply the creation of man. Theomatics was conceived in the mind of God, and for that reason it stands over, above, and beyond everything else. It is in a class by itself. Everything else—no matter what temporary value it may have—is absolute rubbish in comparison (Phil. 3:8).

Only the Living Fountain of waters will ever satisfy our thirst. Only the Bread that comes down from heaven will ever feed our souls. We need to get back to the basics of why God created us—to have fellowship with Him. Understanding the eternal truths that God has placed in His Word is the first step in getting back to that relationship that which was lost before man fell in the garden of Eden. And that is where theomatics comes into play. It is going to help us see the big picture, and put our derailed minds back on track. It will help us see why this world was created, why each one of us exists, and, most importantly, what the glorious future is going to be like. Theomatics will help us understand God's eternal plan and purpose.

To finalize this chapter, I would like to quote a statement by evangelist Billy Graham.

> We are so distracted today—watching television, listening to music on our headphones—that we don't stop to think anymore. Technology has transformed the world, and technology is not yet finished. Change is going on and on. Technology hasn't solved the problem of death. It hasn't solved the problem of evil. (*Decision Magazine*, November 1977, p. 3)

No matter how advanced man becomes, he will never solve the critical issues of life. Mark this fact down. He will never defeat death through technology. He will never be able to overcome sin, evil, and wickedness, through technology (technology will simply make it more easily accessible). He will never find God or prove His existence through technology. He will never be able to create life, or a single living cell, through technology. He will never understand the mysteries of Jesus and His relationship to the heavenly Father through technology. He will never be able to cross into or enter the spiritual dimension through technology. *The information superhighway is not the highway to heaven.*

Man is so proud of all that he has achieved, but to God who created the billions of galaxies, all the atoms and molecules, and every form of life that exists, all this stuff that we are so enamored with means nothing to Him. God looks down from His throne and barely yawns.

If man keeps heading in the direction he's going (and the Bible says that he will) all will end in total confusion. That is what the word Babel or Babylon means—It means *confusion*. It is the full ripening of man's knowledge—apart and devoid of any knowledge of his Creator. God told our first parents that if they ate the forbidden fruit, they "would surely die." When man becomes totally independent and self-sufficient, he will blot God out completely. In the end, he will cease to know why he was created or why he even exists. His spirit and soul may breathe, but he will be spiritually dead.

Should we as Christians be against technology? No! I believe we should use every tool at our disposal for the spread of the gospel. With theomatics research, I virtually live on the computer for at least six hours per day.

This Is My Prayer

My prayer for everyone reading this book is that when you finish, you will stop, kneel down, and say a prayer.

Lord, help me to put you first in my life. Teach me the meaning of prayer. Teach me that knowing you as my Creator *and loving heavenly Father* is the most important thing possible. One of these days they are going to put my body in a coffin and shove me into the ground. At that time all that I have ever achieved, the work I did for the company, the amount of money that I earned, all the things I acquired, all the vacations and pleasures I got out of life, none of those things will matter. Knowing you is all that will count.

If you truly pray that, mean it, and determine that you are going to spend time alone with God—allowing Him to speak individually to your heart—I will feel that this book has accomplished its purpose and goal.

You see, theomatics is a powerful subject. It will carry us right into the very heart and intellect of God. There is the potential to enter vast realms of understanding and knowledge of eternal mysteries—things that even angels desire to look into (1 Pet. 1:12). But what good will this be if we don't have a *relationship* and know God as our Father? Knowledge without relationship is absolute poison; it will bring death. That is precisely why God is not interested in just giving us information. He is far more concerned about our *relationship* with Him than He is in our knowledge.

And that is why as Christians we need to know what it means to make Jesus Lord of our lives. Having Him as Savior is not enough. He must be *both* Savior and Lord.

One of the most amazing facts that was ever revealed to me is that God gets lonely. Imagine that! He actually gets lonely; He created the stars and the galaxies and all the hosts of heaven—everything that exists. And yet without us He is alone. His one consuming wish and desire is to have fellowship and communion. That is why, in the very beginning, God created man "in His image." That is why God called Abraham and started Israel. He wanted to have a friend (James 2:23), and He wants us to be His friends (John 15:14).

And that is why He put theomatics in the Bible. He wanted to reveal Himself to us. He wants to re-create us again in His image; He wants us to be like Him. He wants to have a *relationship* with us. He wants to place His very mind inside of us so that we can understand and think the way He does. That's what the gift of the Holy Spirit is all about—God giving us His very thoughts.

And yet we are more concerned about how the Dallas Cowboys did last Sunday and whether or not our stock went up a few points on the Dow. God forgive us!

Imagine the sadness the Lord must feel as He looks down at the billions of fallen rebellious beings living their lives in absolute rejection of the Creator who made them. They have lost their way. They are wandering stars, walking about in a dry wilderness.

The pain of being desperately alone was felt most by Jesus as He hung on the cross between heaven and earth and cried out, "My God, My God, Why hast thou forsaken me?" I don't think it is fully possible for us to understand that agony He felt. Being eternally separated from God is the most terrible thing possible.

Knowledge and relationship with Him is the most joyful thing possible.

3 The Original Code in the Bible

The Phenomenon Explained in Simple Terms

If you were to walk into any church or religious institution where people study and learn from the Bible and ask them how Christians are supposed to understand God and interpret the Bible, they will probably tell you that in order to do so properly, we must follow what is known of as "the grammatical-historical system." We are supposed to read and interpret the Bible according to two things:

- The rules of grammar:
- The facts of history.

According to this viewpoint, the Bible is to be understood the same way as we would read and understand any other work of literature. We take words and their commonly accepted dictionary definitions, and we couple them with the recorded facts of history—carefully noticing to whom the words were originally addressed and written—and then through a process of historical, traditional, and cultural analysis, arrive at a correct definition of what the text (and God) is attempting to communicate to us. This technique has also been referred to as the "common sense method."

The grammatical-historical system is universally recognized by all religious leaders as the *only* logical and intelligent way—the way God intended—that Christians read and understand the Bible. Modern-day Bible scholars would *never even consider* any other method or system to be valid. In a recent article in *Charisma and Christian Life* magazine denouncing *The Bible Code* by Michael Drosnin, a well-noted seminary professor states, "The Bible is meant to be understood clearly, not to be deciphered."[1] Another scholar states, "*The Bible Code* may encourage people to seek biblical meaning by esoteric methods instead of direct application of the Word."2

This attitude is especially prevalent among fundamentalist and evangelical theologians. One of the best-known evangelical leaders states,

> The words of scripture are to be interpreted the same way words are understood in ordinary daily use. God has communicated his Word to us through human language, and there is every reason to assume he has done it in the most obvious and simple fashion possible. His words are to be understood just as we would interpret the language of normal discourse. 3

These are true statements. In *Theomatics II*, I note that

> With just the simple written words in the Bible, and their simple literal interpretation, God has given us everything we need for both life and Godliness in this present age. Nothing else is essential.

However, That Is Not All That Exists

What we are going to discover with theomatics is that the grammatical-historical comprehension of the words of the Bible—the words that we have come to love and treasure over the centuries—comprises only a very small part of the total picture that the Creator originally had in mind when He composed the Bible.

Much more exists! An enormous plan and an eternal purpose are behind everything present in the Bible. Even though God has given us the conventional means of understanding His message, there is depth of meaning present that could never be understood from just a simple reading of the text. Also present is a numerical system or code of awesome proportions—that will ultimately unlock the deeper and symbolical meanings present.

What is most significant about this assertive statement, is the fact that God did this—it can be proven in the laboratory, according to the highest standards of mathematical science.

Of Major Importance

The critical fact for all Christians to realize is that theomatics will never change or contradict one single thing that the Bible says. The grammatical-historical meaning of the words will mesh perfectly with the numerical code and number system that God has supernaturally placed in the Bible. Everything will fit together flawlessly from one layer to the next. That does not mean, however, that theomatics will substantiate everyone's ideas or interpretations about certain things in the Bible. Much of what people are trying to take literally may not have a literal meaning at all from God's perspective (especially the Book of Revelation).

The important fact is that theomatics will support and *bolster* all the fundamental and essential truths that we as Christians hold dear and sacred. There is nothing to fear from this discovery. Only good things can come from God. The more you study this subject, the more you will realize this fact: theomatics can do nothing but increase your faith and love for the truth.

The Original Code

NOTE: In *Theomatics II* the structural code was explained in more detail, i.e., the "long version." Here it will be the "short version." There is a delicate balance between adequately explaining the essential facts and overwhelming the reader with pages and pages of information.

Learning the ABCs of Theomatics

This chapter will be our training session. I have designed it as a series of steps. There are seven basic, easy-to-understand steps. If you properly understand one, you can easily go on to the next. I have done my very best to explain each step as simply as possible.

STEP 1: The Code

In our language, we have only two basic ways to communicate and express ideas. If you look at a typewriter or computer keyboard, what do you see? Letters (the alphabet) and numbers (1, 2, 3, 4, 5, 6, 7, 8, 9, 0). In our language structure, we communicate just about everything through *words* and *numbers.*

The numbers we use (1, 2, 3, 4, 5, 6, 7, 8, 9, 0) are called Arabic numerals. Those of us living today take the use of these symbols for granted. But here is an interesting fact. For centuries mankind did not have any numbers or digits in their language structure. Instead, for thousands of years, early civilizations used the letters of their alphabets to express numbers.

Have you ever looked at the digits on some watches? A few years ago you may have watched Super Bowl XXIV? What you have of course seen are Roman numerals:

$$I = 1, \ V = 5, \ X = 10, \ L = 50, \ C = 100, \ D = 500, \ M = 1000$$

This same idea or principle is especially true for the languages of the Bible, the ancient Hebrew of the Old Testament and the Greek of the New Testament.

On the following page, you will see the Hebrew and the Greek alphabets, along with the respective number values for each letter in those alphabets.

HEBREW ALPHABET

א	1
ב	2
ג	3
ד	4
ה	5
ו	6
ז	7
ח	8
ט	9
י	10
כ — ך	20 *
ל	30
מ — ם	40 *
נ — ן	50 *
ס	60
ע	70
פ — ף	80 *
צ — ץ	90 *
ק	100
ר	200
ש	300
ת	400

GREEK ALPHABET

α	1
β	2
γ	3
δ	4
ε	5
ς'	6 **
ζ	7
η	8
θ	9
ι	10
κ	20
λ	30
μ	40
ν	50
ξ	60
ο	70
π	80
ο	90 **
ρ	100
σ - ς	200 *
τ	300
υ	400
φ	500
χ	600
ψ	700
ω	800

* These double letters are the same. The second letter is used in place of the first letter when it occurs as the last letter in a word.

** Those who are familiar with New Testament Greek may be surprised to see the addition of the letters *vau* (number value = 6) and *koppa* (number value = 90). The letter *vau* appears in Revelation 13:18 as the numerical value of the number 6 in the number 666. In the early history of the Greek language both these letters existed, but later became extinct. They have always retained their numerical equivalency (see *Webster's Dictionary*).

These Codes Are a Matter of Historical Record

This code is more established and verifiable than even our own English alphabet. In other words, there is nothing arbitrary (or new) about it. It was fixed and etched in stone thousands of years ago.

> NOTE: There are hundreds of sources available that will confirm the validity of these codes. (See note 4, p. 241) Theomatics makes no claim to have discovered this numerical system. What theomatics has discovered, however, are some of the *principles* concerning *how* this code was designed to function. Nothing before has ever operated on the *collective* principles demonstrated in theomatics.

In order to confirm the Greek number code as it is shown, you need to look no further than *Webster's Dictionary*. The Greek alphabet and the numerical equivalents can be found in the back of most editions under the section "Special Signs and Symbols." This usage of letters for numerical values, goes back into the earliest times of ancient Greece.

The Hebrew number code was in use many centuries before Christ. Where and how it originated is not known. If you were to look into a present-day Hebrew Bible, you would find the actual chapter and verse numbers given in Hebrew letters instead of numbers.

Every Jewish scribe and rabbi is as familiar with this code as they are their own existence. Some Jews have believed for thousands of years that there is a Divine or mystical significance to these numerical values. This ancient tradition (among other things) is known of as the Kabbala. Much of the Kabbala is regarded by Christians and others as mystical nonsense. Most devout Jews do not view it as mainstream, but simply a fascinating quest.

Another term used to describe this numerical system is *gematria*.

The Denary System

Based upon my research, I have concluded that the entire theomatic structure in the Bible was formulated and set up to operate on the same *denary system* that is commonly in use today by all civilizations. Everything is based upon 10s, 100s, and 1000s.

The numerical structure of the Hebrew and Greek alphabets operates on the denary system. If you look carefully at the Hebrew and Greek alphabets, you will discover that the first ten letters of each alphabet are numbered 1 through 10. The second group is numbered 10 through 100, and the third group is numbered 100 to 400 for the Hebrew alphabet and 100 to 800 for the Greek alphabet. All of this was arranged in a systematic way. The numerical values are not haphazard; they follow a very concise arrangement.

STEP 2: Every Word Has a Numeric Value

Not only does each letter in the Hebrew and Greek alphabets have a number or numeric value attached to it, but *each word has a value as well.*

To illustrate this, let's take the word for *Jesus* in Greek, which is Ιησους (pronounced *ee-ay-sooce*). By following the chart for the Greek number code and adding the numbers for all the letters in this word, we obtain the following total:

I	=	10
η	=	8
σ	=	200
o	=	70
υ	=	400
ς	=	200
TOTAL	=	888

Another common word in Greek is *kosmos* (κοσμος), or world. When the numbers for the letters in this word are added together, the value is 600.

κ	=	20
o	=	70
σ	=	200
μ	=	40
o	=	70
ς	=	200
TOTAL	=	600

This formula applies to every single Hebrew and Greek word in the Bible. Each has its own number, or theomatic, value.

Phrases Also Add Up

Complete thoughts and sentences also have number values. To illustrate this, let's take the very first verse of the Bible: "In the beginning God created the heaven and the earth."

296	407	395	401	86	203	913
הארץ	ואת	השמים	את	אלהים	ברא	בראשית
earth	and	heaven	***	God	created	in-beginning

The theomatic value for each word is directly above it. We add all these numbers together (296 + 407 + 395 + 401 + 86 + 203 + 913) for a total of 2701. Thus, the theomatic value of the first verse of the Bible is 2701.

Incidentally, you may have noticed that the words above seem to be backward. They are not. Hebrew is read from right to left, instead of left to right—just the opposite of English.

Putting It All Together

When I began my research about twenty years ago, I did something which to my knowledge had never been done before. In order to effectively pursue the study of theomatics, a research tool was needed, one that would save hours of labor and at the same time open up the complete theomatic design in the Word of God. This tool was a *Theomatic Greek-English New Testament.* Since no such tool existed at the time, it was necessary to develop one.

Shown on the next page is one of over one thousand pages comprising the entire New Testament. Underneath each Greek word (or words) is the English equivalent. Above each Greek word is the appropriate number value, written in my own handwriting.

Using a calculator, this entire work took almost eight hundred hours to complete, yet by today's standards it is primitive. In recent years, all this data has been programmed into a massive computer database. The database includes every Hebrew and Greek word in the Bible, its numerical value and the equivalent English translation along with a great deal of other pertinent data.

In addition to the databases, there is a complete research and software package that does all the number crunching and general research (see appendix A, *Theomatics II*).

Eternal Secrets and Mysteries

All of the eternal mysteries of the ages have been imbedded into the Bible by God—based upon these numerical values of historical record. Every single word mentioned in Scripture, every truth, down to the minutest detail, has been placed there according to this system. The fact that God did all of it can be scientifically proven in a laboratory according to the highest standard of scientific testing procedures (see chapters 11 and 12 of this book).

THEOMATICS: On What Basis?

Before moving on to step 3, we will take a short detour. As you have been reading about the concept of the numerical values for the letters and words of the Bible, this thought may have occurred to you: On what is all of this based? Where do you get proof that God had anything to do with the assignment of number values to the Hebrew and Greek alphabets—*and then to the words of the Bible?* Where is the verse in the Bible that tells us that such a phenomenon as theomatics exists? If theomatics is true, why didn't Jesus and the apostle Paul just openly tell us about it? These questions are certainly valid, and they demand an answer.

but he that came down from heaven, *even* the Son of man which is in heaven.

14 And as Moses lifted up the serpent in the wilderness, even so must the Son of man be lifted up:

15 That whosoever believeth in him should not perish, but have eternal life.

16 For God so loved the world, that he gave his only begotten Son, that whosoever believeth in him should not perish, but have everlasting life.

17 For God sent not his Son into the world to condemn the world; but that the world through him might be saved.

18 He that believeth on him is not condemned: but he that believeth not is condemned already, because he hath not believed in the name of the only begotten Son of God.

19 And this is the condemnation, that light is come into the world, and men loved darkness rather than light, because their deeds were evil.

20 For every one that doeth evil hateth the light, neither cometh to the light, lest his deeds should be reproved.

21 But he that doeth truth cometh to the light, that his deeds may be made manifest, that they

---

70 25 770 1091 525 70 680
Ο ΕΚ ΤΟΥ ΟΥΡΑΝΟΥ ΚΑΤΑΒΑΣ, Ο ΥΙΟΣ
the [one] out of - heaven having come down, the Son

770 1510 31 1030 1648 2155
ΤΟΥ ΑΝΘΡΩΠΟΥ. 14 Και καθως Μωυσης υψωσεν
of man. And as Moses lifted up

420 630 55 308 953 1770 1978
ΤΟΝ ΟΦΙΝ ΕΝ ΤΗ ΕΡΗΜΩ, ΟΥΤΩΣ ΥΨΩΘΗΝΑΙ
the serpent in the desert, so to be lifted up

19 420 530 770 1510 61 281 70
ΔΕΙ ΤΟΝ ΥΙΟΝ ΤΟΥ ΑΝΘΡΩΠΟΥ, 15 ΙΝΑ ΠΑΣ Ο
it behoves the Son - of man, that everyone

1845 55 501 613 865 991
ΠΙΣΤΕΥΩΝ ΕΝ ΑΥΤΩ ΕΧΗ ΖΩΗΝ ΑΙΩΝΙΟΝ,
believing in him may have life eternal.

1770 104 355 70 284 420
16 ΟΥΤΩΣ ΓΑΡ ΗΓΑΠΗΣΕΝ Ο ΘΕΟΣ ΤΟΝ
For thus ³loved - ¹God the

450 1305 420 530 420 296
ΚΟΣΜΟΝ, ΩΣΤΕ ΤΟΝ ΥΙΟΝ ΤΟΥ ΜΟΝΟΓΕΝΗ
world, so as the Son the only begotten

884 61 281 70 1845 215 821
ΕΔΩΚΕΝ, ΙΝΑ ΠΑΣ Ο ΠΙΣΤΕΥΩΝ ΕΙΣ ΑΥΤΟΝ
he gave, that everyone believing in him

48 500 61 613 865 991
ΜΗ ΑΠΟΛΗΤΑΙ ΑΛΛ' ΕΧΗ ΖΩΗΝ ΑΙΩΝΙΟΝ.
may not perish but may have life eternal.

470 104 686 70 284 420 530
17 ΟΥ ΓΑΡ ΑΠΕΣΤΕΙΛΕΝ Ο ΘΕΟΣ ΤΟΝ ΥΙΟΝ
For ²not ⁴sent - ¹God the Son

215 420 450 61 188 420 450
ΕΙΣ ΤΟΝ ΚΟΣΜΟΝ ΙΝΑ ΚΡΙΝΗ ΤΟΝ ΚΟΣΜΟΝ,
into the world that he might judge the world,

61 61 1017 70 600 14 1171
ΑΛΛ' ΙΝΑ ΣΩΘΗ Ο ΚΟΣΜΟΣ ΔΙ' ΑΥΤΟΥ.
but that ³might be saved ¹the ²world through him.

70 1845 215 821 470 496
18 Ο ΠΙΣΤΕΥΩΝ ΕΙΣ ΑΥΤΟΝ ΟΥ ΚΡΙΝΕΤΑΙ·
The [one] believing in him is not judged;

70 48 1845 466 380
Ο ΜΗ ΠΙΣΤΕΥΩΝ ΗΔΗ ΚΕΚΡΙΤΑΙ, ΟΤΙ
the [one] not believing already has been judged, because

48 1155 215 370 231 770 958
ΜΗ ΠΕΠΙΣΤΕΥΚΕΝ ΕΙΣ ΤΟ ΟΝΟΜΑ ΤΟΥ ΜΟΝΟΓΕΝΟΥΣ
he has not believed in the name of the only begotten

880 770 484 709 8
ΥΙΟΥ ΤΟΥ ΘΕΟΥ. 19 ΑΥΤΗ ΔΕ ΕΣΤΙΝ Η
Son - of God. And this is the

540 380 370 1500 537 215 420
ΚΡΙΣΙΣ, ΟΤΙ ΤΟ ΦΩΣ ΕΛΗΛΥΘΕΝ ΕΙΣ ΤΟΝ
judgment, that the light has come into the

450 31 351 80 1120 221
ΚΟΣΜΟΝ ΚΑΙ ΗΓΑΠΗΣΑΝ ΟΙ ΑΝΘΡΩΠΟΙ ΜΑΛΛΟΝ
world and ³loved - ¹men ⁴rather

370 860 8 370 1551
ΤΟ ΣΚΟΤΟΣ Η ΤΟ ΦΩΣ· ΗΝ ΓΑΡ ΑΥΤΩΝ
²the ⁵darkness ⁶than the light; for was(were) of them

309 301 109 281 104 70 932
ΠΟΝΗΡΑ ΤΑ ΕΡΓΑ. 20 ΠΑΣ ΓΑΡ Ο ΦΑΥΛΑ
evil the works. For everyone evil things

1431 265 370 1500 31 490 1021
ΠΡΑΣΣΩΝ ΜΙΣΕΙ ΤΟ ΦΩΣ ΚΑΙ ΟΥΚ ΕΡΧΕΤΑΙ
doing hates the light and does not come

450 370 1500 61 48 301 109
ΠΡΟΣ ΤΟ ΦΩΣ, ΙΝΑ ΜΗ ΕΛΕΓΧΘΗ ΤΑ ΕΡΓΑ
to the light, lest is(are) reproved the works

1171 70 89 1010 358 11 1021
ΑΥΤΟΥ· 21 Ο ΔΕ ΠΟΙΩΝ ΤΗΝ ΑΛΗΘΕΙΑΝ ΕΡΧΕΤΑΙ
of him; but the [one] doing the truth comes

450 370 1500 61 1473 1171 301
ΠΡΟΣ ΤΟ ΦΩΣ, ΙΝΑ ΦΑΝΕΡΩΘΗ ΑΥΤΟΥ ΤΑ
to the light, that may be manifested of him the

The Historical Basis

First, there is a strong historical basis for the assignment of numerical values to the Hebrew and Greek alphabets. The numerical values are established and commonly known and accepted. In other words, it is standardized. Yet none of this in itself "proves" that any concept such as theomatics exists, i.e., that there is some sort of supernatural element or phenomenon operating in the Bible based upon this system. On the surface, nothing is indicated by the numerical values other than the fact that ancient civilizations used letters to represent numerals. Also, the historical precedent proves that this Author did not arbitrarily come up with this standard.

Suppose that I were to use a completely different, or arbitrary, assignment of numbers to the letters of the Hebrew and Greek alphabets. Suppose that I insisted that the way God revealed this to me was by sending down an angel with the assignment of numerical values written "on golden plates."

So obviously, there must be a basis for all of this that has historical precedence and is academically credible. In addition, *there is evidence for the entire numerical system right in the "original" text of the Bible itself.*

The Chester Beatty Papyrus

When the books of the New Testament were written in the first century after Christ, no such thing as paper existed. Instead, a kind of "paper" made from a sedge plant called papyrus was used. This plant grew abundantly in the Nile River Delta and reached a height of fifteen feet or more. When bound in bundles, the long stems could be used to make rafts or canoes; this plant also gave man his first cheap and practical writing material. The papyrus was cut into thin slices, placed crisscross on a board, beaten together, and pressed until the natural glue from the plant bound the pieces into a strong, thin form of paper.

All the earliest manuscripts of the New Testament were written on papyrus. (Some older Old Testament manuscripts were written on leather.) Some of the documents from this early period are still extant, and they are considered to be the most treasured and priceless artifacts in existence—the earliest known copies of the New Testament.

One such manuscript is in Dublin, Ireland, in a collection of manuscripts owned by a Chester Beatty (designated p47). It is unquestionably the earliest known copy of the Book of Revelation. The date of this particular papyrus has been placed in the third century, or somewhere between 250 and 300 A.D.[5]

The most significant thing about this particular manuscript is that it gives all the numbers in the Book of Revelation with number, or theomatic, values. Every single number in the Book of Revelation is shown with the letters of the Greek alphabet. For example, the number 7, referred to many times in Revelation, is expressed with letter ζ, which

has a numerical value of 7. The number 12 would be expressed by the two letters ιβ (10 + 2 = 12), and so on.

Revelation 13:18 is, of course, the verse that describes the number of the beast—666. On the previous page is one of the pages from Revelation chapter 13. Notice the number 666 with an arrow pointing to the right. Follow the arrow to the right for about half an inch, and you will see the following symbol with a line over it: χξϛ'. This is the number 666 given with theomatic values. The first letter χ has a value of 600, the second letter ξ has a value of 60, and the third letter ϛ' has a value of 6. The total equals 666.

Verse 1 of chapter 14 immediately follows. It describes how the Lamb stood on Mount Zion, and with Him there were 144 thousands. If you look at the picture of the papyrus again, you will see, beneath the 666, the number 144 with an arrow pointing to its right. Follow this arrow for about half an inch, and you will see the symbol ρμδ. This is the number 144 given with theomatic values. Immediately following the number values is the Greek word for "thousands." The number 144 appears again in verse 4 at the bottom.

This numerical concept is found not only in the Chester Beatty Papyrus, but also in a number of other New Testament manuscripts. However, in later families of manuscripts the numbers are expressed in words instead of numerical symbols. (More discussion on this is given in appendix D of *Theomatics II*, which deals with the whole issue of Greek New Testament text.)

This concept of assigning number values to the letters of the alphabet is a well-documented historical and *biblically based* practice. But again, this in itself is no proof for the existence of theomatics. That brings us to a very important statement.

The Scientific Method is the Only Way to Know for Sure

Chapter 11, which is entitled "Theomatics and the Scientific Method," explains that the only way we can truly know whether this system is valid is by taking the data into the laboratory and using computers to test the theomatics hypothesis in an unbiased and scientific manner. Through this process we are able to discover whether God implanted a code; whether or not theomatics is true, if there is indeed *an inherent and deliberate structure to the letters and words of the canon of Scripture* (the sixty-six books of the Bible) based upon this numerical system. That the Good Lord has provided us with textual evidence, such as the Chester Beatty Papyrus, is only icing on the cake. It gives us the basis, a *biblically based* precedent, for the allocation of numerical values to the letters of the alphabet.

Back to the Question of Jesus and Paul

So why didn't Jesus or the apostle Paul just tell us all about it? The answer? Maybe God in His sovereignty did not want man delving into this before the proper time. If God had revealed it centuries ago, there is a good possibility it could have wreaked complete havoc in the theological world and been counterproductive to God's purposes. (Can you imagine Christians sitting in pews analyzing everything the pastor says with their calculators?)

Jesus or Paul could not have told us that theomatics existed in the Bible because the New Testament was not even written at the time they would have made the statement.

The Old Testament *had* been completed at the time of Christ, but as theomatics will clearly show, no one would be able to clearly see or understand the phenomenon without putting the two halves together.

In Chapter 7 we will find that the Bible does indeed tell us all about theomatics, because, as will be shown, *every number mentioned openly in the Bible text jibes with and corresponds to all the numerical values for the letters and* words. The whole thing is proven by what the text specifically states—right out in the open!

A Quick Review

Before we look at step 3, let's do some quick reviewing. In step 1 we saw how each letter in the Hebrew and Greek alphabets has a numerical, or theomatic, value assigned to it. Furthermore, by adding all the number values for the letters in a word, we find that each word has its own distinct numerical value (step 2). And last, by adding up all the number values in a phrase of two or more words, we find that each phrase (or combination of words within a phrase) also has its own numerical, or theomatic, value.

STEP 3: Multiples

This concept is many-faceted, but its essence is this: *Everything in theomatics operates on the principle of multiples and multiple structures based upon prime numbers.* The factors within multiple structures and the manner in which all numbers relate to one another by factoring are the principles by which God has organized the theomatic structure.

There are many complicated aspects to multiples that I will not have time to fully discuss in this book. For now I will present a very simple explanation of what multiples are.

Consider the number 300. The number 300 is a multiple of 100, 100 times 3 equals 300 (100 x 3 = 300). In other words, 300 is a multiple of 100 because it can be divided evenly by 100. The same holds true of the number 700. It is a multiple of 100 because it too can be divided by 100 (100 x 7 = 700). Likewise, the numbers 500, 1200, 200, 1000, and 17,800 are all multiples of 100.

At this time there is only one important item to remember. Later when I present the theomatic designs, I will show that "all" Bible topics have key number(s) assigned to them by God. For example, if you examine specific references to Jesus the Son of God, you will find that they all contain multiples of the same number. The many different references to Satan are all structured around multiples of another number.

STEP 4: Clusters

The principle or phenomenon of clusters is one of the most profound aspects of theomatics. The last step showed how everything in theomatics operates by multiples of certain key numbers. *Step 4 demonstrates the clustering of numbers around these multiples.* The easiest way to explain and illustrate this concept is with the following illustration, that shows all the numbers from 96 to 104.

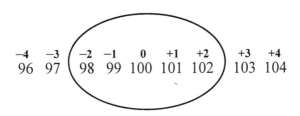

As you can see, the number 0 in the center of the circle represents the number 100. On each side of the number 100 are the numbers 98, 99 and 101, 102. All five numbers (98, 99, 100, 101, 102) form a cluster of the multiple 100.

These circles or clusters are rather like shooting a basketball through a hoop. If we were to examine the many different references to Jesus and Satan their number values would all fall into the appropriate circles or clusters. Here is an example.

Let's say that we had a phrase in Greek with a theomatic value of 799. This feature would fall within the cluster of the multiples of 100, because 800 is a multiple of 100, and the numbers 798, 799, 800, 801, and 802 form the cluster. Another example would be the number 2602. A phrase with a theomatic value of 2602 would fall within the cluster, because 2598, 2599, 2600, 2601, and 2602 form the cluster. Everything in theomatics operates on this principle.

One example in creation demonstrates the principle of clusters. In the universe, galaxies are all structured around clusters of stars. The largest concentration of stars exists toward the center of the galaxy. But farther out from the center, the stars become fewer and fewer.

Since theomatics operates on the same principle, the greatest percentage of features presented in this book are exact multiples or within −1 or +1 of the exact multiples. Fewer still are within −2 and +2. A very small percentage (approximately 2 percent) are within −3 or +3. The numbers all cluster around the precise multiples, and this is the same principle by which God designed the galaxies.

Clustering Proves the Whole Theomatic Concept

When the theomatic patterns are tested by computer in a scientific manner, clustering or a concentration of numbers would be impossible, if theomatics did not exist. The clustering phenomenon, statistically speaking, is amazing and totally miraculous. This book devotes an entire chapter to a discussion of this (chapter 12). Clustering scientifically proves the whole theomatic concept. If the world's scientific community knew about these findings, studied them, and comprehended them, it would change forever the world that we live in.

Also it is important to point out that only one aspect of theomatics manifests itself with the clustering. *In order for theomatics to work properly and the patterns to exist at all, each word must have an exact and precise value.* Every numerical value must be perfect and right on target; it cannot vary by one or two numbers.

STEP 5: The Grammar of the Hebrew and Greek Languages

So far we have covered four steps: *(1) the theomatic number codes, (2) each word and phrase having its own numeric value, (3) multiples, and (4) clusters.*

Step 5 is lengthy and involved (in *Theomatics II*, a much-enlarged discussion is provided). There are a number of factors concerning the Hebrew and Greek languages that are important to understand.

Ancient Hebrew

Hebrew is one of the most ancient languages in existence. It comes from the Semitic language group. The word *Semitic* is derived from *Shem*, the name of one of Noah's sons after the flood. As the language of the Old Testament, Hebrew evolved slowly and has remained virtually unchanged for thousands of years. A more modern version of Hebrew is the official language of Israel.

Hebrew is a beautiful language. It is also a rather simple language in its structure. To those just starting out to learn Hebrew, the shapes of the letters and the manner of pronunciation can be somewhat intimidating. It takes a degree of effort to learn the fundamentals. As I previously mentioned, Hebrew reads "backward," from right to left, opposite to the way English is read.

Hebrew is a consonantal language. It is unique in that it has no vowels. Since Hebrew has no vowels, no one knows for sure how words were pronounced during biblical times. Those living in ancient Israel simply knew what words traditionally were supposed to sound like.

Ancient Greek

The Greek language of the Bible comes from a group of languages called *Indo-European* or *Indo-Germanic*. Unlike Hebrew, Greek is more dynamic and has always been in a state of change and evolution. In historic progression, it went from (1) its primitive state, to (2) Classical Greek (the Greek of Plato and Socrates), to (3) Hellenistic Greek (the time of the Bible), to (4) Byzantine Greek, and finally to (5) Modern Greek, which is spoken today in Greece.

Our interest lies in Hellenistic Greek, which is the Greek used during biblical times. In the past, scholars had been puzzled by the Greek language of the New Testament because it has some very unique characteristics. Many people throughout the centuries referred to it as a "language of the Holy Spirit." However, later investigations revealed that the Greek of the New Testament was a form of the common "marketplace Greek" of the people of Jesus' day. This is why it is presently known as *Koine Greek*, which means "common Greek." It was a language rarely used in writing and was mostly a spoken or street-language.

In Reality—Two Heavenly Languages

At the beginning of chapter 1, I stated that in order for theomatics to be possible, "God created two 'heavenly' languages—Hebrew and Greek—and placed them unknowingly into human culture and finally into the vocabulary of the Bible." Very simply:

Every word in the Bible was designed by God, from eternity past, to be part of a very organized and systematic grammatical structure. It had to have an exact spelling that was predetermined before the word ever evolved and came into use in human culture. It had to have a precise spelling with the right combination of letters so that these letters would all add up to an exact and predetermined numerical value; but just as important, it also had to make sense, from a linguistic standpoint, by following the proper "rules" of grammatical structure.

But that was just the beginning. Not only did God give each word an exact and accurate spelling with its proper numeric value, He also had to consider how and where that word would be placed and fit into the text—next to the other words on both sides of it and with their exact spellings and numerical values. Not just words, but phrases and all portions thereof, had to add up to the proper numbers. As we shall see, it gets so complicated that it is doubtful there are computers, at least on this earth, capable of working out the mathematical complexities it would take to put grammar, words, and adjacent words together, *with spiritual truth* and make everything work out perfectly numerically. You will see this fact demonstrated.

A Simple Illustration

The following analogy is a simple way to illustrate this. Have you ever watched a large brick building under construction? Surrounding the building is a complete network of scaffolding, planks, tarps, masons, and bricklayers. The entire thing looks like a mess. However, after the job is complete and each brick has been neatly laid, the scaffolding is removed, the brick is cleaned, and a beautiful structure is the result.

Every word existing in the Hebrew and Greek languages—throughout history—could be compared to this network. The words that do not end up in the Bible text (the discards) could be considered "scaffolding." However, once the structure has been completed, the scaffolding is torn down and all that is left is the finished structure with every brick (word in the Bible) in its proper location.

Theomatics operates on logic and principles that are totally heavenly in origin. God had one objective in mind: to bring forth via the numerical structure—in an unmistakable way—spiritual, eternal, and absolute truth.

The Cases

How many ways are there to spell the word God in the English language? The answer is simple: there is only one way. The word *God* is spelled *G-o-d*. This is not true in the Greek language. In fact, for just about every single noun in Greek, there are at least four or five possible spellings. These spellings are called *cases*, and each fulfills a basic grammatical purpose (that I will not go into here). Each word has a basic root, or stem, and the ending of the word, or suffix, is the variable.

(θεος) Theos (θεου) Theu (θεω) Theo (θεον) Theon

To further illustrate this, along with one minor theomatic example, let us compare the two words "God" and "Holy." There are probably no two words in all of scripture more synonymous than these two words. God is holiness, and holiness is God. Every single spelling for God and every single spelling for Holy match up perfectly.

	GOD		HOLY	
Nominative Case	θεος =	284	αγιος =	284
Genetive Case	θεου =	484	αγιου =	484
Dative Case	θεω =	814	αγιω =	814
Accusative Case	θεον =	134	αγιον =	134
Vocative Case	θεε =	19	αγιε =	19

As you can see, the basic word root remains the same; the only thing that changes is the ending. This is true with almost every Greek noun. If one were to spell "God" in the plural, as "Gods," it would also have four different spellings. *With this principle, God has provided Himself with a language that is extremely flexible.* In a few moments I will show why.

Greek verbs are even more flexible than Greek nouns. For every Greek verb root, there is an abundant supply of prefixes and suffixes. These variations give the verb its tenses. The tense of a verb is the characteristic that shows its action or state of being (such as present, past, future, etc.).

The less-flexible Hebrew language is still complex, with numerous spellings for most words. Hebrew operates on a complex system of roots, or root words, with variations of prefixes and suffixes. Many variations are possible.

The Article

The articles of Hebrew and Greek are indeed fascinating. The words "a," "an," and "the" are known as *articles*. The two articles "a" and "an" are indefinite articles, while "the" is definite. The Greek language has only a definite article. This fact is highly significant.

However, there is only one thing you have to remember: "There are no 'rules' for the use of the article in Greek."[5] The Greek article has absolutely no meaning (beyond the translated meaning of "the.") Because it is only definite, it can add emphasis and act as a pointer, but it has no other significance.

In John 11:4, Jesus is referred to as "the Son of God." The Greek words for "the Son of God," with the articles, are ο υιος του θεου. But in Mark 15:39, Jesus again is referred to as "the Son of God." In this verse, the words "the Son of God" appear without the articles (υιος θεου), but the translation remains exactly the same. Therefore, a Greek phrase has the same meaning with or without the article, and the same is true of Hebrew.

What Does All This Mean?

As you have been reading these words concerning the Greek and Hebrew articles, one question may have been going through your mind: If the articles have no discernible meaning, why did God place them in the text of the Bible? *He put them there because of theomatics!* The reason Hebrew and Greek are structured the way they are is that they are theomatic languages.

All the various articles, along with the multitude of possible spellings for words have different numerical, or theomatic, values. What God does is simply use the right combination or mixture of words (with their various spellings), along with the different articles, to compose or construct a sentence, phrase, or thought that equals the determined numerical value(s).

Theomatics would be totally impossible with any other kind of language, such as English, and once this discovery becomes widely understood it should explain many, if not most, of the inexplicable questions concerning the grammatical structure of these two languages. There is an entire section in *Theomatics II* (appendix C) for Greek scholars that is thoroughly documented and discusses all of this in detail.

STEP 6: Putting It All Together

Step 6 shows many aspects related to the complexity of theomatics and discusses facts concerning how the structure was put together. Including all that information here would present extremely laborious reading. (Please refer to *Theomatics II* for a detailed explanation of this step, pp. 39-42.)

STEP 7: *Rules and Guidelines for Theomatics Research*

This is the final step. It presents the rules for theomatics research. Again, this is covered in more detail in *Theomatics II*. There is a specific guideline that must be followed at all times. I have called it "the golden rule of theomatics."

Every single word or phrase that is used for a theomatic feature must come right out of the text in exactly the same manner as God put it there. No words may be changed or added at any time for any reason. All words to be used for a theomatic feature must be lifted out of the text exactly as they appear in the original manuscript.

The one variable in theomatics is to sometimes leave out the numerical value for the article (which has no translatable meaning). Conjunctions can be ignored only if they appear on the front end of a phrase, not if they break the sentence in the middle. Words are always in juxtaposition (side-by-side), but there are some exceptions when the clear-cut meaning of two or more words leap frogs over other words. Let us look at just one brief example of this.

An outstanding theomatic example is found in the very first verse of the Bible. Most English translations read, "In the beginning God created the heavens and the earth." In the original Hebrew the words actually read, "In the beginning created God." The word "created" comes before the word "God." By taking the two words "In the beginning God" and skipping over the word "created," the theomatical result without the zeros, is the number 1. In the beginning there was only one God.

IN THE BEGINNING GOD   1000 — or just 1

Gen. 1:1 בראשית אלהים׳

This type of thing must be done sparingly and only when there is *no question* as to its distinct clarity of meaning.

Which Translation?

Have you ever wondered why there are so many English translations of the Bible on the market? The reason for this is the way Hebrew and Greek are structured grammatically. Ideas can be expressed in many different ways when a verse is translated into English. As there are so many possible shades of meanings, all the translators are basically saying the same thing, only with a different word choice.

This book will show hundreds of examples. It would be impossible to use one standard translation in presenting these findings. Many times the Hebrew or Greek words are arranged in a completely different order than the words in the English translations. Therefore, in this book I shall quote a verse as it would *interlineate* straight out of the Hebrew or Greek text. Interlineation means quoting the words in the order they appear in the original language. In a few instances, this may sound awkward, but it is the only accurate way it can be done.

The best way to check my translation firsthand would be to purchase an Interlinear Hebrew/Greek/English Bible. That way you can see exactly what is going on.

Remember that theomatics is not a truth to be understood in English. It is meant to be understood in the original languages.

Format and Layout of Features

You have just graduated. Now that you are familiar with the basic steps or concepts, we are ready to begin a full presentation. There are, however, a few basic things that should be explained concerning the format of the features or theomatically analyzed phrases. All examples will be shown in the following manner.

THE LAMB'S BOOK OF LIFE   1200 x 3
Rev. 13:8 τω βιβλιω ζωης αρνιου

THE DISCIPLES OF HIM   144 x 12 (12 x 12 x 12)
Mat. 12:49 μαθητας αυτου"

In the above examples, two numbers follow each English translation: 1200 x 3 for "the Lamb's book of life" and 144 x 12 for "the disciples of Him," referring to the twelve disciples of Jesus. The first numbers indicated (1200 and 144) are the key numbers and primary factors or multiples for that particular topic. Look at the first feature above. The number, or theomatic value, of the phrase "the Lamb's book of life" is exactly 3600, or 1200 x 3, the key number in this case being 1200. The secondary factor is the number 3.

The next feature is a little different. The value for the two Greek words meaning "the disciples of Him" is 1730, and this is within the cluster of 2 of the multiple of 144 x 12 (144 x 12 equals 1728). At the end of the Greek phrase there is a mark ("). All clusters will be thus indicated, either by a ('), if within the range of –1 or +1, or by a ("), if within the range of –2 or +2.

As a final note, the Greek text used is the straight Nestle Text (twenty-fifth edition), without any variants. If a variant is used, it will always be indicated before the verse reference; (nv) means Nestle Variant, and (mt) means the Majority Text or a Majority Text variant was used. See appendix D of *Theomatics II* for a complete discussion on the text.

4 Theomatics Demonstrated

Seeing Is Believing

Right now there are a thousand places I could begin this chapter. There are hundreds of studies in my files, any one of which would be highly impressive. This subject is so enormous! So far we have barely scratched the surface.

Pulling a Rabbit Out of the Hat

As I looked into my files to try and decide what to show first, an idea occurred to me. Why should I take the "best stuff," derived after years of research, and use it as the first example? Why not be more realistic? Why not pick something out of mid-air—almost at random—something that would be considered less than spectacular (by theomatic standards), and simply show the reader the common and the ordinary?

So right after I had written the first paragraph above, I bowed my head and prayed for wisdom. Without hesitation, the word *love* popped into my head. So I reached into the box "blindfolded," and decided to check out this word in the Greek New Testament. Never before, at any time, had I done a systematic study on the subject of love in the Bible.

Let me state emphatically, this was the first and only experiment that I attempted. What you are about to read was not even known a short time ago. I am going to write this chapter like a jazz musician who improvises as he goes. This is very important, because you will see first-hand the manner in which literally thousands of theomatic patterns have unfolded themselves over the years.

The evidence for theomatics is so overwhelming—it saturates the Bible from cover to cover—that once a person get the knack for seeing and understanding the structure and finds the right keys, the mathematical patterns will literally explode and open up right before their very eyes!

Phileo, Eros, and Agape

In the English language, there is only one word to describe all types of love, the word l-o-v-e. This generic term can be used in many different ways. At the time the New Testament was written, there were basically only two words in the Greek language that could be used to express love.

One was *phileo*. This word described an affectionate type of love that existed between humans, person to person. It is the word from which the name Philadelphia comes—the "city of brotherly love."

The other word used was *eros*. This was more of a sensual or sexual type of love—an erotic love between two people.

So the men who wrote the New Testament were faced with a dilemma. Neither of these two words was adequate for expressing a godly or divine type of love. What happened next is extremely significant. The Holy Spirit prompted the New Testament writers to actually *invent* a brand-new word. They called it *agape,* and it is descriptive of God's love. It depicts His love for us and our love for Him. It also applies to God's love as Christians express it one toward the other.

The Word Agape

The Greek word *agape* (αγαπη) appears approximately 119 times as a noun. The verb form, *agapao* (αγαπαω), which is used more loosely in its context, occurs approximately 124 times. We are going to examine just the noun.

According to *Moulton & Geden's Concordance to the Greek New Testament*, this word occurs ten times in the gospels and eight times in the Book of Romans. Here is a list of the first eighteen occurrences in the New Testament: Matt. 24:12; Luke 11:42; John 5:42, 13:35, 15:9, 15:10a, 15:10b, 15:13, 17:26; Rom. 5:5, 5:8, 8:35, 8:39, 12:9, 13:10a, 13:10b, 14:15, 15:30.

Heavenly in Origin

As we progress, we are going to learn that God has attributed certain symbolical and spiritual characteristics to specific numbers. In other words, the specific numerical values of individual words and phrases will express theological concepts and ideas.

As stated earlier, "theomatics operates on logic and principles that are totally heavenly in origin." This means that if we are going to properly understand this discovery it is crucial to make careful observations and draw conclusions based upon those observations. Any investigation will require a form of logic that is highly *inductive*.

The Number 31

Over the years, as I have performed research, I have observed over and over that the number 31, which is a prime number, is clearly associated with the concepts of holiness and purity. It speaks of that which is completely pure in the eyes of God. For example, there is a structure of 31 and 310s to do with the saints clothed in white garments. The number 31 saturates references to the blood of Jesus, and predominates in phrases that portray Jesus as the perfect "Lamb of God." The word lamb (αρνιω) has a value of 961, which is 31 x 31. I briefly touched on this 31 pattern in chapter 12 of *Theomatics II*.

The Number 93

Agape (αγαπη) has a numerical value of 93. This number factors out to 31 x 3. What we are now going to observe, as we investigate all these references to *agape,* love, is that the number 93 (and sometimes 310) will occur over and over again—beyond the mathematical laws of chance. In fact, we will begin to see one small piece of an amazing picture start to emerge as we look at each verse in the Bible. Please keep in mind that I am analyzing each passage as this book is actually being written.

After looking over the following references, we will summarize what has been shown.

One More Comment

From a scientific or statistical standpoint, this pattern would be somewhere down the list in impressiveness. On a scale of 1 to 10, I would rate it a 4. Though the following could easily hold up under a major scientific analysis with absolute ground rules and established controls, I would not even consider it a candidate for scientific evaluation. There is other statistical data far more impressive. Even so, the mathematical pattern is clearly present and very compelling.

One important fact that should be stated, is that the *average* length for all examples shown in this chapter is only 2.40 Greek words (not counting articles or conjunctions that begin a phrase): These will be extremely short and explicit phrases.

Reference 1 — Matthew 24:12

And because lawlessness will be increased, the love of many will grow cold.

The following consists of only three Greek words.

THE LOVE OF MANY WILL GROW COLD   93 x 30
Mat. 24:12 ψυγησεται η αγαπη πολλων"

Reference 2 — Luke 11:42

Woe to you Pharisees, because ye tithe the mint and the rue and every herb, and neglect justice and the love of God.

THE LOVE OF GOD 93 x 15
Luke 11:42 αγαπην του θεου"

Reference 3 — John 5:42

In speaking to the Jews, here are the words of Jesus.

But I have known that ye do not have the love of God in yourselves.

The manner in which the following works out theomatically is very clear and concise. The entire phrase as quoted above is 93 x 41. However, in this brief demonstration, I am trying to present the shortest and most concise words possible that either include or relate to the word "love." In the original Greek, the word arrangement reads "that love of God not ye have in yourselves."

LOVE OF GOD NOT 93 x 12
John 5:42 αγαπην θεου ουκ'

Reference 4 — John 13:35

By this all men will know that ye are my disciples, if love ye have for one another.

IF LOVE YE HAVE 93 x 12
John 13:35 εαν αγαπην εχητε'

LOVE YE HAVE FOR 93 x 12
αγαπην εχητε εν

Reference 5 — John 15:9

As loved me the Father, I also loved you. Remain in love mine.

The word "love" appears three times in this verse; however, the last reference is the only one using *agape*. The first two references use the verb form.

REMAIN IN LOVE 93 x 6
John 15:9 μεινατε εν αγαπη'

Look at the distinct nature of just these two words, and how the 93 pattern unmistakably appears.

REMAIN IN 93 x 5
μεινατε εν'

Some people may be asking, do the two verb forms in this passage fit the 93 pattern? The first time the verb for love is used, this happens.

LOVED ME THE FATHER   961 (31 x 31)
ηγαπησεν με ο πατηρ"

The pattern is clearly present, but not everything is 93 or 31 x 3. Please bear in mind that 31 is the key prime number here relative to love, not just 93. There are many 31s present in these passages, and I am simply not taking the time to show all of them, just the *prevailing consistency* that exists with the 93s. The 93s are occurring more often than the other 31 multiples, but other portions that may seem to "miss" the 93s, *still contain* this 31 pattern, as well as other inherent and relative patterns.

Now let's examine the second occurrence of the verb.

I ALSO LOVED YOU   93 x 19
καγω υμας ηγαπησα'

References 6 and 7 — John 15:10

If the commandments of me ye keep, ye will remain in love of me. As I have kept my Father's commandments and abide in His love.

We already saw how the words "remain in love" worked out to this 93 pattern. The interesting feature from this verse is the word "keep." Jesus stated that if a person will keep His commandments, he will remain in His love.

KEEP   930
John 15:10a τηρησητε'

And the last part of this verse states, "As I have kept my Father's commandments and abide in His love." The only pattern in this passage was simply the word *agape*.

LOVE (*agape*)   93
John 15:10b αγαπη

There is an entirely different verb form in Greek for the word "love"—it is spelled completely different from *agape*. Guess what occurs?

Now there was leaning on Jesus' bosom one of his disciples, whom Jesus loved.

LOVED   93
John 13:23 ηγαπα

Reference 8 — John 15:13

> Greater love than this has no man, than he should lay down his life for his friends.

The following is the most specific thing possible. It is one word in Greek. "Greater love than this has no man."

THAN THIS 93 x 13
John 15:13 ταυτης

HAS 310 x 2
εχει

The Greek word meaning "than this" has the same value as the following. The great love that Jesus was talking about is laying down His life for His friends.

FRIENDS 93 x 13
John 15:14 φιλους'

Jesus had previously stated that "greater love than this has no man." The word "has" is 310 x 2. Another Greek spelling for the word "friends" has the same sum total. This is one example of the indescribable logic seen so often in theomatics.

FRIENDS 310 x 2
John 15:14 φιλοι

HAS 310 x 2
εχει

Reference 9 — John 17:26

> I made known to them thy name, and I will make it known, that the love with which thou lovest me may be in them, and I in them.

The following six English words come from three Greek words.

THE LOVE WITH WHICH THOU LOVEST 93 x 7
John 17:26 αγαπη ην ηγαπησας'

LOVE 93
αγαπη

WITH WHICH THOU LOVEST 93 x 6
ην ηγαπησας'

We will now jump to the Book of Romans and the next series of references. It is strange how neither the noun nor the verb for *agape*—which occurs 241 times in the New Testament—appears not one single time in the entire Book of Acts.

Reference 10 — Romans 5:5

And hope does not disappoint us, for the love of God has been poured out in our hearts.

Of course the words "love of God," as we previously saw, worked out to 93 x 15. The following nine English words come from only three Greek words plus one conjunction.

FOR THE LOVE OF GOD HAS BEEN POURED OUT   93 x 25
Rom. 5:5 οτι η αγαπη θεου εκκεχυται'

Reference 11 — Romans 5:8

For God shows His own love toward us, in that while we were yet sinners, Christ died for us.

SHOWS HIS OWN   93 x 7 x 4
Rom. 5:8 συνιστησιν εαυτου

Reference 12 — Romans 8:35

Who will separate us from the love of Christ?

SEPARATE US FROM THE LOVE   93 x 26
Rom. 8:35 ημας χωρισει απο αγαπης

The words "love of Christ" do not contain a 93, but they still have the 31 pattern present. The number 8 is one of the major key numbers to do with *Jesus*, which has a value of 888.

THE LOVE OF CHRIST   310 x 8
της αγαπης χριστου'

Reference 13 — Romans 8:39

Nor height nor depth nor any other creature will be able to separate us from the love of God in Christ Jesus our Lord.

A computer search of the last part of the above verse revealed almost a dozen multiples of 93 in all the various phrase segments. Here is the most explicit example. Look at the value of the second feature below.

WILL BE ABLE TO SEPARATE US FROM   3100
Rom. 8:39 δυνησεται ημας χωρισαι απο'

FROM THE LOVE OF GOD   930
Rom. 8:39 απο αγαπης θεου"

LOVE OF GOD   93 x 15
Luke 11:42 αγαπην του θεου"

Reference 14 — Romans 12:9

Let love be genuine; hate what is evil, hold fast to what is good.

LET LOVE BE GENUINE   93 x 15
Rom. 12:9 αγαπη ανυποκριτος'

What could be more incredible than the following?

GENUINE   93 x 7 x 2
ανυποκριτος'

As we watch these patterns unfold themselves, isn't it amazing, that something this profound and significant, with implications that are absolutely earth-shattering and conclusive, something that is right there in the text and can be so easily verified—is virtually unknown to the entire religious, scientific and academic worlds?

Reference 15 — Romans 13:9,10

Thou shalt love thy neighbor as thyself. Love to one's neighbor does not work evil.

THOU SHALT LOVE THY NEIGHBOR   93 x 22
Rom. 13:9 αγαπησεις τον πλησιον σου

The next phrase interleaved from Greek states, "Love to one's neighbor evil not works." It could have been translated as "to one's neighbor love not evil works." The following arrangement is clearly in the context of meaning and the theomatic design that exists in this verse.

LOVE NOT EVIL (works)   93 x 8
Rom. 13:10a αγαπη κακον ουκ

NOT EVIL   93 x 7
κακον ουκ

Reference 16 — Romans 13:10

Love to one's neighbor does not work evil; love is therefore the fulfillment of the law.

LOVE IS THEREFORE THE FULLFILMENT   93 x 18
Rom. 13:10b πληρωμα ουν αγαπη"

IS THEREFORE THE FULFILLMENT   93 x 17
πληρωμα ουν"

Reference 17 — Romans 14:15

If your brother is being hurt by what you eat, you are no longer walking according to love.

ACCORDING TO LOVE   93 x 5
Rom. 14:15 κατα αγαπην

Reference 18 — Romans 15:30

I beseech you therefore brethren, by our Lord Jesus Christ and by the love of the Spirit to strive with me in your prayers to God on my behalf.

BRETHREN   310 x 2
Rom. 15:30 αδελφοι

BY THE LOVE   310
δια αγαπης"

THE LOVE OF THE SPIRIT TO STRIVE   930 x 5
της αγαπης του πνευματος συναγωνισασθαι"

Let's Analyze This

We have now completed our examination of the first eighteen occurrences of the word "love" in the New Testament. It is important to point out one very important fact concerning the manner in which the above was shown.

In all experiments and tests that are done *every single Bible passage* that refers to a certain word or topic, must be looked at and analyzed. The hits must be shown right alongside the misses. That is why it is important to list and write down *all* possible references *before* any findings are made. That is the correct scientific approach. That way skeptics and doubting Thomases cannot accuse theomatics of being arbitrary and only showing the "good stuff," i.e., selective data.

There Are Still 101 Passages Left

Another objective way to do an experiment is to randomly or systematically select a limited number of passages containing the key word and *afterwards* test those. What I decided to do for the rest of the New Testament was to start counting after Romans and write down each tenth occurrence of *agape*. The following ten verses were the only ones from the rest of the New Testament that I tested: 1 Cor. 13:13; 2 Cor. 8:8; Eph. 1:15; Phi. 1:16; 1 Thess. 3:12; 1 Tim. 6:11; Heb. 6:10; 1 John 3:17; 1 John 4:18; Rev. 2:4).

Reference 19 — 1 Corinthians 13:13

And now abideth faith hope love, these three; but the greatest of these is love.

BUT THE GREATEST IS LOVE   93 x 11
1 Cor. 13:13 μειζων δε η αγαπη'

Reference 20 — 2 Corinthians 8:8

I speak not by commandment, but by occasion of the forwardness of others, and to prove the genuiness of your love.

These are the words of the apostle Paul. The last portion of the above verse, in Greek actually reads, "And of your love the genuineness proving."

AND OF YOUR LOVE THE GENUINENESS   93 x 19
2 Cor. 8:8 και υμετερας αγαπης γνησιον'

THE GENUINENESS PROVING   93 x 15
2 Cor. 8:8 γνησιον δοκιμαζων"

Reference 21 — Ephesians 1:15

For this reason, because I have heard of your faith in the Lord Jesus and the love to all the saints.

LOVE TO ALL THE SAINTS   93 x 18
Eph. 1:15 αγαπην εις παντας αγιους

Reference 22 — Philippians 1:16

Some indeed preach Christ from envy and rivalry, but others from goodwill. The [latter] do it from love, knowing that I am here but for the defense of the gospel.

The above exhibited one six-word phrase that was 930 x 2, but I did not feel it was short and explicit enough to show.

Reference 23 — 1 Thessalonians 3:12

And may the Lord make you increase and abound in love unto one another and to all men.

ABOUND IN LOVE   93 x 14
1 Thess. 3:12 περισσευσαι αγαπη"

ABOUND IN   93 x 13
περισσευσαι"

Reference 24 — 1 Timothy 6:11

But as for you, man of God, shun all this; aim at righteousness, godliness, faith, love, steadfastness, gentleness.

As a rule in theomatics, there will never be a pattern with a word such as "love" simply present in a long list with other items. In such instances there are are no words either before or after the word "love" that relate to it.

Reference 25 — Hebrews 6:10

For God is not so unjust as to overlook your work and the love which you showed for his sake in serving the saints.

AND THE LOVE WHICH YOU SHOWED   93 x 15
Heb. 6:10 και της αγαπης ης ενεδειξασθε'

Reference 26 — 1 John 3:17

But if anyone has the world's goods and sees his brother in need, yet closes his heart against him, how does the love of God remain in him?

HOW DOES THE LOVE OF GOD REMAIN   93 x 19
1 John 3:17 πως αγαπη θεου μενει'

Reference 27 — 1 John 4:18

"There is no fear in love, but perfect love casts out fear."

THERE IS NO FEAR IN LOVE   93 x 22
1 John 4:18 φοβος ουκ εστιν εν αγαπη'

The above reference to *agape* is the one that was included in our list of each ten references. However, this particular verse has two references to *agape*. The second one states that "perfect love casts out fear."

PERFECT LOVE CASTS OUT   93 x 15
1 John 4:18 η τελεια αγαπη εξω βαλλει

The following example is not in our list of verses to examine, but I simply had to show it. The above verse contains still a third reference to *agape*.

…but perfect love casts out fear, because fear has punishment. And the one fearing has not been perfected in love.

PERFECTED   93 x 19
τετελειωται'

Reference 28 — Revelation 2:4

In the Book of Revelation, Jesus addresses the church at Ephesus. The value here is 93 x 31.

But I have this against you, that you have left your first love.

LEFT YOUR FIRST LOVE   93 x 31
Rev. 2:4 αγαπην σου πρωτην αφηκας"

Conclusion

At this point I could show at least a hundred more examples with the number 93 from both the Old and New Testaments. In the next chapter, an analysis will be presented that will help the reader understand more about what has just been shown.

5 Putting the Pieces Together

Explaining How Theomatics Works

Years ago someone shared a little puzzle with me called a magic square. The magic square is really nothing more than a simple mathematical formula, but what it does is amazing. Although the following example is in no way intended to be a complete explanation of how the theomatic structure operates, it will illustrate the basic idea.

Shown below are sixteen squares. Many numbers can be used. For this example we will use the formula for the number 34. By combining the right numbers (from 1 to 16) in each square, the following results are observed:

1 8	2 11	3 14	4 1
5 13	6 2	7 7	8 12
9 3	10 16	11 9	12 6
13 10	14 5	15 4	16 15

All the numbers in the four horizontal rows add up to 34.

All the numbers in the four vertical rows add up to 34.

The four squares in each corner add up to 34.

The four squares in the very center add up to 34.

The diagonal squares all add up to 34.

All opposite squares on the edges add up to 34.

In the magic square, just about every symmetrical pattern of four squares adds up to 34. The theomatic design in the Bible could be likened to a gigantic magic square. The major difference is that instead of the various combinations of words equaling the same number (34), they would come out to the predetermined values.

Perhaps another similar illustration is a crossword puzzle. Instead of each square holding a number, it contains the letter of a word. Just like the magic square, all the letters must intersect perfectly in all directions for a crossword puzzle to work.

In theomatics the numerical values for the words and various phrase segments are arranged in proper order, to enable the designs relative to each spiritual truth to fit and flow together—in all directions. When different words, or combinations thereof, are in juxtaposition (side-by-side), they will add up to the right numerical values, just as the magic square exhibits the right numbers when each number has been properly placed inside the right square.

Let's look at a few examples of how this works.

Light Coming into the World

Here is a simple phrase taken from John 3:19:

And this is the judgment, for light has come into the world, and men loved darkness rather than light.

380	370	1500	537	215	420	450
οτι	το	φως	εληλυθεν	εις	τον	κοσμον
For		Light	has-come	into		the-world

Again, above each word is the appropriate numerical value. The words that are underlined in Greek (το and τον) are articles that "modify" the words immediately after them. They have no translatable meaning.

In this passage each individual word has its own significant numerical value. Take the word "light." It has a theomatic value of 1500. However, with the article (το φως) it has a value of 1870 (1500 + 370 = 1870). Therefore, the word "light" equals both 1500 and 1870. The same thing is true of the word "world" (κοσμον), which equals 450 and 870. The Greek verb "has come" (εληλυθεν) has a value of 537. The preposition "in" (εις) has a value of 215.

Every combination of words in this phrase has various numbers passing through it. When all the words are added together, the entire phrase equals 3872. However, there are other numbers present in this total phrase. Without the two articles, the value of the phrase would be 3082. However, with just the first article, the value would be 3452. With just the second article, the value of the phrase would be 3502.

There are even more combinations when all the possibilities are examined.

What Does This Mean?

Inside this one simple phrase are many highly significant theomatic patterns—all of which relate to the whole. For now, let us examine just one of them.

In both my previous books, there were entire chapters showing how the number 150 had significance relative to the topic of light, lamps, eyes and seeing, and other related concepts. The number 150 (along with 100 and 225) literally saturates most major passages in scripture dealing with these subjects. The pattern and consistency are absolutely mind boggling. I am tempted to present some of the data here, but it may be difficult to put on the brakes.

Examining the above phrase from John 3:19, we find this simple pattern.

FOR	LIGHT	HAS	COME	INTO	WORLD	3452 or	**150** x 23 + 2
	LIGHT	HAS	COME	INTO	WORLD	2702 or	**150** x 18 + 2
FOR	LIGHT	HAS	COME	INTO		3002 or	**150** x 20 + 2
	LIGHT	HAS	COME	INTO		2252 or	**150** x 15 + 2
FOR	LIGHT					2250 or	**150** x 15
	LIGHT					1500 or	**150** x 10
		HAS	COME	INTO		752 or	**150** x 3 + 2
		HAS	COME	INTO	WORLD	1202 or	**150** x 8 + 2
					WORLD	450 or	**150** x 3

In this one phrase of only four words (with one conjunction and two articles), there are nine features that cluster around multiples of the number 150. Just about every possibility worked out to 150. This type of phenomenon is seen repeatedly in numerous passages. *So many multiples of 150 would be impossible without God's flexibility mechanism for the articles and conjunctions.*

The probability or mathematical chance of this phrase containing nine multiples of 150 (or any other number that size) is very unlikely. But that is just the beginning. There are at least a dozen other apparent patterns in this phrase clustering around other large key numbers. These all relate to and specifically cross-reference other theological concepts, topics, themes, and numerical structures from other portions of the Bible.

Just like the magic square, all these numbers come together in *perfect balance* with the biblical theomatic structure and the manner in which the whole relates specifically to this one phrase. I call this concept the *orchestration of theomatics*. Chapter 10 of *Theomatics II* discusses this aspect.

Keeping Things Simple

It would be very easy to engage in a lengthy and complicated discussion intended to show how the whole theomatic structure was put together and how it operates. Hundreds, if not thousands, of examples could be analyzed, along with unbelievable and mind-boggling consistencies. In *Theomatics II*, almost three thousand individual examples are given.

It was mentioned early on that this book was going to be simple. So I do not want to bog down the reader in too much detail. I will be brief and show just a few illustrations. None of this is intended to be scientifically or statistically conclusive. The goal of this chapter is for the reader to simply see *how* the whole thing was intended by God to work. There are no doubt many aspects to all this that have not yet been discovered.

Let's Return to the Example of Agape/Love

All the examples of 93 shown in the previous chapter represent only one piece of the puzzle, in fact, a very small piece. There are a number of other phrase combinations present—the ones that did not work out to a multiple of 93. Again, *every word and phrase present contains values that relate to the overall picture of what each passage represents.*

In the last chapter, we discussed how the most basic spelling of the word "love" (*agape*) equaled 93. Let's look now at all three spellings of this word, each with the appropriate article. This produces a grand total of six numbers in all. In this instance, all of the following appear somewhere in the New Testament.

LOVE 93	LOVE 100
αγαπη	η αγαπη'
LOVE 144	LOVE 500
αγαπην'	την αγαπην'
LOVE 294	LOVE 800
αγαπης'	της αγαπης'

Every one of the above numbers fits into the overall theomatic design of the Bible. We'll discuss that aspect in a second. First, let's analyze each individual number.

With the article the value of agape is 100.

LOVE 100
η αγαπη'

One is the most simple and basic number possible. We saw in chapter 3 how the expression "In the Beginning God" had a value of 1000, or without the zeros, just 1. Everything to do with God in His most simple and singular form is exemplified by the number 1. The fact that the word "love" works out to 1 illustrates that true, genuine love can exist only in one God. As Christians we worship and serve one God.

The number one also brings forth the concept of that which is holy, pure and undiluted. The love of the One God is absolutely pure.

LOVE 500
την αγαπην'

Now another number that I have extensively catalogued is 500. There are a group of passages all related to God being the one and only God, and for some strange reason, the numbers all come out to just 500 (and multiples of 500). The pattern is outstanding. Here, we find that one of the spellings of love also has a value of 500. This again fits into the one and only aspect. (Note: If I took the time to show this pattern and its consistency, all would make perfect sense to the reader.)

The next obvious pattern above is the number 144. This is without question the major number in theomatics dealing with *all* of God's chosen people, the elect, the saints, the Church, the Bride of the Lamb, and so forth. It saturates this topic all through the Bible. Both *Theomatics* and *Theomatics II* had entire chapters that discussed this number 144, which is 12 x 12. The Book of Revelation talks about the "144 thousands," which can only be a *representative* number for all of God's people from all ages, the "great multitude which no man could number" (Rev. 7:9). For that reason we find that the love of God is with His people who belong to Him.

LOVE 144   LOVE OF GOD 144 x 4
αγαπην'   αγαπη θεου'

Two numbers of the six for love remain. One of the most significant numbers associated with the perfection of God's people is 7, and more specifically 14. The square of 7, or 49, is also very important (see *Theomatics II*, pp. 342-344). A whole presentation could be made relative to this pattern.

LOVE 294 (14 x 7 x 3) (7 x 7 x 6 or 49 x 6)
αγαπης'

The last word for love yields 800. This number 8 is unmistakably linked to Jesus, who established the gospel of grace based upon faith. Look at the following examples.

LORD   800
κυριος

JESUS   888
Ιησους

LOVE   800
της αγαπης'

The new order that Jesus established was also based upon resurrection, and He arose on the first day of the week (or eighth day). The number 8 follows 7, which is the Sabbath or seventh day.

THE DAY HE WILL BE RAISED UP   800
Mat. 20:19 ημερα εγερθησεται

Circumcision (or a new life) took place on the eighth day, and there is a whole pattern of 8s surrounding that topic as well.

The word *Sabbath* in Hebrew has a value of 700. Is it any coincidence that the following expressions all come out to 700? It will be difficult for any hard-nosed skeptic (who knows the Bible) to look at the following three expressions and say that the way these numbers work out theomatically is pure coincidence.

THE SABBATH   700
Exo. 16:23 "שבת

MOUNT SINAI   700
Gal. 4:25 Σινα ορος'

THE LAW   700
Eph. 2:15 τον νομον

Mankind could not be saved by the keeping of the law. He could be saved only by faith and that is why the number 8 follows 7 and Sunday follows Saturday or the Sabbath. *Faith superseded the requirement of keeping the law as the means of salvation.* With the old system of law, there was no love. It was do or die. But with faith, there is love. That is why the following words have values of 8.

FAITH   800
πιστις

LOVE   800
της αγαπης'

JESUS   888
Ιησους

Perfection and the Number 7

Let's examine just a few examples and see more concerning the divine logic behind this phenomenon and how it works. Look at this example from Romans 8:39.

Nor height nor depth nor any other creature will be able to separate us from the love of God in Christ Jesus our Lord.

Earlier it was shown how the words "love of God" worked out to 93 x 15, or 1395. In that example, the word "love" was spelled as *agape* (αγαπη) and had a value of just 93. However, in the above verse in Romans, the expression "love of God" works out to 777. Here *agape* is spelled *agapes* (αγαπης) with an ς (or sigma) on the end. This gives it a value of 293.

LOVE OF GOD 777
Rom. 8:39 αγαπης θεου

We learn from this example that it would have been impossible for God to achieve the 777 result unless the word "love" had a value of 293. The word "[of] God" has a value of 484, and when that number is added to 293, the total is 777. This is the reason for multiple spellings. If love or God could be spelled only one way (as in English), this rigidity would prevent theomatics from working. That is the reason for all the different spellings; it gives the entire structure the necessary flexibility.

In Luke 11:42 we find that the expression "love of God" appears with the third spelling, *agapen* (αγαπην). Watch what happens now.

LOVE OF GOD 700 x 2
Luke 11:42 αγαπην του θεου'''

Even though God's love is based upon faith and love and the number 8, it is also founded upon God's law and perfection. His law is perfect, and His love is also perfect.

The law of the Lord is perfect, converting the soul.

PERFECT 490 (70 x 7)
Psa. 19:7, Gen. 17:1 תמים

It is amazing that the Hebrew word for "perfect" or complete perfection, is 490 or 70 x 7—the square of the number 7. Look at the two features of 70 in the following.

There is no fear in love; but perfect love casteth out fear: because fear hath torment. He that feareth is not perfected in love.

PERFECTED IN 70 x 26
1 John 4:18 τετελειωται εν'

PERFECT 70 x 5
1 John 4:18 τελεια'

I could show at least a dozen examples of how all this ties into the number 7 and the complete perfection of God's love.

Some people may find fascinating the fact that the following expression works out to 666. The number 666 has been associated with

Satan (see Rev. 13:18). However, it is a prevalent number in theomatics to do more with this present world system (p. 497, *Theomatics II*).

LOVE OF GOD 777
Rom. 8:39 αγαπης θεου

WRATH OF GOD 666
Col. 3:6 οργη θεου'

Here again, in order for "wrath of God" to work out to 666, the word "wrath" had to have a value of 182'; coupled with "of God," which is 484, total 666.

Let's Analyze This

As we look into this whole phenomenon, we find the magic square principle at work. Each word was designed with its own specific numeric value. That value has a specific or general meaning attached to it. Most importantly, the value of each word was designed to ultimately fit into the proper place in the text, next to other words with their own predesigned values.

The more one examines the complexity of all the words and phrases, the more doubtful it becomes that there are computers, at least on this earth, capable of working out the mathematical intricacies of putting grammar, words, and adjacent words together, *along with spiritual truth*, to make everything work out perfectly numerically and theologically.

What is even more awesome is that we begin to see how the entire Old Testament, which was written in Hebrew, fits together with the New Testament, which was written in Greek. Theomatically, the Bible is one contiguous masterpiece, even though the two halves are in completely different languages and cultures. That fact will be demonstrated shortly.

All of this is based upon some form of supernatural knowledge— mathematical laws and principles that are totally new and foreign to this earth—that exists in the mind of the heavenly Father. Every event, every person born, every detail necessary to put the Bible together, was preplanned and prearranged by God in eternity past, carried out in history and time, and then numerically encoded in ways that the mind of man is just now beginning to see and fathom.

Wonderfully, God is now going to open up at least a tiny portion and share it with us. No doubt this is something that will occupy a great deal of our time in eternity to come, as we learn about the heart and mind of our heavenly Father and the eternal principles according to which Jehovah, or Jesus, created the material universe and all other spiritual dimensions.

Back to Our Example

Let's look further at the example in Romans 8:39.

Nor height nor depth nor any other creature will be able to separate us from the love of God in Christ Jesus our Lord.

It was shown above that the expression "love of God" from this verse totaled 777, the number of perfection. But look what happens when the word "in" is attached to this phrase—pointing to the fact that the love of God is *in* Jesus.

THE LOVE OF GOD IN   800 x 2
Rom. 8:39 αγαπης του θεου εν"

LOVE   800
της αγαπης'

There are two multiples of 800 in just three words. How is this possible? The first phrase above does not have the article preceding the word "love" or *agapes*. That is what is necessary for the entire three-word phrase to work out to 800 x 2. But just the word "love" by itself *did* require the article in order for *it* to work out to 800.

Mathematically, it would be very difficult to do the above without the mechanism of the flexibility of the article (and still show all the other mathematical patterns that must be present). The amazing thing about the articles is that they have absolutely no translatable meaning, and there is no Greek scholar on the face of the earth who can provide any consistent explanation as to why the article appears in some places and not in others (See appendix C, pp. 619-624, *Theomatics II*). Grammatically speaking, it is used arbitrarily and at random. But now, with theomatics, we learn that its intended purpose was not grammatical; it was placed in the text so that theomatics would work.

The Number of Power

We are now going to look at some other short portions of Romans 8:39, and see how they fit together.

There are two numbers that seem to saturate almost every passage with the concept of light, power, authority, action, force, ability, etc. as its theme. The primary numbers that appear on a regular basis are 150 (as we saw earlier) and 225, which is 15 x 15. Multiples of 100 are also prevalent. Again, in both *Theomatics* and *Theomatics II*, there are entire chapters that discuss 150 and 225. Anyone who is at all familiar with theomatics will immediately recognize the significance of these two numbers that seem to always crop up.

They unmistakably appear as well in this passage at the juncture where *force* and *action* are present.

> Nor height nor depth nor any other creature will be able to separate us from the love of God in Christ Jesus our Lord.

WILL BE ABLE TO SEPARATE   225 x 12   FROM   150
Rom. 8:39 δυνησεται χωρισαι'   απο'

The significant fact is that this pattern is present *along with all the other patterns* that must also mesh together within these few words.

The Patterns of Separation

In my research, I have observed numerous instances in which the number 2 speaks of division, separation, or tearing something apart. There is a whole structure of 200 and 222 surrounding this concept. It also appears with the topic of war.

> Nor height nor depth nor any other creature will be able to separate us from the love of God in Christ Jesus our Lord.

WILL BE ABLE TO SEPARATE US FROM 2220
THE LOVE OF GOD IN
Rom. 8:39 δυνησεται ημας χωρισαι απο της αγαπης θεου εν'

FROM THE LOVE OF GOD IN 222 x 9
απο της αγαπης θεου της εν'

FROM THE LOVE OF GOD IN 2000
απο της αγαπης θεου της εν'

FROM THE LOVE 222 x 2
απο αγαπης'

All the above phrases contain the word "from." This is the key word that refers to the tearing-apart concept, and that is why it is included in the portions that work out to 222 and 2000.

The 86/172 Pattern

The Greek word "separate" (χωρισαι) by itself has a value of 1720. What could this number possibly represent? Breaking it down to its largest prime number, it factors out to 430 x 4. It is also 860 x 2.

SEPARATE 1720
Rom. 8:39 χωρισαι'

A quick spot-check brought up one other reference in this same chapter that speaks of being separated from the love of God.

> Who shall separate us from the love of Christ? Shall tribulation, or distress, or persecution, or famine, or nakedness, or peril, or sword?

WHO SHALL SEPARATE 172 x 13
Rom. 8:35 τις χωρισει'

Here, the word "separate" is spelled slightly different in Greek. In Romans 8:39, it had a value of 1720. In verse 35 it equals 1725—not a multiple of 172. But when 1725 is linked to the word "who shall," which has a value of 510, guess what? The result is 2236, or 172 x 13.

This Is Yet Another Major Design

In practically every major reference examined from the entire Bible, that involved God separating, the pattern of 86/172 literally exploded—an absolutely wondrous design. My plan was to show a few examples and then conclude this chapter.

When I tried to put it into a few short examples, it got so long that before I knew it, I had written an entire chapter.

Conclusion

Everything in theomatics operates on a profound system of *rules of association*. At this point we could look at numerous other patterns and topics within this one verse of Romans. The magic square for each passage is many times bigger than what we have discussed here. Enough has been shown to simply illustrate the most basic manner in which everything fits and works. A great deal of time would be required before "everything" that is present in this passage would be both deciphered and assimilated.

6 Moses Parts the Red Sea

And the Waters Are Separated

Now is the time to begin looking at a truly powerful design in theomatics. What has been shown so far could at best be described as mediocre. The major fact to bear in mind in examining these various patterns is that the ones presented are just a "random" sampling out of literally thousands of design structures that exist in both the Old and New Testaments. As it was stated earlier, we have barely scratched the surface. At a slow yet progressive pace, we are learning more and more concerning the logic of how the Divine mind works in putting all of this together. Again, it will require a highly inductive process of making keen observations and drawing conclusions based upon those observations.

Brace yourself to think new thoughts and examine a form of logic that is thoroughly "out of this world." Even though God used historical people and events to compose the Bible, the total scenario was simply the acting out of a Divine plan—conceived in eternity past with the intended purpose of ultimately bringing forth eternal and absolute truth. Those who seek to understand God's revelation based strictly upon the rules of grammar and the facts of history will miss the *substance* of what the Word of God is *ultimately* all about.

The Hebrew Old Testament

You will now see the exciting aspect of theomatics. The Bible was written not in just one language but in two completely different languages. Yet the God who inspired and wrote the one is the same God who inspired and wrote the other, and He also placed the same exact theomatic structure in the Hebrew that He did in the Greek. The same patterns or theomatic structures will exhibit themselves throughout both testaments. It is one contiguous book numerically.

In fact, it is in the original Hebrew that the real keys to the theomatic structure lie. When Bible scholars interpret the Bible, they use what is known as "the law of first mention." It means that one should look many times at the first mention of something in the Bible in order to find the key to its meaning. That principle applies to theomatics. The pattern that follows is a case in point.

The Number 172

The last chapter was concluded by showing that the Greek word for "separate" (*chorizo*), from Romans 8:39, had a value of 1720, and the expression "who shall separate," was 172 x 13.

SEPARATE 1720
Rom. 8:39 χωρισαι'

WHO SHALL SEPARATE 172 x 13
Rom. 8:35 τις χωρισει'

The counterpart word in Hebrew, used numerous times, has a similar value.

SEPARATED 172
Psa. 78:13 בקע

This is Yet Another Major Design

In practically every major reference that I examined, the pattern of 86/172 literally exploded—an absolutely stupendous happening.

The primary word for *God* in Hebrew (Elohym) has a numerical value of 86. There is a whole structure around the Heavenly Father based upon 43 and 86. The number 43 is a prime number, and 43 x 2 = 86. Throughout Scripture, many times, God separates or divides. In Genesis, God separated or divided the light from the darkness. He separated or divided the waters from the waters. When the Israelites crossed the red sea, the waters were separated and divided. In the Gospels, Jesus separates the sheep from the goats. The wheat and tares were separated from each other. Christians are commanded by God to separate themselves from sinners. Everywhere you look, the number 86 or 172 (86 x 2) saturates the key words and short explicit phrases concerning separation.

And God said, Let there be an expanse between the waters.

BETWEEN THE WATERS 172 x 3
Gen. 1:6 בתוד מים"

BETWEEN 86 x 5
בתוד"

Let's look at the complete verse.

And God said, 'Let there be an expanse between the waters, and let it be to separate between waters from waters.

TO SEPARATE BETWEEN 172
Gen. 1:5 יהי מבדיל בין'

SEPARATE 86
מבדיל

This pattern is also found in passages that talk about God separating light from darkness and night from day.

God set them in the expanse of heaven to give light upon the earth, to govern the day and night, and to separate the light from the darkness.

AND TO SEPARATE THE LIGHT FROM 86 x 5
Gen. 1:18 ולהבדיל בין האור ובין'

AND TO SEPARATE 86
ולהבדיל'

THE LIGHT FROM 172 x 2
בין האור ובין"

We are now establishing a consistency that is mind-boggling. The statistical probability of these short explicit phrases containing all these multiples of 86 would be ridiculously remote if the numbers were random (which of course they are not). We'll consider this possibility in chapter 11 on the scientific method.

From now on, virtually every passage we look at will be saturated with 86 and 172. When a person unlocks a pattern in the Hebrew Old Testament by finding the right "key number to the concept," the consistency is overwhelming.

Exodus gives the well-known account of how Israel crossed the Red Sea after being chased by Pharaoh's army. As the Israelites stood by the shore, crying out to God for help, the Lord told Moses to lift his hand over the sea. When he did, God split and separated the waters, and the Israelites walked through the middle of the sea on dry ground. The pursuing Egyptians subsequently drowned when the waters came crashing back over them.

Every passage in the entire Bible that speaks of this miracle of the parting of the waters was carefully examined. Our concern here is to examine the most explicit words possible describing the *actual separation* of the waters.

And Moses stretched his hand over the sea, and all that night Jehovah drove back the sea with a strong East wind, and turned the sea into dry land.

DROVE BACK THE SEA 172 x 3
Exo. 14:21 'יולד את ים

TURNED THE SEA INTO 86 x 5
ישם ים ל

Now let's look at the complete verse.

And all that night Jehovah drove back the sea with a strong East wind, and turned the sea into dry land. And were divided the waters.

Here is the Hebrew word for "divided," or "separated."

DIVIDED 172
Exo. 14:21 בקע
Compare Psa. 78:13

And the waters were to them a wall on their right and left.

THE WATERS WERE TO THEM 172
Exo. 14:22 "המים להם

TO THEM A WALL ON THEIR RIGHT AND LEFT 86 x 9
'להם חמה מימינם ומשמאלם

The nine English words above come from four Hebrew words.
Now look what happens when Moses again stretches forth his hand. The waters that were separated (172) return to their place (172)—the same numbers are still present in the text.

And so Moses stretched forth his hand over the sea, and the sea went back to its place at daybreak.

THE SEA WENT BACK TO ITS PLACE 860 (172 x 5)
Exo. 14:27 'ישב ים לאיתנו

And the waters flowed back and covered the chariots and horsemen; the entire army of Pharaoh... not one of them survived... And Israel saw the Egyptians lying dead on the shore.

THE WATERS FLOWED BACK AND COVERED 172 x 3
Exo. 14:28 'ישבו המים ויכסו

And the ensuing song of praise that the children of Israel sang is one example among many of how this pattern runs all through the account.

I will sing to the Lord, for He is highly exalted. The horse and its rider he has hurled into the sea. The Lord is my strength and my song.

STRENGTH 86
Exo. 15:2 עזי

It was through God's strength that the waters were parted. The result of the waters parting was Pharaoh's army being drowned in the sea. This next example is very significant.

> The Lord is a man of war. The Lord is His name. Pharaoh's chariots and his army He has hurled into the sea. The best of Pharaoh's officers are drowned in the Red Sea.

DROWNED 86
Exo. 15:4 טבעו

Here is the next specific mention of the waters being separated.

> In greatness of your majesty you threw down the ones opposing you. You unleashed your burning anger; it consumed them like stubble. At the blast of your nostrils they piled up the waters, they stood firm like the raging wall.

The following twelve English words come from only six Hebrew words that explicitly and completely describe the separation of the waters.

THEY PILED UP THE WATERS, THEY STOOD 860 (172 x 5)
FIRM LIKE THE RAGING WALL
Exo. 15:8 נערמו מים נצבו כמו נד נזלים'

LIKE THE RAGING WALL 86 x 3
כמו נד נזלים '

The Hebrew word "piled up" has a value of 366 or 122 x 3. There is a whole structure of 122 in theomatics relative to God collecting and gathering waters—all based on the number 122.

> At the blast of your nostrils they piled up the waters, they stood firm like the raging wall. The deep waters congealed in the heart of the sea.

THE DEEP WATERS CONGEALED 172 x 6
קפאו תהמת

The above feature is powerful. The Hebrew word for "congealed" means "to shrink and thicken." That is exactly what happened when God separated the waters. The word "congealed" is another direct term expressing the separation of the waters that took place.

Look at this next explicit example of Jehovah splitting the waters.

> When Pharaoh's horses, chariots and horsemen went into the sea, the Lord brought the waters of the sea back over them.

THE LORD BROUGHT   172 x 2
Exo. 15:19   וישב יהוה

The following will need no explanation.

> The Lord brought the waters of the sea back over them. But the children of Israel walked on dry ground through the middle of the sea.

WALKED ON DRY GROUND THROUGH   860 (172 x 5)
THE MIDDLE OF THE SEA
Exo. 15:19   "הלכו ביבשה בתוד ים

THROUGH THE MIDDLE   86 x 5
"בתוד

It was in the *middle* of the sea that the waters were split and separated.

The story continues as Moses led the children of Israel away from the Red Sea and into the wilderness. Let us examine one more pattern from Exodus before continuing. Here is the previous verse 11.

> But you blew with your breath and the sea covered them. They sank like lead in the mighty waters. Who is like you among the Gods, Oh Lord? Who is like you—majestic in holiness, awesome in glory, working wonders?

LIKE YOU 86	**GOD 86**
Exo. 15:11 כמכה'	אלהים

After all we have seen, is the following a surprise? It was God's power, through Moses, that enabled the miracle of the parting of the waters to take place.

> And when the people saw the great power the Lord displayed... they feared the Lord and put their trust in Him and in Moses His servant.

MOSES HIS SERVANT   86 x 5
Exo. 14:31   במשה עבדו'

MOSES   172 x 2
משה'

It was not the arm of Moses that caused the waters of the Red Sea to part; it was God's arm manifested through Moses. Look at the following from the song the children of Israel sang after the victory. The numerical value is the same as that for Moses—172 x 2.

All the inhabitants of Canaan shall melt away. Fear and dread shall fall upon them; by the power of your arm they shall be as still as a stone; till thy people pass over, O LORD.

BY THE POWER OF YOUR ARM 172 x 2
Exo. 15:16 "בגדל זרועד

References in Other Parts of the Bible

There are a few references in the Old Testament to the parting of the Red Sea. After the spies returned to Joshua from their exploration of the promised land, this is what had been told to them by one of the heathen residents of Palestine.

I know that the Lord has given this land to you and a great fear of you has fallen on us, so that all who live in this country are melting in fear because of you. We heard how the Lord He dried up the waters of the Red Sea for you when you came out of Egypt.

Look at the value of the following:

WE HEARD HOW HE DRIED UP 1720
Jos. 2:10 כי שמענו את אשר הוביש

Nothing could be more clear and straightforward than the following. The verse actually reads in Hebrew, "We heard how He dried up the Lord the waters of the Sea Red."

HOW HE DRIED UP THE WATERS OF THE SEA 1720
את אשר וביש את מי ים

The words in Hebrew, "He dried up the Lord" actually mean "the Lord dried up the waters." The Lord dried them up by separating them. The following feature has the same value as the words "by the power of your arm," from Exodus 15:16.

THE LORD DRIED UP 172 x 2
וביש יהוה

DRIED UP THE WATERS 86 x 9   WATERS 90
וביש את המי   מים

Psalms 78:23 contains the most explicit feature.

He divided the sea and let them through it, and made stand the waters like a wall.

HE DIVIDED 172
Psa. 78:13 בקע

MADE STAND THE WATERS LIKE 86 x 3
יצב מים כמו

What is interesting about the example above is that the value is 86 x 3. Look at the following examples, also from Psalms, where both features are 86 x 3 as well.

To the one dividing the Sea Red into halves. His love endures forever.

DIVIDING THE SEA 86 x 3
Psa. 136:13 "גזר ים

HALVES 86 x 3
"גזרים

Here is yet another verse in Psalms.

You split open the sea by your power; you broke the heads of the monsters in the waters.

YOU SPLIT OPEN 86 x 3 x 5
Psa. 74:13 "אתה פוררת

SPLIT OPEN THE SEA BY YOUR POWER 172 x 6
"'פוררת בעזך ים

Our last example again comes from Psalms. The Lord rebuked the sea and that is what caused it to split apart.

And He rebuked the Sea Red and it dried up, and He led them through the depths as the desert.

AND HE REBUKED THE SEA 172 x 2
Psa. 106:9 "ויגער בים

Israel Crosses the Jordan River

The type of event that took place at the Red Sea did not happen just once. God performed the miracle a second time when the children of Israel crossed over the Jordan River to go into the Promised Land.

In this story, God commanded the priests, who were bearing the ark of the covenant to step foot in the river. At that moment, God split the waters and the river dried up.

We are now going to look at the specific Hebrew words that describe God splitting the river in the middle.

For the Lord your God dried up the waters of Jordan from before you until you had crossed over.

DRIED UP THE WATERS OF JORDAN   172 x 6
Josh. 4:23   וביש את מי ירדן'

Of course, as we saw earlier in this chapter, the words "dried up the waters" (also in the above) equal 86 x 9.

> "Dried up the waters of Jordan from before you until you had crossed over, just as Jehovah your God did to the Red Sea, when He dried it up from before us until we had crossed over."

DID TO THE RED SEA   86 x 7
עשה לים סוף'

WHEN HE DRIED IT UP FROM   860 (172 x 5)
אשר וביש מ'

Now look at the most specific words possible for describing separating the waters of the Jordan River.

> And as soon as the priests who carry the ark of the Lord, the Lord of all the earth, set foot in the waters of Jordan, the waters of the Jordan will be cut off the waters the ones flowing from above will stand in a heap.

The Hebrew word meaning "will be cut off," could have been translated "will be separated." When the waters were cut off, they divided themselves.

WILL BE CUT OFF THE WATERS   86 x 9
Josh. 3:13   "יכרתון מים

WILL BE CUT OFF   172 x 4
"יכרתון

The following translation is equal to five words in Hebrew.

THE ONES FLOWING FROM ABOVE WILL   172 x 4
STAND IN A HEAP
"הירדים מלמעלה ויעמדו נד אחד

STAND IN A HEAP   172
עמדו נד

There are other less significant phrases—all multiples of 86—that could be shown. Here is one more.

> Now the priests who carried the ark stood in the middle of the Jordan until everything the Lord had commanded Joshua was done by the people, just as Moses had directed Joshua.

STOOD IN THE MIDDLE OF JORDAN   860 (172 x 5)

Josh. 4:10 עמדים בתוך הירדן'

IN THE MIDDLE   86 x 5

בתוך "

Elijah Separates the Waters

There is one other occasion in the Old Testament where the waters are divided. The story occurs when Elijah crosses the Jordan River just before he was taken to heaven in a whirlwind.

> Elijah took his cloak, rolled it and struck the waters and they divided to here and to there.

ROLLED IT AND STRUCK THE WATERS AND   860 (172 x 5)
THEY DIVIDED TO HERE AND TO THERE

2 Kings 2:8 יגלם ויכה את מים ויחצו הנה והנה'

The above long phrase is equal to six words in Hebrew. Here is the most distinct feature possible, two Hebrew words.

THEY DIVIDED TO HERE   172

יחצו הנה"

The words "struck the waters" did not add up to 172. But in another part of the Bible, in Exodus, we see the pattern emerge. Only this time, instead of the waters being divided, they are changed.

> And Moses and Aaron did so, as the LORD commanded; and he lifted up the rod, and struck the waters in the river... and turned all the waters that were in the river to blood.

AND STRUCK THE WATERS   172 x 6

Exo. 7:20 ויך את המים אשר'

AND TURNED ALL   172

יהפכו כל'

The Pattern in the New Testament

Now our attention turns to the Greek New Testament. There are three references in the New Testament to the crossing of the Red Sea, none of which specifically refer to or mention God separating the waters. The book of Acts contains this phrase concerning Moses. Here is a good illustration of the most fundamental usage of the number 86 in theomatics.

This man led them out, having performed wonders and signs in Egypt and in the Red Sea.

AND IN   86
Act. 7:36 και εν

IN THE RED SEA   86 x 13
εν ερυθρα θαλασση'

The name *Moses* was 172 x 2, or 344 in Hebrew. Guess what the numerical value is for the name *Moses* in Greek?

MOSES   1720 (344 x 5)
Act. 7:37 ο Μωυσης"

The second passage that contains a possible hit is in 1 Corinthians.

And I want you to know, brethren, that our fathers were all under the cloud, and all through the sea passed.

ALL THROUGH THE SEA   86 x 3 x 7
1 Cor. 10:1 παντες δια της θαλασσης"

The above is not only a multiple of 86 x 3, but also of 7. The number 7 is universally recognized by Bible scholars as "the number of completion" in Scripture. This secondary factor of 7, I have noticed, usually appears when the text is referring to a complete number of something. The example above describes *all* who went through the sea.

Back to the Theme of Separation

This design of 86/172 will literally leap out in the New Testament when short, specific phrases concerning God separating anything and everything are looked at. Here we are going to examine mostly the 172 hits. Virtually everything came up 172 with just a few working out to 86 (or odd multiples).

There are at least six specific instances where Divine separation is mentioned.

- The sheep are separated from the goats.
- The wheat is separated from the tares.
- The wheat and chaff are separated.
- The good and bad fish are separated on the shore.
- Satan's kingdom falls because it is a house divided.
- The sword divides and separates.
- The righteous are separated from sinners.
- Jesus is separated from His Heavenly Father on the cross, and his garments are divided. The veil of the temple is torn in half.

The Sheep Are Separated from the Goats

The judgment that takes place before the tribunal of Christ is in a well-known passage in Matthew.

> And will be assembled before him all the nations, and He will separate them from one another as the shepherd separates the sheep from the goats.

FROM ONE ANOTHER   172 x 12
Mat. 25:32 απ αλληλων"

The last part of the above verse states that "He will separate them from one another as the shepherd separates the sheep from the goats."

THE SHEPHERD SEPARATES   172 x 12
ο ποιμην αφοριζει'

The one portion of this passage that specifically speaks of the separation, between the sheep and the goats, is verse 41.

> Then shall he say also unto them on the left hand, Depart from me, ye cursed, into everlasting fire, prepared for the devil and his angels.

The word "me" from the phrase "depart from me," is in the genetive case in Greek and could have been translated "Depart from of me." Here it indicates the action of separation *away* from Christ. This is just one example of how the 172 design is imbedded in the design structure of the words.

OF ME   172 x 3
Mat. 25:41 εμου'

The Wheat Separated from the Tares

The pattern of 172 in this passage is astounding.

> Another parable put he forth unto them, saying, The kingdom of heaven is likened unto a man which sowed good seed in his field: But while men slept, his enemy came and sowed tares among the wheat, and went his way. But when the blade was sprung up, and brought forth fruit, then appeared also the tares.

TARES   86
ζιζανια

"Tares" will fit this pattern because the tares themselves will be separated *away* from the wheat.

Here now is the first mention of the separation process.

So the servants of the householder came and said unto him, Sir, didst not thou sow good seed in thy field? from whence then hath it tares? He said unto them, An enemy hath done this. The servants said unto him, Wilt thou then that we go away and collect them?

The last phrase in Greek reads, "Wilt thou therefore that going away we collect them."

WILT THOU WE COLLECT THEM 172 x 15
Mat. 13:28 θελεις συλλεξωμεν αυτα'

COLLECT THEM 86 x 27
Mat. 13:28 συλλεξωμεν αυτα

But he said, Nay; lest while ye are collecting the tares, ye root up also the wheat with them.

COLLECTING THE TARES 172 x 8
συλλεγοντες ζιζανια"'

Let both grow together until the harvest: and in the time of harvest I will say to the reapers, Collect ye first the tares.

AND IN 86
και εν

THE TIME OF HARVEST I WILL SAY 1720 x 2
καιρω του θερισμου ερω

At the harvest the wheat and tares were to be collected, bound, and separated.

Collect ye first the tares, and bind them in bundles to burn them: but gather the wheat into my barn.

COLLECT YE 172 x 6
συλλεξατε'

BIND 172 x 3
δησατε"

Now this story abruptly ends, but later in the chapter, the disciples come to Jesus and ask Him to explain the parable of the tares of the field.

He answered and said unto them, He that soweth the good seed is the Son of man; The field is the world; the good seed are the children of the kingdom; but the tares are the children of the wicked one; The enemy that sowed them is the devil; the harvest is the end of the world; and the reapers are the angels. As therefore the tares are collected and burned in the fire; thus it will be at the completion of the age.

THEREFORE THE TARES ARE COLLECTED 172 x 11
Mat. 13:40 ουν συλλεγεται τα ζιζανια'

As therefore the tares are collected and burned in the fire; thus it will be at the completion of the age.

THUS IT WILL BE AT COMPLETION OF AGE 172 x 26
Mat. 13:40 ουτως εσται εν συντελεια αιωνος'

IT WILL BE 172 x 3
εσται

Going back to the above verse, look at these words.

THE HARVEST IS THE COMPLETION 86 x 19
θερισμος συντειλεια'

The Son of man shall send forth his angels, and they shall collect out of his kingdom all the things leading to sin, and them which do iniquity.

COLLECT ALL THE THINGS LEADING TO SIN 86 x 29
Mat. 13:41 συλλεξουσιν παντα τα σκανδαλα'

ALL 86 x 5
παντα"

This happens with the two most specific Greek words.

COLLECT THE THINGS LEADING TO SIN 172 x 12
συλλεξουσιν τα σκανδαλα'

And shall cast them into a furnace of fire: there shall be wailing and gnashing of teeth. Then shall the righteous shine forth as the sun in the kingdom of their Father. Who hath ears to hear, let him hear.

CAST THEM INTO A FURNACE OF FIRE 1720 x 2
Mat. 13:42 βαλουσιν αυτους εις καμινον πυρος

One other passage must be shown as it relates to this theme. It occurs in Revelation.

And another angel came out from the altar, which had power over fire; and cried with a loud cry to him that had the sharp sickle, saying, Thrust in thy sharp sickle, and gather the clusters of the vine of the earth; for her grapes are fully ripe.

AND GATHER THE CLUSTERS   172 x 13
Rev. 14:18 και τρυγησον βοτρυσας'

And the angel thrust in his sickle into the earth, and gathered the vine of the earth, and cast it into the great winepress of the wrath of God.

AND GATHERED THE VINE   172 x 8
και ετρυγησεν αμπελον"

Let's jump back to verse sixteen from this story.

And he that sat on the cloud thrust in his sickle on the earth; and the earth was reaped.

WAS REAPED   172 x 2
Rev. 14: 16 εθερισθη"

From the above passage in Revelation, I have shown a fraction of the 86/172 pattern that is present.

The Wheat and Chaff Are Separated.

The third occurrence of God separating occurs in the passage where Jesus talks about separating the wheat from the chaff.

His fan is in His hand, and He will thoroughly cleanse His threshing floor and gather His wheat into the barn, but the chaff He will consume with fire unquenchable.

THOROUGHLY CLEANSE   172
Mat. 3:12 διακαθαριει'

CONSUME WITH FIRE   172 x 9
Mat. 3:12 κατακαυσει πυρι

Absolutely nothing could be more significant than the fact that the Greek verb meaning to "thoroughly cleanse" adds up to 172. It is on the threshing floor that the wheat and chaff were separated from each other.

I did a quick spot-check to see if there were any other verses in the New Testament referring to wheat being divided or separated. This passage where Jesus speaks to Simon Peter, immediately drew my attention.

And the Lord said, Simon, Simon, behold, Satan hath desired to have you, that he may sift you as wheat.

SIFT YOU   172 x 11
Luke 22:31 υμας του σινιασαι'

The Good and Bad Fish Are Separated on the Shore

Wheat and chaff are separated on the threshing floor. There is another surface place where something else is divided—the seashore.

> Again, the kingdom of heaven is like a net cast into the sea and of every kind gathering; when it was full, men drew it onto the shore, and sat down and sorted the good into vessels but cast out the bad.

ONTO THE SHORE   172 x 3
Mat. 13:48 επι τον αιγιαλον"

SHORE   172
αιγιαλον'"

And just like the tares, it is the bad fish that are separated and thrown away.

CAST OUT THE BAD   172 x 9
τα σαπρα εξω

> Thus it will be at the completion of the age. The angels will go forth and will separate the evil men from the midst of the righteous.

AND WILL SEPARATE THE EVIL MEN   172 x 24
FROM THE MIDST
Mat. 13:49 και αφοριουσιν τους πονηρους εκ μεσου"

EVIL MEN FROM THE MIDST   1720
πονηρους εκ μεσου"

Satan's Kingdom Falls Because It Is a House Divided

In the Gospels Jesus spoke of the fall of Satan's kingdom and how this would happen if Satan was divided. He likened it to a house divided against itself.

> Every kingdom against itself divided cannot stand, and a house against a house falls.

EVERY KINGDOM AGAINST ITSELF DIVIDED   172 x 14
Luke 11:17 πασα βασιλεια εφ εαυτην διαμερισθεισα'"

HOUSE AGAINST A HOUSE   172 x 4
Luke 11:18 οικος επι οικον'"

Every kingdom divided against itself is brought to desolation; and every city or a house divided against itself shall not stand.

A HOUSE DIVIDED 172 x 4
Mat. 12:25 οικια μερισθεισα'''

If Satan also be divided against himself, how shall his kingdom stand?

DIVIDED AGAINST HIMSELF 1720
Luke 11:18 εφ εαυτον διεμερισθη"

The Sword that Divides

Probably the most famous verse in the New Testament about division is this one.

For the word of God is living, and powerful, and sharper than any two-edged sword, piercing even to the dividing asunder of soul and spirit, and of the joints and marrow, and is a discerner of the thoughts and intents of the heart.

This passage contains numerous 86s in phrases describing the Word of God and dividing asunder. Here is the spectacular example: the sword that divides.

THE TWO-EDGED SWORD 172 x 9
Heb. 4:12 μαχαιραν διστομον'

The passage also states, "For the Word of God is living." Its value is the same as that of the two edged sword.

FOR THE WORD OF GOD 172 x 9
ο γαρ λογος θεου'

LIVING 860 (172 x 5)
Ζων'''

And he had in his right hand seven stars: and out of his mouth proceeds a sharp two-edged sword.

PROCEEDS A SHARP TWO-EDGED 172 x 11
Rev. 1:16 διστομος οξεια εκπορευομενη'

Repent; or else I will come unto thee quickly, and will fight against them with the sword of my mouth.

THE SWORD 172 x 6
Rev. 2:16 τη ρομφαια"

And there went out another horse that was red: and power was given to him that sat thereon to take peace from the earth, and that they should kill one another: and there was given unto him a great sword.

GREAT 86
Rev. 6:4 μεγαλη'

And out of his mouth proceeds a sword sharp, that with it he should smite the nations.

PROCEEDS A SWORD 1720
Rev. 19:15 εκπορευεται ρομφαια"

I was ready to conclude this portion when the thought occurred to me, What about the Old Testament? Here is the first mention of a sword in the Bible, in only three words in Hebrew. The purpose of this flaming sword was to separate Adam and Eve from having access to the tree of life.

So he drove out the man; and he placed at the east of the garden of Eden Cherubims, and a flaming sword flashing all around, to keep the way of the tree of life.

A FLAMING SWORD FLASHING ALL AROUND 172 x 7
Gen. 3:24 להט החרב מתהפכת

THE FLAMING SWORD 86 x 3
להט החרב '

General References
A Greek concordance shows a total of six words used in the New Testament to express *separation* or *division*. Most of these were used only once or twice. Two of the most common were *merizo* (μεριζω) and *diamerizo* (διαμεριζω). Every possibility in the New Testament was carefully examined, and almost every one contained a 172. Let's look at the majority of these.

The following comes from the well-known story of the prodigal son.

And the younger of them said to his father, Father, give me the portion of goods that falleth to me. And he divided unto them his living.

AND HE DIVIDED 172 x 2
Luke 15:12 ο δε διειλες'

In the Book of Acts, the early Christians also did some dividing.

And sold their possessions and goods, and divided them to all men, as every man had need.

AND DIVIDED THEM   172 x 6
Act. 2:45 και διεμεριζον αυτα"

The word *divide,* of course, is a synonym for separate, the verb form. Here is yet another spelling of *separate*, the verb form. Earlier it was shown in Romans that "separate" had a value of 1720.

Therefore come out from the midst of them and be ye separate, saith the Lord.

BE YE SEPARATE   172 x 7
2 Cor. 6:17 αφορισθητε'

As our High Priest and example, Jesus was also separated from sinners.

For it was fitting that we should have such a High Priest, holy, blameless, undefiled, separated from sinners, exalted above the heavens.

UNDEFILED, SEPARATED FROM   172 x 17
Heb. 7:26 αμιαντος κεχωρισμενος απο'

In the above passage, Christ is separated from sinners. Is the following therefore any surprise? Sin is the one thing that separates man from God.

SIN   860 (172 x 5)
John 1:29 την αμαρτιαν'

Let's examine three specific references to God Himself dividing.

But we will not boast of things without our measure, but according to the rule which God divided to us in measure.

GOD DIVIDED TO US IN MEASURE   1720
2 Cor. 10:13 εμερισεν ημιν θεος μετρου"

This next example is probably the most distinct in the entire Bible.

For I say, through the grace given unto me, to every man that is among you, not to think of himself more highly than he ought to think; but to think soberly, according as God divided to every man the measure of faith.

AS GOD DIVIDED   1720
(mt) Rom. 12:3 ως ο θεος εμερισε'

Only to each as divided the Lord, to each as God has called, so let him walk.

TO EACH AS DIVIDED THE LORD   172 x 21
(mt) 1 Cor. 7:17 εκαστω ως εμερισεν ο κυριος'

On the day of Pentecost fire came down from heaven and divided itself into individual "tongues of fire."

Appeared to them being divided tongues as of fire.

APPEARED TO THEM BEING   1720 x 3
DIVIDED TONGUES AS
Act. 2:3 ωφθησαν αυτοις διαμεριζομεναι γλωσσαι ωσει'

It is interesting to observe the various manners in which the 172 pattern manifests itself. The following is a case in point.

And he took the cup, and gave thanks, and said, Take this, and divide it among yourselves.

YOURSELVES   172 x 8
Luke 22:17 εαυτους

What was it that the disciples were to "take" and "divide" among themselves?

TAKE   172 x 2   THE CUP   172 x 4
λαβετε'   ποτηριον

Here is another interesting example. Paul speaks about an unbelieving marriage partner.

But if the unbeliever separates, let him remain unmarried.

UNBELIEVER   172 x 5
1 Cor. 7:15 απιστος'

The following is also very interesting.

Hath Christ been divided?

CHRIST 172 x 9
1 Cor. 1:13 ο Χριστος"

In the Book of Luke, a man speaks out from the multitude to Jesus, in yet another interesting example of the 172 pattern.

And one of the company said unto him, Master, speak to my brother, that he divide with me the inheritance.

WITH ME 860 (172 x 5)
Luke 12:13 μετ εμου

WITH 172 x 3
μετ'

Abraham tithed to God by dividing off a tenth part.

For this Melchisedec, king of Salem, priest of the most high God, who met Abraham returning from the slaughter of the kings, and blessed him; To whom also Abraham divided a tenth part of all.

DIVIDED A TENTH PART OF ALL 172 x 13
Heb. 7:2 δεκατην απο παντων εμερισεν'

The book of Revelation describes the fall of the City, Babylon the Great.

And was divided the city great into three parts.

AND WAS DIVIDED THE CITY 860 (172 x 5)
Rev. 16:19 και εγενετο πολις'

Jesus on the Cross

Now I would like to share what I think is the most fascinating and poignant, and also the most unmistakable and spectacular example of the 172 pattern. When Jesus was crucified, the Roman soldiers could not decide who would get the Lord's garments.

And they crucified him, and divided his garments, casting lots.

AND DIVIDED HIS GARMENTS, CASTING LOTS 1720 x 2
(mt) Mark 15:24 και διαμεριζονται τα ιματια αυτου βαλλοντες κληρον'

And it was the casting itself that divided them.

CASTING 172 x 4
βαλλοντες

Here is another account of the same event from the Gospel of Luke. Even though we are generally not examining the 86 in the New Testament, the following pattern is one example among many.

"And dividing the garments of Him, they cast lots."

AND DIVIDING 86 x 5
Luke 23:34 διαμεριζομενοι δε'

The dividing of Jesus' clothing is also described in John's Gospel.

They said therefore among themselves, Let us not rend it, but cast lots for it, whose it shall be.

CAST LOTS FOR   1720
John 19:24 λαχωμεν περι'

IT SHALL BE   172 x 3
εσται

The Hebrew words "cast lots" also fit this pattern.

CAST LOTS   86 x 3
Joel 3:3 ידו גורל'

> That the scripture might be fulfilled, which saith, They divided my garments among them, and for my vesture they did cast lots. These things therefore the soldiers did.

The above verse from John, is quoting a prophetic passage from the Old Testament Book of Psalms.

> They divided my garments among them, and cast lots upon my vesture.

THEY DIVIDED MY GARMENTS   172
Psa. 22:19 יחלקו בגדי'

As I was writing this paragraph, this thought occurred to me: What about the passage where, on the cross, Jesus cries out, "My God, My God, Why hast thou forsaken me?" Was not the cry of the Lord due to the fact that He had been separated (temporarily) from His heavenly Father?

WHY HAST THOU FORSAKEN   172 x 6
Mat. 27:46 ινατι εγκατειλπες"

The moment Jesus died on the cross, he also became separated from His physical body. That is the reason for the following phenomenon.

> And when Jesus had cried with a loud voice, he said, Father, into thy hands I commend my spirit: and having said thus, he expired.

HE EXPIRED   860 (172 x 5)
Luke 23:46 εξεπνευσεν

Here are two indescribable features. When Jesus died, something supernatural took place in the temple—a separation and division.

> "And the veil of the temple was rent in two from the top to the bottom."

WAS RENT IN TWO   1720
Mark 15:38 εσχθσθη εις δυο'

WAS RENT   172 x 6   IN TWO   172 x 4
εσχθσθη'   εις δυο'

At the time just before Jesus expired and released His spirit, and the veil of the temple was rent, the Bible tells us that the sun went dark and there was great darkness over the earth.

Now from the sixth hour darkness occurred over all the earth.

Throughout my life, I had been taught that hell in the Bible, more than anything else, represented eternal separation from God. What could be more descriptive of separation than darkness?   Throughout the Gospels, Jesus refers to the unprofitable servant who would be cast into complete outer darkness.

And cast the unprofitable servant into outer darkness.

DARKNESS   860 (172 x 5)
Mat. 25:30 σκοτος

In the book of Revelation, nothing could be more final than what the Bible calls "the second death." This entire phrase contains at least four 172s.

This death the second is, the lake of fire.

DEATH THE SECOND IS, THE LAKE OF FIRE   172 x 19
Rev. 20:14 θανατος δευτερος εστιν λιμην πυρος

THE SECOND IS   1720
ο δευτερος εστιν'

7   The 153 Fishes in the Net

Oil Seeping From the Rocks

This chapter is a condensed version of chapter 3 of *Theomatics II*. I include it here because it provides a genesis account of how I became involved with theomatics—the story of how all of this was discovered.

The following will also open up to our understanding the manner in which the plain words of Scripture fit the big picture. The Bible "tells" us—overtly and right out in the open—the fact that theomatics exists.

A Metaphor for Theomatics

The oil, or petroleum, industry is a vital industry throughout the world. Virtually all forms of transportation depend on the fuels refined from petroleum. Many byproducts, such as plastics, are derived from petroleum. Probably no other industry has a greater effect on the world's overall economy.

Crude oil is usually found very deep in the earth. Oil companies invest millions of dollars drilling in places such as jungles, offshore, and the Arctic regions in order to discover the "black gold." The amount of oil that lies beneath the surface of the earth is enormous, yet it is usually difficult to obtain and seldom seen on the surface.

The way that oil was first discovered, however, is quite revealing. In a few locations, man noticed that seeping out from rocks was a putrid-smelling, brackish liquid or sticky tar. Although mankind did not see a great deal of value in it, there were some uses. It could burn in lamps, and the tar could be used to seal the bottoms of boats. (This no doubt was the "tar and pitch" used to float the woven basket in Egypt, containing the baby Moses.)

So the way all the vast oil reserves of the world were discovered was due to the fact that in just a very few locations, oil made its way to the surface where it could eventually be seen.

Theomatics was discovered in a similar manner.

Oil Seeping Out of the Rocks

The theomatic structure in the Bible can be compared to the vast oil reserves that lie beneath the surface of the earth. On the surface there is no discernible way of seeing theomatics, or knowing about its existence, because it is so deeply buried. Since Bible students relate to God's Word only according to the rules of grammar and the facts of history, the idea that there is some sort of numbering system, or code, embedded deep below the surface is the furthest thing from the minds of most scholars. Since they have no direct way of knowing that something like this exists, they are obviously not looking to find it.

Hundreds of Numbers!

Yet sprinkled throughout the Bible, hundreds of times, the text refers to many different numbers. Numbers appear everywhere in the Old and New Testaments: Adam lived 930 years, there were 12 tribes of Israel, they spent 40 years in the wilderness, Jesus was in the wilderness 40 days, Abraham had 318 servants, Solomon had 666 talents of gold, Daniel's 70 weeks' prophecy, Jesus taught 5,000 people by the seashore, the man lame for 38 years healed by Jesus, the woman bound by Satan for 18 years, the 46 years it took the Jews to build the temple that Jesus said He would tear down in 3 days, 276 souls saved from the apostle Paul's shipwreck, 7 golden lampstands in Revelation, 144 thousands sealed in the Book of Revelation, and so on.

Here is the key. *Every number that appears openly in the text of the Bible is a key number for the theomatic structure. It is oil coming to the surface and seeping out of the rocks. It is the VISIBLE part of the whole theomatics code that God originally put in the Bible. It is God saying to us—"Look! This is what I have done! Can't you see it?"*

Revelation 13:18, states,

> Here is wisdom. Let him who has understanding *calculate* the number of the beast, for it is the number of man, and its number is 666.

Why would God command us to do something (such as calculate), if it were not possible? He would have to first give us the key or the code if He expected us to carry out His command.

Note: Chapter 20 of *Theomatics II* thoroughly discusses this passage that talks about the number 666.

This Is By No Means a New Idea

For centuries, hundreds of Bible scholars have believed and taught that the numbers mentioned openly in the Bible text must certainly contain some sort of deeper symbolic or spiritual significance—they are not in the Bible haphazardly or by chance. Other more conservative theologians have warned Christians to stay away from too much speculation and simply look at the Bible numbers as being nothing more than historical data (see complete discussion in *Theomatics II*, pp. 139-142) This unenlightened and so called "conservative" approach, as we shall soon see, is thoroughly in error.

Every number in the Bible—used in a historical and quantitative sense—contains a deliberate *symbolic* function that was designed to express eternal truths. Once the proper interpretation is made of a particular number's significance, it will open up a whole array of theomatic patterns *incorporated within* the actual numerical values of the letters and words. *In fact, only by inductively comparing the numbers mentioned in the text to the consistency found with the numerical values themselves will fully reveal the meaning and significance of the numbers.*

The Disciples Go Fishing

One of the more fascinating passages of Scripture is John 21:11, wherein the disciples go fishing shortly after the resurrection of Jesus.

> And Simon Peter went up and drew the net to land, full of great fishes, one hundred and fifty-three; and although there were so many, the net was not torn.

This number 153 has taxed the ingenuity and minds of some of the greatest Bible students over the centuries. Many have felt that there must be something deeply significant and important about this number in a symbolic sense. Why would the number of fishes caught be such a specific and strange number? Why not a nice even round number, like 100 or 150? *Why did someone take the time to even count the exact number of fishes in the first place?* Why did God specifically call out this number?

Many commentators have seen in this number some reference to the saved as being of a finite and particular number, even down to the last one; thus, they make up not a large round number but a smaller and odd number: 153.

This is How It All Started

At age twenty-four, when the Holy Spirit began prompting me to investigate this subject, I began by researching the works of the late Dr. Ivan Panin. Ivan Panin was a Russian Jew who was a professor at Harvard University in the late 1800s. He converted to Christianity after discovering a mathematical pattern in the original Greek language of the New Testament. He called his discovery "Bible Numerics" and subsequently devoted over fifty years researching and writing many tracts and publications. He died in 1942. His works are still well known all over the world and eagerly sought after.

There is virtually no similarity between what he did with "Bible Numerics" and theomatics. (A lengthy discussion of this is found in chapter 7 of *Theomatics II*, pp. 155-159.)

I had driven down to California and obtained 40,000 pages of Ivan Panin's original calculations and research papers on microfilm from well-known chemical scientist Dr. Albert Nobell, who lived in the little "one-horse town" of Coloma, California, east of Sacramento. (Interestingly, Coloma was the original gold discovery site for the great California gold rush of 1849. It was also the birthplace of theomatics.)

Ivan Panin had lived with Albert Nobell before his death in 1942. Shortly thereafter, George Pepperdine, the founder of Pepperdine University in California, donated $50,000 (a considerable sum during the 1940s) to research Ivan Panin's lifework. In order to perform the investigation, a number of Hebrew and Greek scholars were retained along with a statistician. The investigation was never formally concluded.

When the investigation terminated, the general consensus among the researchers was that some sort of significant phenomena probably did exist in the Bible, but that it was virtually impossible for the investigators to get a handle on it. Panin's method was just too arbitrary and unscientific.

When I visited with Dr. Nobell in 1975, he told me that his conclusion was similar, that a supernatural element did exist, but that I should completely discard Dr. Panin's method and pursue a different approach. He reiterated, "if there is a supernatural element, it would probably only be found with *just the numerical values in conjunction with the related theological meanings of Scripture.*" This was a radical departure from Panin's Bible Numerics.

He gave me a brief study he had completed. In it were two numerical features that caught my eye.

More Than Just a Coincidence

In John 21:11, the text says that "Simon Peter went up and drew the net to land, full of great fishes, one hundred and fifty-three."

In the Greek language, the word for "fishes" (ιχθυες) has a numerical value of 1224. This number factors out to 153 x 8. But what is most interesting is that the numerical value for "the net" (το δικτυον) is also 1224, or 153 x 8. Was this a coincidence, considering that the text explicitly mentioned that the disciples had caught 153 fishes?

FISHES   153 x 8
Luke 9:13 ιχθυες

THE NET   153 x 8
John 21:11 το δικτυον

As I was looking this over, a thought occurred to me: Perhaps other references to fishes and fishing would exhibit this same pattern?

I Will Make You Fishers of Men

The well-known words of Jesus from Mark 1:17 immediately popped into my mind. This without a doubt is the best-known, the most loved, and the most significant verse possible related to fishes and fishing in the entire Bible.

> And Jesus said to them, follow Me, and I will make you to become fishers of men.

Guess what happened when I looked up "fishers of men"?

FISHERS OF MEN   153 x 14
Mark 1:17 αλεεις ανθρωπων'

I immediately raced for my concordance. What happened afterward became history. Oil had started coming out of the rocks.

The Number 17

Before we can fully visualize and see this pattern, it is important to understand the number 153 and the numbers that relate to it.

As a general rule, one can always discover the major number relative to a particular topic or theme by determining the largest prime number, or "key primary factor," in that number. A prime number is a number that can be divided only by itself and 1. For example, the numbers 1, 2, 3, 5, 7, 11, 13, 17, 19, 23, 29, and 31, are all prime numbers. You cannot divide any other numbers into them.

The largest prime number within the number 153 is 17 (17 x 3 x 3 = 153); 153 also exhibits some unique and fascinating characteristics, one of which is the fact that all the numbers from 1 to 17 add up to 153.

$$1+2+3+4+5+6+7+8+9+10+11+12+13+14+15+16+17 = 153$$

What I discovered in going through nearly every reference to fishes and fishing in the entire Bible was that these two numbers, 153 and 17, were positively *pervasive*. Multiples of 153, 170, and 289 (17 x 17), along with several others, saturated virtually every major reference to this topic; but 17 by itself is the *key number* for fishes and fishing in the Bible.

In John 21:11, the text states, "Simon Peter went up and drew the net to land, full of great fishes, one hundred and fifty-three."

DREW THE NET TO LAND, FULL OF GREAT FISHES,   153 x 54
ONE HUNDRED AND FIFTY-THREE
John 21:11 ειλκυσεν δικτυον εις την γην μεστον ιχθυων
μεγαλων εκατον πεντηκοντα τριων'

In Greek, the words of this verse are arranged in a different order than English translations generally use. The original text reads "and drew the net to land full of fishes, of great one hundred and fifty-three."

DREW THE NET TO LAND FULL OF FISHES 153 x 31
John 21:11 ειλκυσεν δικτυον εις την γην μεστον ιχθυων'

OF GREAT ONE HUNDRED AND FIFTY THREE 153 x 23
μεγαλων εκατον πεντηκοντα τριων

Since 17 by itself is a key factor, along with the number 153, the number 170 also prevails in this passage. The word for "fishes" taken directly from this passage is spelled differently in Greek than the word ιχθυες, which is 1224, or 153 x 8. Here, the word is ιχθυων, which has a numeric value of 1870', or 170 x 11.

FISHES 170 x 11
John 21:11 ιχυθων'

There are a number of other multiples of 153 and 170 within other combinations of the above phrase. Again, almost all of these passages are dominated by multiples of 153 and 170.

DREW THE NET TO LAND 170 x 13
John 21:11 ειλκυσεν δικτυον εις την γην"

THE NET 153 x 8   THE NET TO 153 x 7
το δικτυον   δικτυον εις"

TO LAND FULL OF FISHES GREAT 170 x 11 x 2
εις γην μεστον ιχθυων μεγαλων'

FISHES 170 x 11   LAND 11
ιχυθων'   γη

An Important Comment

In *Theomatics II*, almost thirty pages dealt with this 153 pattern relative to fishes and fishing. In the longer version I explained many other patterns—besides 153/170—flowing through these passages. In order to keep this presentation as simple and straightforward as possible, we will limit the discussion to a few of the more outstanding examples of the 153/170 pattern.

A Multitude of Fishes

Above, the word "fishes" in Greek equals 1224, or 153 x 8, as does "the net." The most significant feature possible relative to this topic (other than "fishers of men") is from Luke 5:6:

And when He [Jesus] had ceased speaking to the multitudes, he said to Simon, Put out into the deep and let down your nets for a catch. And Simon answered, Master, we toiled all night and caught nothing! But at thy word I will let down the nets. And when they had done this they enclosed a great multitude of fishes.

AT THY WORD   1224 (153 x 8)
Luke 5:6 επι ρηματι σου

THY WORD I WILL LET DOWN THE NETS   153 x 8 x 4
τω ρηματι σου χαλασω τα διστυα'

WORD   153 x 3
ρηματι

What happened when Simon Peter obeyed the Word of the Lord? The story tells us that they "enclosed a great multitude of fishes."

MULTITUDE OF FISHES   1224 x 2 (153 x 8 x 2)
ιχθυων πολυ'

The word for "multitude" by itself is 289 x 2, and 289 = 17 x 17, which is the square of 17.

MULTITUDE   289 x 2 (17 x 17 x 2)   OF FISHES   170 x 11
πολυ"   ιχθυων'

Therefore, in "multitude of fishes," there are three patterns: one a multiple of 153, another of 170, and a third of 289 (17 x 17). Here again, we see the magic square principle at work.

NOTE: Any time you have a square of a number, such as 12 x 12 = 144 or 17 x 17 = 289, the square *accentuates the importance and significance* of the number. It concentrates the emphasis of 17.

The longer portion of this passage from Luke 5 states, "And this doing they enclosed a great multitude of fishes."

DOING [THEY] ENCLOSED A GREAT   153 x 31
MULTITUDE OF FISHES
Luke 5:6 ποιησαντες συνεκλεισαν πληθος ιχθυων πολυ"

Interestingly, this five-word phrase has the same value (153 x 31) as "drew the net to land full of fishes."

A Draught of Fishes

Let's back up a little. Two verses earlier during this story in Luke, Jesus had told Simon Peter to "let down your nets for a catch." The word for "catch" in Greek can be translated as "draught" (pronounced *draft*). This means the "pulling in or drawing in of a large amount or multitude of fish."

DRAUGHT (or A CATCH)   153
Luke 5:4 αγραν"

In this passage, Jesus tells the disciples to "let down your nets." We have already seen how the word "net" by itself is 153 x 8. The expression "your nets," in the plural, is a multiple of 289, or 17 x 17.

YOUR NETS   289 x 7   (17 x 17 x 7)
δικτυα υμων"

There is one other verse from this story that applies. After they caught the great multitude of fishes,

> Simon Peter fell at the knees of Jesus, saying Depart from me, for I am a sinful man, O Lord. For he was astonished, and all that were with him, at the draught of fishes which they caught.

The value of 289 x 15 is very significant, because it factors out to 17 x 17 x 15. The number 15 is the number of power in theomatics. This indicates the tremendous size or strength of the catch!

AT THE DRAUGHT OF FISHES [THEY] CAUGHT   289 x 15
Luke 5:9 επι τη αγρα των ιχθυων συνελαβον
(Text note: there are three variant readings for the article η—"which"—from all MSS. None produces a pattern.)

AT THE DRAUGHT   170 x 3   OF FISHES   170 x 11
επι τη αγρα"   ιχθυων'

FISHES [THEY] CAUGHT   153 x 25
των ιχθυων συνελαβον"

A related passage that exhibits a similar number of 153 x 15 in relation to a large haul of fish is found in one of the parables that Jesus gave.

> The kingdom of God is like a net cast into the sea and of every kind gathers. And when it was filled bringing it up onto the shore, and sitting down [they] collected the good into vessels, but cast out the bad.

AND WHEN IT WAS FILLED BRINGING IT UP   153 x 15
Mat. 13:48 ην οτε επληρωθη αναβιβασαντες'

The last part of the above verse states that after they brought it up, they "collected the good into vessels."

THE GOOD INTO VESSELS   289 (17 x 17)
(mt) καλα εις αγγεια'

Before moving on, let's go back to the original story of John 21. In verse 6 Jesus says, "Cast in the right parts of the boat the net, and ye will find." This phrase is 153 x 27. But what is interesting is that the word "parts"—the *location* they would catch the 153 fishes—has a value of just 153.

THE NET   153 x 8
John 21:6 το δικτυον

PARTS   153
μερη

Here is another key in theomatics. One would think that the Greek verb "ye will find" (ευρησετε) would produce a 153/170 pattern. Instead the word works out to 1024, a seemingly irrelevant number. But this number produces the following feature:

YE WILL FIND   1024
ευρησετε'

$$1024 = 2 \times 2 \times 2 \times 2 \times 2 \times 2 \times 2 \times 2 \times 2 \times 2$$

This is 2 to the 10th power. This concept is prevalent when the thought being brought forth is that of *fulfillment* or a *concentrated emphasis.* I have observed this phenomenon repeatedly throughout my research.

The next mention of fishes is in verse 8, after Simon Peter has cast himself into the sea.

But the other disciples in the little boat came dragging the net of fishes.

DRAGGING THE NET OF FISHES   170 x 13 x 2
John 21:8 συροντες το δικτυον ιχθυων"

DRAGGING THE NET   170 x 15
συροντες το δικτυον'

There are other structures of 17 within many of the significant phrase combinations. The number 119 is highly significant and factors out to 17 x 7. The number 7 always speaks of "completeness" in the Bible, and 17 x 7 would indicate a *complete* number of fish. From the phrase "dragging the net of the fishes" comes the following.

THE NET OF THE FISHES   17 x 7 x 13 x 2
το δικτυον ιχθυων'

One thing that occurs repeatedly is the secondary factor of 13. The next verse states,

> When therefore they disembarked onto land, they see a coal of fire lying and a fish lying on, and bread.

AND A FISH LYING ON   153 x 13
John 21:9 και οψαριον επικειμενον

> Jesus said, bring now from the fishes which ye caught.

THE FISHES WHICH [YE] CAUGHT   289 x 15 (17 x 17 x 15)
John 21:10 των οψαριων ων επιασατε"

The phrase above has the same exact value of 289 x 15, as in the phrase from Luke 5:9: "at the draught of fishes they caught." Furthermore, the word "which" from the phrase "the fishes which ye caught," directly points back to "fishes."

WHICH   170 x 5
ων

Jumping to Luke 24:42, we find a related incident in which Jesus eats a cooked fish. This is Luke's account of this same incident in John.

> And while they still disbelieved for joy [at His resurrection], and wondered, he said to them, have ye any food here? And [they] handed to him a fish [the one] broiled.

We saw from the John 21:9 account that "and a fish lying on" was 153 x 13. But in Luke these words are found.

HANDED TO HIM A FISH   289 x 13
Luke 24:42 επεδωκαν αυτω ιχθυος"

A FISH BROILED   170 x 13   [ONE] BROILED   153 x 6
ιχθυος οπτου'   οπτου"

In the John 21 account, the story concerning the fish cooking on the coals continues:

> Comes Jesus and takes the bread and gives also to them the fish likewise.

GIVES TO THEM THE FISH LIKEWISE 170 x 25
John 21:13 διδωσιν αυτοις οψαριον ομοιως

GIVES TO THEM THE FISH   153 x 20 (170 x 18)
διδωσιν αυτοις οψαριον

Peter Goes Fishing Again

An outstanding parallel design to this topic is found in Matthew. The setting is different, but it was still Simon Peter who went fishing.

(24) And when they had come to Capernaum, those who received the temple tax came to Peter and said, "Does your Teacher not pay the temple tax?" (25) He said, "Yes." And when he had come into the house, Jesus anticipated him, saying, "What do you think, Simon? From whom do the kings of the earth take customs or taxes, from their own sons or from strangers?" (26) Peter said to Him, "From strangers." Jesus said to him, "Then the sons are free. (27) Nevertheless, lest we offend them, go to the sea, cast in a hook, and the coming up first fish take. And when you have opened its mouth, you will find a piece of money; take that and give it to them for Me and you."

The following pattern will speak for itself. If God could perform the miracle described in this story, then the following is quite understandable.

AND THE COMING UP FIRST FISH   153 x 19
Mat. 17:27 και αναβαντα πρωτον ιχθυν᾽

THE FIRST FISH   170 x 17 (289 x 10)
τον πρωτον ιχθυν᾽

And here is the Greek word for *fish* in the singular.

FISH   153 x 7
ιχθυν᾽᾽

Casting a Net into the Sea

The pattern of 153/170 occurs in many references to the net. We will at this time limit ourselves to a couple of features. Matthew 13:47:

Again, the kingdom of heaven is like a net cast into the sea, and of every kind gathering.

LIKE A NET   153 x 3
Mat. 13:47 ομοια σαγηνη᾽᾽

When Jesus first found the disciples and called them, it says that they were

Casting a net into the sea, for they were fishermen.

CASTING A NET INTO THE SEA   153 x 20 (170 x 18)
Mat. 4:18 βαλλοντας αμφιβληστρον εις την θαλασσαν

CASTING A NET INTO   170 x 13
βαλλοντας αμφιβληστρον εις

FOR THEY WERE FISHERMEN   153 x 4
ησαν γαρ αλεεις"

THEY WERE FISHERMEN   170 x 3
ησαν αλεεις

And of course,

FISHERS OF MEN   153 x 14
Mark 1:17 αλεεις ανθρωπων'

Jesus states, "I will make you to become fishers of men." Without the pronoun "you," the clear cut meaning and pattern of 17 is present.

MAKE TO BECOME FISHERS   1700
ποιησω γενεσθαι αλεεις"

There is one more still in Luke 5:2.

While the people pressed upon Him to hear the Word of God, He was standing by the lake Gennesaret, and saw two boats standing by the lake; but the fishermen had gone from them and were washing their nets.

THE FISHERMEN   170 x 2
Luke 5:2 οι δε αλεεις

WASHING THEIR NETS   1720
επλυνον τα δικτυα'

The 172 pattern appears because they were removing and separating the dirt from their nets. They were washing them. This is just one among thousands of examples of theomatics phenomena. If we did not know what 1720 meant and stood for, the above example would be meaningless.

Loaves and Fishes

It is at this point that we pick up the pace.

Of all the references to fishes in the New Testament, the majority of those in the Gospels concern the story of the loaves and fishes.

And taking the five loaves and two fishes, looking up to heaven he blessed and broke the loaves, and gave to the disciples that they might set before them. And the two fishes he divided to all.

LOAVES 153 x 7	THE LOAVES 170 x 12
Mark 6:41 αρτους	Mark 6:44 τους αρτους'

I do not know why the 153 pattern prevails in many phrases having to do with the loaves. My emphasis here is only on the fish aspect of this design, so I will omit showing these pattern with "loaves." However, there must be a legitimate reason for the 153/170 pattern and the connection between loaves and fishes.

A most significant phrase from Mark 6:41 immediately follows:

THE TWO FISHES [HE] DIVIDED TO ALL 153 x 16
Mark 6:41 δυο ιχθυας εμερισεν πασιν"

THE TWO 289 x 5 (17 x 17 x 5)
τους δυο'

The next related passage is found in Luke 9:13. Look at how these next two features link theomatically with the above!

They [the disciples] said, we have no more than five loaves and two fishes—unless we are to go and buy food for all these people.

TWO FISHES 1700	THE TWO 289 x 5 (17 x 17 x 5)
Luke 9:13 ιχθυες δυο"	Mark 6:41 τους δυο'

FISHES 153 x 8
ιχθυες

And He took the seven loaves and gave thanks, broke them, and gave them to His disciples to set before them, and they served the multitude, and they had fishes a few, and blessing them he told them to serve these also.

AND [THEY] HAD 153 x 5	HAD FISHES 17 x 8 x 13
Mark 8:7 και ειχον'	ειχον ιχθυδια'

The words "and they had," point directly to the word "fishes." That is why it contains the 153 pattern.

The next feature is probably the most clear-cut possible after just the word "fishes," or "fish."

Took therefore the loaves Jesus, and having given thanks distributed to the ones lying down, likewise also of the fishes as much as they wanted.

OF THE FISHES 153 x 19
John 6:11 εκ των οψαριων'

A Summary Listing

Before we move on to the Old Testament, let us rearrange the most distinct features from above. When this is done, the powerful consistency of that which God has done with theomatics should be obvious.

FISHES   153 x 8
Luke 9:13   ιχθυες

FISH   153 x 7
Mat. 17:27   ιχθυν"

OF THE FISHES   153 x 19
John 6:11   εκ των οψαριων'

THE TWO FISHES [HE] DIVIDED TO ALL   153 x 16
Mark 6:41   δυο ιχθυας εμερισεν πασιν"

THE TWO FISHES   1700
Luke 9:13   ιχθυες δυο"

THE TWO   289 x 5 (17 x 17 x 5)
Mark 6:41   τους δυο'

AND THE COMING UP FIRST FISH   153 x 19
Mat. 17:27   και αναβαντα πρωτον ιχθυν'

THE FIRST FISH   170 x 17   (289 x 10)
Mat. 17:27   τον πρωτον ιχθυν'

MULTITUDE OF FISHES   153 x 16
Luke 5:6   ιχθυων πολυ'

MULTITUDE   289 x 2   (17 x 17 x 2)
Luke 5:6   πολυ"

DRAUGHT   153
Luke 5:4   αγραν"

AT THE DRAUGHT   170 x 3
Luke 5:9   επι τη αγρα"

OF FISHES   170 x 11
Luke 5:9   ιχθυων'

FISHES [THEY] CAUGHT   153 x 25
Luke 5:9   των ιχθυων συνελαβον"

THE FISHES WHICH [YE] CAUGHT   289   (17 x 17 x 15)
John 21:10   των οψαριων ων επιασατε"

AND WHEN IT WAS FILLED BRINGING IT UP   153 x 15
Mat. 13:48   ην οτε επληρωθη αναβιβασαντες'

THE GOOD INTO VESSELS   289   (17 x 17)
(mt) Mat. 13:48   καλα εις αγγεια'

AND A FISH LYING ON 153 x 13
John 21:9 και οψαριον επικειμενον

A FISH BROILED 170 x 13
Luke 24:42 ιχθυος οπτου'

GIVES TO THEM THE FISH 153 x 20 (170 x 18)
John 21:13 διδωσιν αθτοις οψαριον

DREW THE NET TO LAND FULL OF FISHES 153 x 31
John 21:11 ειλκυσεν δικτυον εις την γην μεστον ιχθυων'

THE NET 153 x 8
John 21:11 το δικτυον

DRAGGING THE NET OF FISHES 170 x 13 x 2
John 21:8 συροντες το δικτυον"

DREW THE NET TO LAND 170 x 13
John 21:11 ειλκυσεν δικτυον εις την γη"

YOUR NETS 289 x 7 (17 x 17 x 7)
Luke 5:4 δικτυα υμων"

CASTING A NET INTO THE SEA 153 x 20 (170 x 18)
Mat. 4:18 βαλλοντας αμφιβλητρον εις την θαλασσαν

FOR THEY WERE FISHERMEN 153 x 4
Mat. 4:18 ησαν γαρ αλεεις"

THEY WERE FISHERMEN 170 x 3
Mat. 4:18 ησαν αλεεις

THE FISHERMEN 170 x 2
Luke 5:2 οι δε αλεεις

FISHERS OF MEN 153 x 14
Mark 1:17 αλεεις ανθρωπων'

A Scientific Comment

Listed above are 30 examples. From a scientific perspective, in evaluating the proof for the existence of theomatics, the significant statistic is that the average length of each phrase is only 2.26 Greek words (not counting articles or conjunctions). These are extremely short phrases; for a skeptic to try and disprove or debunk the above with random numerical values and showing that these examples were arbitrarily selected and carefully presented—that would be next to impossible. (See chapter 11 on the Scientific Method.)

The Hebrew Old Testament

The first time fish are mentioned in Genesis, the Hebrew word for "fish" is not used. Instead, the Bible talks about creatures who live in the sea.

And God said, let the water teem with living creatures, and let the birds fly above the earth across the expanse of heaven. So God created the sea creatures the great ones.

The Hebrew words for the above if translated literally read,

And said God, let teem waters [with] creatures of breath living.

CREATURES OF BREATH   170 x 6
Gen. 1:20 שרץ נפש

CREATURES LIVING   153 x 4
שרץ חיה'

So God created the sea creatures the great ones.

GOD CREATED THE SEA CREATURES   170 x 5
Gen. 1:21 יברא אלהים תנינם'

CREATED SEA CREATURES   153 x 5
יברא תנינם"

SEA CREATURES   17 x 8 x 7
תא תנינם'

In Leviticus there is yet another reference to fishes, but the word used here is "creature" as well.

These are the regulations concerning animals, birds, and every creature living moving in the waters.

AND EVERY CREATURE LIVING   170 x 3
Lev. 11:46 כל נפש חיה'

CREATURE LIVING   153 x 3
נפש החיה'

Amazingly, all three passages from the Old Testament that speak of creatures living in the waters contain *both* a 170 and a 153. Let's now jump to the Greek New Testament. Here is yet one more pair of 170 and 153.

Then the second angel sounded, And something like a great burning mountain was thrown into the sea, and became the third part of the sea blood. And died the third part of the creatures in the sea having souls.

THIRD PART OF CREATURES IN SEA   153 x 35
Rev. 8:9 τριτον των κτισματων των εν θαλασσης

THIRD PART OF CREATURES   170 x 15
τριτο κτισματων'

The Word "Fishes" in Hebrew

The first time the word "fish" or "fishes" is used in the Hebrew Old Testament is Genesis 1:26.

> And God said, Let us make man in our image, in our likeness, and let them rule over the fish of the sea and the birds of the air..."

RULE OVER FISH OF THE SEA   170 x 4
Gen. 1:26 'ירדו בדגת ים

OVER FISH OF THE SEA   153 x 3
בדגת ים

The preposition meaning "over" is one Hebrew letter (ב—numeric value = 2). It attaches right to the word "fish." Without it, the words "fish of the sea" still fall within the cluster of 153 x 3.

FISH OF THE SEA   153 x 3
"דגת ים

A verse in Ezekiel relates perfectly to the above.

> The fish will be of many kinds, like the fish of the great sea very.

This entire phrase is 1224, or 153 x 8. Here are the distinct words.

FISH OF THE GREAT SEA   170 x 3
Eze. 47:10 דגת הים הגדול

And of course the words "fish of the sea" equal 153 x 3.
Let us move on to the second time the word "fish" is used in the Old Testament. It occurs in Exodus 7:18 during the ten plagues of Egypt.

> And the fish that is in the Nile will die, and the river will stink; the Egyptians will not be able to drink its water.

Here is the primary Hebrew spelling for "fish."

FISH   17
Exo. 7:18 הדגה

Absolutely nothing could be more incredible than this after what we have seen from the New Testament. The word for "fish" in Hebrew has a singular value of just 17!

But what about the Hebrew word for "fishes" in the plural? Genesis 9:2 says: "and upon all the fishes of the sea." Here, the word for "fishes" is spelled with entirely different Hebrew letters! But the numeric value is still the same as that of the singular. Both the words "fish" and "fishes" have the same exact value of 17.

FISH 17   **FISHES 17**
Exo. 7:18 הדגה   Gen. 9:2 דגי

In one location, Psalms 105:29, the word is spelled differently in Hebrew. Along with the untranslatable particle, which acts similarly to the article, the value is 170 x 5.

FISH 170 x 5
Psa. 105:29 "את דגתם

Now the above verse in Genesis 9 is talking about "all the fishes of the sea."

UPON ALL FISHES OF THE SEA 119 (17 x 7)
כבל דגי ים

ALL FISHES OF THE SEA 119 (17 x 7)
"כל דגי ים

The number 7 is universally God's number of fullness and completeness, thus—"all" fishes of the sea. But in the book of Ezekiel, the text states.

> I will pull you out from among your streams, with all the fish sticking to your scales.

ALL THE FISH 153 x 3   **ALL 49 (7 x 7)**
Eze. 29:4 "כל דגת   'כל

The word for net in Hebrew is *cherem* (חרמו).

NET 17 x 15
Hab. 1:15 חרמו

There is an extensive reason why the word "net" is a multiple of 17 x 15. This is discussed in *Theomatics II*. At this juncture I could show a whole structure of 150 and 225 (15 x 15) having to do with casting a net into the sea. The text is filled with the 150/225 pattern (see discussion pp. 51, 52, 56 of *Theomatics II*).

Do you remember the feature from the fish story in Luke chapter 5, where the word "draught" had a value of just 153? The word "draught" meant "a large catch of fish." In Numbers the text talks about catching fishes in the sea.

Would they have enough if all the fish of the sea were caught for them.

IF ALL THE FISH   170 x 3
Num. 11:22   אם את כל דגי

WERE CAUGHT   153
יאסף"

In the New Testament, we saw how the pattern of 153 relating to nets was pervasive. There is one major reference in the Old Testament to casting a net into the waters.

The fishers also shall mourn, and all they who cast into the Nile a hook shall lament, and they that cast the nets upon the waters shall languish.

ALL THEY WHO CAST INTO THE NILE   170 x 4
Isa. 19:8   כל משליכי

ALL THEY WHO CAST   153 x 3
כל משליכי"

CAST THE NETS UPON   170 x 9
פרשי מכמרת על פני

CAST THE NETS UPON   153 x 10
פרשי מכמרת על פני

In the Old Testament there are a few passages that concern "fish spears." This was evidently a technique of catching fish by spearing them.

Can you fill his hide with harpoons, or with fish spears his head?

WITH FISH SPEARS   153 x 2
Job. 41:7   ובצלצל דגים'

Therefore watch yourself very carefully, so that you do not become corrupt and make for yourselves an idol like any creature that moves along the ground or any fish in the water below.

ANY FISH IN THE WATER   153
Deu. 4:18   כל דגה במים'

The word *multitude* (in Greek) had a value of 289, or 17 x 17. Here is a passage from Ezekiel.

And [there] will be a great multitude of fish.

WILL BE A GREAT MULTITUDE OF FISH   289 (17 x 17)
Eze. 47:9   היה הר גה רבה מאד

FISH   17
הדגה

Another explicit reference is in Psalms 8:9:

What is man that thou art mindful of him. You made him ruler over the works of thy hands. You put everything under his feet. The birds of the air, and the fish of the sea that swim the paths of the seas.

THE FISH OF THE SEA THAT SWIM   170 x 2
Psa. 8:9   דגי ים עבר

THE FISH THAT SWIM   289 (17 x 17)
דגי עבר

In Exodus, the children of Israel are complaining about having to eat so much manna.

If only we had meat to eat! We remember the fish which we ate in Egypt at no cost—also the cucumbers, melons, leeks, onions and garlic. But now we have lost our appetite.

THE FISH WHICH WE ATE   170 x 6
Num. 11:5   את הדגה אשר נאבל

THE FISH WHICH   153 x 6
את הדגה אשר

Four times the Old Testament talks about the "fish gate."

Now after this he built a wall without the city of David, on the west side of Gihon, in the valley, even to the entering of the gate of fishes.

THE ENTERING OF THE GATE OF FISHES   170 x 4
2 Chr. 33:14   ולבוא בשער הדגים

THE ENTERING OF THE GATE   153 x 4
לבוא בשער

In the Old Testament, the words "fish" and "fishes" appear thirty times. The pattern of 153/170 hits practically every significant reference.

The only major references left from the Old Testament concern the story of Jonah. There is a larger discussion of that in *Theomatics II*.

The Multitudes by the Sea

Everywhere I looked there was the 153/170 design. To conclude this section on the Old Testament, I will present the most significant theomatic feature, relative to this design, in the entire Bible. It indicates that God uses the term "fishes" as a *symbol* for mankind. The complete phrase is 170 x 11.

Thou makest man like fishes of the sea, like sea creatures that have no ruler.

MAKEST MAN LIKE FISHES OF THE SEA   153 x 6
Hab. 1:14   ותעשה אדם כדגי הים

MAN LIKE FISHES OF SEA   17 x 8   **FISHES   153 x 8**
אדם כדגי הים '   ιχθυες

FISHES   17
דגי

In Luke 5 from the New Testament, just after the disciples pulled in the great draught of fishes,

Jesus said to Simon, fear not, from now on men thou wilt be taking alive.

NOW ON MEN   170 x 13
Luke 5:10   νυν ανθρωπους

Throughout the New Testament there are many references to "all men." In almost all of these instances the word "men" is not even in the text, but the English translators have added it because it is implied. 1 Corinthians 9:22 talks about "all men."

ALL MEN   170 x 2
1 Cor. 9:22   πασιν'

When a computer search is made of every reference from the New Testament to the Son of Man, the number of 170s that come spilling out is absolutely mind-boggling. I could write an entire chapter on the number 170 and references to the Son of Man.

Perhaps you have been wondering what the true significance of the fishes is. Theomatics will provide a definite clue. In *Theomatics II*, two things were shown extensively in the chapter on the 153 fishes.

- The numbers 153 and 170 represent vast numbers or multitudes of people.

- A whole structure links the number 170 and the sand of the sea. Of course, God told Abraham that his descendants would be as numerous "as the sand of the sea."

Multitudes of People

Throughout His ministry on earth, Jesus was constantly pressed by great multitudes of people. Biblical scholars have always recognized that waters, or the sea, are *figurative or symbolic* of mankind (see Rev. 17:15).

I have time and space in this book to examine only four examples relative to this topic. This design on the 153 pattern is pervasive and clearly establishes a definite, *symbolic relationship* between the great multitudes of fishes and the multitudes of people that followed Jesus.

The first thing to note is that the vast majority of times the Bible refers to the multitudes following Jesus, instances such as the five-thousand being fed by the loaves and fishes, *these events take place by the seashore!* There is obviously an incredible array of symbolic and hidden eternal truths in these stories—matters and related facts that no one has even thought of. The words "great multitudes" from the following passage appear throughout the New Testament.

And great multitudes followed Him from Galilee.

GREAT MULTITUDES   153 x 7
Mat. 4:25 οχλοι πολλοι'

The word "great" in the above passage actually means "a multitude" or "many." The passage could read a "multitude of multitudes," "many multitudes," or "great multitudes."

MULTITUDES   289 (17 x 17)
πολλοι'

In Mark 3:8 the text refers to a "great multitude of people."

MULTITUDE   289 x 2 (17 x 17 x 2)
πολυ"

Matthew speaks of simply "the multitude."

THE MULTITUDE   153 x 17 (also 289 x 9)
Mat. 15:35 τω οχλω'

8 A Sampling of Theomatics

How Many Patterns Are There?

W e have seen three diverse examples of theomatics presented in a relatively thorough manner. In chapter 4 the pattern of 93 and 310 was shown; in chapter 5, the numbers 86 and 172; in the last chapter, 153, 170, and 289.

Now that you have a basic understanding of the nature of this subject—the rationale behind how theomatics works—here is more of a wide-angle view.

Every Number has Meaning

Ultimately, every number in the entire numerical spectrum will fit into theomatics. There will eventually be patterns based upon 132, upon 350, upon 711, upon 98, upon 161, upon 223, and so forth. Every single number that exists will be a player in the overall scheme. In chapter 10 of *Theomatics II* there is a general discussion on this.

Not only are there common denominators between all the various passages related to specific topics or similar usages of Hebrew and Greek words, there are entire *groups of numbers* common to each passage as well. It is not just uncovering the single factors that run through each passage, but knowing how *all* the numbers fit together and orchestrate in unison that is the key to theomatics. I have somewhat neglected these aspects here; the purpose of this book is to keep things simple and straightforward.

This chapter will be a quick description and summary of numerous theomatic patterns and structures. It will give you a sampling of the numerous consistent patterns that have been catalogued.

We begin by looking at just one example of the type of thing I see happening every day as I perform research—I have many hundreds of things like this in my files.

If the World Hates You

Just the other evening, as I was preparing to retire, I looked down at an open page in my interlinear and saw the following verse in the Gospel of John.

The world cannot hate you, but me it hates, because I witness concerning it that its works are evil.

I noticed that the word "hate" had a value of 315. This stuck out because the value of 315 is very significant. It carries the concept of power (3150 = 225 x 14). But 315 also intersects one of the more sinister numbers in theomatics, 63—the serpent number, i.e. 315 is 63 x 5. I have done an entire statistical study on 63 and the subject of serpents, venom, and death by serpents, all structured around 63, 315, and 630s.

I immediately looked at the second occurrence in this phrase to the word "hate,"and it had a value of 265. But when it is joined with the word "me" in reference to Jesus, this is what happened.

ME IT HATES   315
Joh 7:7 εμε μισει

HATE   315
μισειν

As always, this little discovery immediately let me know that I was most likely on to something. It must be a key! So I looked up every reference to the world hating Christ and His Father, and every reference to the world hating Christians.

The statistical and mathematical probability of all the following short and simple phrases having a factor the size of 315 is minute.

In Greek two words are used for hate or hatred. *Miseo* (μισεο) occurs thirty six times, and *exthra* (εχθρα) occurs five times. Only a few of all these actually refer to the world hating Christ, the Father, and Christians. Virtually every major reference that I examined panned out to 315.

Jesus said this to His disciples:

AND YE WILL BE HATED BY ALL NATIONS   315 x 13
Mat. 24:9 και εσεσθε μισουμενοι υπο παντων εθνων'

Jesus also told his disciples this:

YE WILL BE HATED BY ALL MEN   315 x 10
Mat. 10:22 εσεσθε μισουμενοι υπο παντων

And Jesus said again to His disciples:

Blessed are ye when men hate you.

WHEN MEN HATE YOU   315 x 12
Luke 6:22 οταν μισησωσιν υμας οι ανθρωποι

In light of the above, the following is interesting.

MEN   315 x 6
1 John 5:9 ανθρωπων

This next phrase appears many times in the New Testament.

If the world hates you, ye know that me before it has hated.

THE WORLD HATES YOU   315 x 5
John 15:18 ο κοσμος υμας μισει'

Now comes this from John Chapter 17, the prayer Jesus gave before He went to the cross.

I have given them thy word, and the world hated them, because they are not of the world even as I am not of the world.

AND THE WORLD HATED THEM   315 x 8
John 17:14 και κοσμος εμισησεν αυτους

HATED THEM   315 x 6
εμισησεν αυτους'

1 John again refers to the world hating Christians, but this time the order of the Greek words used is completely different.

Do not marvel brothers, if hates you the world. We know that we have been removed out of death into life.

HATES YOU THE WORLD   315 x 5
1 John 3:13 μισει υμας ο κοσμος'

But then Jesus turns around and says this to his disciples.

But I say to you that hear, Love your enemies, do good to those who hate you.

DO GOOD TO THOSE WHO HATE YOU   315 x 10
Luke 6:27 καλως ποιειτε μισουσιν υμας"

In those references of the world hating God and Christ, I could quickly peruse only a handful. We of course saw first off the reference in John 7:7. Here are the words of Jesus in John 3:20. Jesus, of course, is the Light of the world.

Everyone doing evil hates the light and does not come to the light.

EVERYONE DOING EVIL HATES THE LIGHT 315 x 14
John 3:20 πας φαυλα πρασσων μισει φως'

The next feature is outstanding, even though the breakdown of the thematic pattern is strange-sounding. Here it is quoted straight from the Greek.

Know ye not that friendship of the world hatred of God is.

KNOW YE NOT THAT 315 x 4
Jam. 4:4 ουκ οιδατε οτι

FRIENDSHIP OF THE WORLD HATRED 315 x 9
φιλια του κοσμου εχθρα'

If I had not done among them the works which no one else did, they would not have sin; but now they have seen and both hated me and the Father of me.

HATED ME AND THE FATHER 315 x 5
John 15:24 μεμισηκασιν εμε και τον πατερα'''

Here is the last example. Nothing could be more straightforward.

The one hating me, also hates my Father.

HATES MY FATHER 315 x 4
John 15:24 πατερα μου μισει''

There is one passage that uses the word "despised," in reference to hating God. It appears twice, in 2 Peter 1:10 and Jude 8, as "those who despise dominion." Despising dominion is the same thing as hatred for God.

DESPISE DOMINION 315 x 7
(mt) Jude 8 κυριοτητα αθετουσι'

The surface of this topic and the associated numbers has barely been scratched. Let's stop at this point.

A Sampling List

Below are just some of the number structures and patterns shown in my previous two books, *Theomatics* and *Theomatics II.* This will give you an idea of a few of those subjects that have to date been researched and classified.

- **The number 111 and the birth of Christ.**

This is one of the first major patterns discovered. It has been extensively researched and enlarged since I wrote the original *Theomatics.* Virtually every single passage related to the birth of Christ is accompanied by the number 111—short explicit phrases to do with the child Jesus, the babe in the manger, the fruit of Mary's womb, etc. Over fifty references to the blessed event exhibit this 111 pattern. (See chapter 3 of the original *Theomatics.*)

- **Man created in God's image and the number 425.**

An outstanding design, where almost every reference to the image of God and man being created in that image comes out to 425. (See chapter 4 of *Theomatics II.*)

- **Satan and the number 276.**

Almost every single reference to Satan contains a multiple of the number 276—over eighty explicit references. (See chapter 5 of *Theomatics II.*)

- **Satan cast out of heaven and the number 122.**

References to Satan throughout the Old Testament all work out to 122, and virtually all references to the casting down and defeat of Satan are saturated with 122 as well. (See chapters 5 and 21 of *Theomatics II.*)

- **The wrath of God and the number 190.**

A complete scientific study was done on all the references to the wrath of God in the Book of Revelation; that pattern was shown in the "Scientific Method" chapter of *Theomatics II.* (See chapter 8.)

- **Jehovah God in the Old Testament and the number 13.**

Chapter 9 of *Theomatics II* extensively discusses this design in reference to Jehovah God, mostly from Exodus 3, where God appears to Moses in the burning bush. Multiples of 130, 182, and 169 dominate just about every major phrase combination. A pattern of 210 relative to the eternal nature of God is also shown.

- **Right hand and 130.**

Everything to do with the right hand of Jesus, and Jesus sitting on the right hand of God, is permeated by the number 130. (See chapter 9, *Theomatics II*.)

- **The numbers 150 and 225, light, darkness, and power.**

This is one of the most powerful designs embedded in nearly every passage that deals with related concepts of light, eyes, darkness, blindness, power, strength, glory, ruling and reigning, etc. (See chapter 11 of *Theomatics II* for a limited example of this pattern.)

- **The number 1000, ruling and reigning.**

There is a whole structure linked with ruling and reigning with Christ, all based upon multiples of 1000, as well as the other numbers related to these concepts. (See chapter 22 on the millennium and the conclusion of chapter 23 of *Theomatics II*).

- **The new birth and the number 830.**

A very impressive pattern of 830s surrounds being born again and the new birth. (See chapter 11 of *Theomatics II*.)

- **The number 110 and the grass of the field.**

Everything related to the flesh of man as being temporal is equated with the grass of the field that is here today and gone tomorrow—an amazingly consistent pattern. (See chapter 11 of *Theomatics II*.)

- **The number of Judas Iscariot, 171.**

Just about everything to do with Judas Iscariot has a multiple of 171 in it. (See chapter 11 of *Theomatics II*.)

- **The day of the Lord and the number 77.**

References to the day of the Lord and the day of judgment are literally saturated with 77. (See chapter 11 of *Theomatics II*.)

- **The number of all God's elect, 144.**

The number 144 is unquestionably the major number associated with all of God's people from all ages. The "144 thousands" in the Book of Revelation is a symbolic and representative number for all God's children, i.e., "spiritual Israel." (Chapter 12 of *Theomatics II* covers this along with a number of other related patterns.)

- **The number 240 and perfection.**

Revelation talks about twenty-four elders around the throne of God. The number 240 permeates those passages that concern perfection and spiritual maturity. (Chapter 12, *Theomatics II*.)

- **The Holy City New Jerusalem, streets of gold, and 140/700.**

This outstanding and most incredible pattern covers the Holy City and the subject of gold. (See chapter 12, *Theomatics II.*)

- **The numbers 1260 and 420.**

Revelation describes the time of 1,260 days and 42 months. These are symbolic expressions, and numerous patterns show their representative nature. Aparently they have nothing to do with literal earth time. (See Chapter 17, *Theomatics II.*)

- **The number of the Antichrist, 222.**

Every single reference to the Antichrist and adversary works out to 222. (See chapter 18, *Theomatics II.*)

- **The "number of the beast" is not 666.**

Twenty is perhaps the most revealing chapter in *Theomatics II.* Most Greek manuscripts of Revelation 13:18 give the number of the beast as 666. But some of the best manuscripts instead show the number 616. Theomatics proves which reading is the correct one—the one that contains the Divine stamp of approval. There is some historical evidence that the number John wrote originally was 616 but that early Christian scribes changed it to 666 in order to make Nero the supposed beast of Revelation. Nero is 666 in Hebrew. (See chapter 20, *Theomatics II.*)

- **The number 140 and the mark of the beast.**

This pattern is overwhelming from a scientific perspective. Every single reference to the "number of the beast," "mark of the beast," and "image of the beast" is saturated with 140. (See chapter 20, *Theomatics II.*)

- **Jesus manifested in glory and the number 1000.**

The vast majority of references to the coming of the Son of Man, and Christ being glorified, come out multiples of 1000. (Chapter 23, *Theomatics II.*)

- **The number 107 and the rapture.**

This is one of the most fascinating patterns ever discovered. Everything to do with the rapture, being caught up, being taken up into the clouds of heaven, the air, etc., works out to the prime number 107. (See chapter 23, *Theomatics II.*)

Patterns Shown on the Internet

There are three patterns currently shown on the Internet or World Wide Web. You can access our web site at: http://www.theomatics.com.

- **The Tree of Life and the number 240.**

- **The Root of the Trees and the number 169.**

- **Satan Deceiving Mankind and the number 180.**

This third design is absolutely stupendous, and one that you will not want to miss. It is quite lengthy, yet there is a great deal more to it than the data on the web site. It will completely blow you away! I simply have not taken the time to put all of it into an exhaustive presentation format.

The Theomatic Archives

Listed below is just a brief random sampling taken from hundreds of individual studies in my files. It will give you a synopsis or "random" cross-view of the variety of patterns that have been discovered.

- **Temple and 130.**

Numerous references to the temple in the New Testament contain a 130 pattern.

- **Cross of Christ and 112.**

Virtually every reference to the cross of Christ contains a 112 multiple.

- **Son of Man and 170.**

References to the Son of Man produces an incredible number of 170s.

- **Sons of God and 49.**

The number 49 hits on just about every single reference to "sons of God"—very short, explicit phrases.

- **Creation of man and 88.**

In the Hebrew, the number 88 saturates references to man being created.

- **Seed of Abraham and 67.**

There is a whole structure regarding Abraham's seed—all based upon a prime of 67.

- **Babylon and 340.**

Multiples of 340 run all through references to Babylon the Great.

- **Death by the sword, 480 and 800.**

A whole structure of being slain and death by the sword—based on 8s.

- **Noah's flood, rain, and 83.**

Everything to do with the flood and rain falling contains a phenomenal 83 structure.

- **Stars and the number 12.**

The number 120 runs all through references to the stars of heaven. The woman in Revelation 12:1 wears a crown of twelve stars.

- **Serpent and 63.**

Everything to do with poisonous serpents, Satan as the serpent, etc. is saturated with 63s.

- **Foundations and 110.**

Everything to do with foundations contains a 110 pattern.

- **Truth, 640 and 160.**

The numbers 640 (40 x 4 x 4) and 160 (40 x 4) permeate the subject of truth in the Bible.

- **Multiples of 700 all through Revelation.**

The structure of 7 and multiples of 700, 490, etc., stand out in the Book of Revelation.

- **Water of life and 330.**

There is a whole design surrounding purity, pure waters, etc. based on 330s.

- **The subject of sin and 163.**

For some reason, the prime number 163 exists in references dealing with sin and being cleansed from sin.

- **Lazarus coming out of tomb and 244.**

Everything to do with Lazarus's tomb and tombs in general is inundated with 122/244.

- **God's rest and 490.**

The number 490 (70 x 7) appears over and over again in references to entering into God's rest.

- **Temple of man and 460.**

There is an outstanding link between the earthly temple and multiples of 460. It took the Jews forty-six years to build the temple that existed during the time of Jesus.

118 / *The Original Code in the Bible*

- **The mind and intellect and 140.**

A complete study has been done on the mind or intellect—all based upon multiples of 140.

- **Adam the Lord of creation and the numbers 45 and 225.**

A major study has been completed on Adam being the master and "Lord" of creation and having dominion—all based on 45 and 225. Another even more astounding pattern dealing with this topic is all based upon the prime of 113.

- **Conception in the womb and 61.**

There is a whole structure regarding the point at which babies are conceived—all based upon the prime number 61.

- **The Garden of Eden and 124.**

A complete study has been completed on the Garden of Eden and how the original paradise represents the very first temple that God instituted. There is a whole structure of 124 to do with the symbolic nature of the temple of God and the temple in heaven, and how all of that fits in with the pattern laid out in Eden.

- **Adam, dominion, and 113.**

A whole structure of 113 exists with the concept of Adam being created to have dominion.

9 Understanding the Implications

What All of This Is About

Only the Creator Himself knows how far and how deep all of this will ultimately go. It will take a good part of eternity to even begin grasping the volume of eternal truth that is embedded in the theomatic structure (or any other potential and valid code system that may also exist). Already, a huge number of things that previously were not clearly understood are starting to come into focus. This is especially true in the area of so-called "Bible prophecy"—understanding the Book of Revelation (see Chapter 13 of this book). It also applies to the mysteries of the garden of Eden and the original creation of man.

The Logic behind Theomatics

Bible commentators have always liked to believe that the Bible easily interprets itself. What they can read and understand with their own eyes and mentally grasp is all that exists. In many cases the Bible does explain itself. A careful, systematic, and focused study of the grammatical-historical meaning of the words will give us much knowledge—and most certainly all the essential facts and truths that pertain both to life and godliness, the things that God expects us to understand and obey.

Yet—as the very existence of theomatics proves—there is much more to the Bible than what has been previously known. It has often been stated that during a person's lifetime, he or she utilizes less than two percent of the capacity of the brain. Likewise, if you were to add up all the knowledge about the Bible that has ever existed—all the Christian books and commentaries ever written, all the sermons ever preached, all the things ever taught in Bible schools and theological seminaries—it would comprise a minute fraction of the sum total of truth that has been deliberately embedded in the text. *There is a supernatural and heavenly side to this entire picture that has never been fully examined.* As we will discover in chapter 13 on Bible prophecy, many people have greatly misunderstood the Bible because they have tried to perceive it on a human, earthly level. They are trying to make everything in the Bible fit earthly times and events. They do not see the BIG picture behind everything—the eternal plan and purpose of God. We need to learn and understand the Bible from the Creator's point of view.

In *Theomatics II*, I made the following statement.

> The logic that is the architect behind theomatics is far above and beyond, and in some ways totally at odds with, every human and religious philosophy that has ever existed. Even though theomatics can be scientifically proven through the most elementary of means, the power and brains that are behind it are so totally beyond and so completely different from any logic ever conceived in this world that—unless a person approaches this subject in a prayerful and humble spirit, refusing to allow himself to see it through the prism of any prejudice—the knowledge and assimilation of this subject will have little chance of establishing coherence in one's thinking process.

Bear in mind as we examine theomatics that it was put together by the same mind that created the big bang—the billions upon billions of galaxies. The same mind that created black holes, time itself, atoms and molecules and designed every form of life and every detail of the human body. The same mind that created other dimensions—both material and spiritual.

That is why one must approach this subject with simple and childlike faith. One must look to God for total wisdom and understanding and not allow his own thoughts to obstruct the process.

Simple, Yet So Complex

Look at what is probably the single most practical discovery in the history of civilization. Nothing in our society would be possible without the wheel—cars, trains, airplanes, all sorts of machinery. The wheel is the most simple and basic of concepts, yet the manner in which it can be used, the applications, can become incredibly complex.

All of God's truth, at the elementary level, is basic and simple. A little child is able to grasp it. Yet at the same time, this same truth can catapult itself into the most complex "superstructures"—truths that are enormously complex, convoluted, and, at times, incomprehensible.

Begin with the analogy of a fishing line in a giant snarl. Or a net tangled up with knots. When you work out one tangle, it leads to many more. It is difficult to sort out the truth, as there is so much to work with. *The full picture is difficult to see unless much symbolism is understood.* A piece here and there is not sufficient.

Another Example

Take a look inside the cockpit of an airplane. On the surface one can see all the instruments, buttons, and levers. But until one pulls back the instrument panel and looks inside at the thousands of transistors and circuits, jillions of wires running all over the place, and the design theory of how all that connects into the hydraulic lines and other systems, he cannot really understand the *details* of how an airplane functions and works.

Theomatics is going to help show us how it all fits together. There are things connected and wired together throughout the Bible—meanings that relate to other similar passages—that explain what the first passage means, and the others as well.

There are thousands upon thousands of truths embedded in Scripture that no one has even thought of yet, simply because these areas have not been investigated nor revealed. People have not yet perceived the connection—where something here connects and relates to something over there.

Before a person can see what is under the ocean, he must dive into the water. Looking over the pretty blue surface and admiring its beauty will not give the complete picture of what lies beneath.

That is the point at which theomatics is going to take Christians to a whole new level of understanding the Bible. *It will tie all the details and reference points together in ways that are not seen by present methods.* Now we can start to look underneath. Our feet will be planted firmly on the right premises.

The Language of the Symbol

The most significant factor to understanding all this is comprehending the *symbolic principle* that God has placed in the Bible. It is a thousand times more prevalent in Scripture than people have ever imagined. It imbues the Bible from cover to cover. There is not a single word that is not a part of it. It comprises a network of galactic proportions. *Everything in the Bible contains deeper spiritualized meaning.*

What is most perplexing is that the vast majority of evangelical Bible scholars, as well as numerous others, have tried to do everything possible to steer Christians in a direction *away* from looking in the Bible for deeper spiritualized interpretations. *Instead, the preponderant attitude and consensus have been to try and demystify the Bible.* "Take everything literally" we are told. "Don't spiritualize too much. To do so can only open the door to all types of crazy ideas and ridiculous notions. People will have a free-for-all where only the imagination rules."

This reminds me of the story of the man who saw a spider on his foot. In a panic he grabbed his shotgun. The short version of the story is that he got the spider.

Most scholars tend to accept symbolism in the Bible—only where it is unmistakably obvious. For example, Jesus said, "I am the vine and ye are the branches." Obviously, that does not mean that we are supposed to pick grapes off Him. Jesus also stated that He was the "shepherd of the sheep." This obviously does not mean that Christians walk on four legs and grow wool. No biblical scholar would take literally a passage that speaks of mountains singing or the trees clapping their hands (Isa. 55:12). There are hundreds of other places where most commentators would concede that there is *deliberate* symbolism and typology placed in the Bible by God. In other more obscure locations, students are divided on the issue.

A Major Misconception

By not studying and learning the language of the symbol that God deliberately uses, Bible scholars have cut themselves off from 98 percent of the Divine truth that exists in Scripture. Instead, as chapter 13 on Bible prophecy will show, this way of thinking has led straight into the heresy of premillennial dispensationalism—the predominant idea that a literal interpretation is the only thing present. The result is a stunted way of thinking that has almost entirely dominated Christian evangelical thought over the past century and a half.

There is a common and horrible misconception that exists concerning the Bible. Here now is the crux of the matter.

Most Christians believe that God gave us the Bible as a means to communicate information relative to the real world we live in. Therefore, its ONLY practical value, relative to our understanding, is in the applications it has for this life and this world. That is a false premise. Theomatics proves that the Bible really transcends this world and was given to us by God to reveal heavenly and eternal truths. When the Christian church arrives at a complete understanding of these things, it will then be in a position to enter into the fullness of God. Therefore, the Bible is a revelation of God's master plan for all eternity. God simply used the history and culture of this earth, its stories, peoples and events—and placed all that in the Bible—to symbolize and represent things that are eternal. Therefore, the full meaning and impact of at least 98 percent of everything present in the Bible—is yet to come.

Jesus stated that "heaven and earth will pass away [the tangible and temporal], but My Word shall never pass away [the intangible and spiritual]." (Mat. 24:35) A person who does not understand this as the foundation premise for the Bible, will miss everything (including the meaning of theomatics), and find themselves impotent to explain many things in Scripture.

Theomatics will prove that the *language of the symbol* is much more extensive and vast than any of us have ever imagined.

Examples of Symbolism

Even an elementary discussion of this aspect would require half a book. As was previously stated, throughout the Bible God uses earthly things to represent heavenly and spiritual truth. There is not one thing mentioned in the Bible—not one word used in the text—that is not a part of this network.

Here is a random sample (among tens of thousands) of some of the things that God uses symbolically.

Everything in the Genesis account of creation carries a deeper symbolic meaning. Even though the things mentioned took place literally, materially, and historically six thousand years ago, there is a deeper meaning behind *everything* that is mentioned.

- Light represents something
- Darkness represents something
- Waters represent something
- God separating goes beyond the physical act
- Adam represents and is a type of something
- So is Eve
- The serpent is symbolical (Satan and the devil)
- So is the forbidden fruit
- The garden or earthly paradise is more than just a physical place
- The plants and green growth represent many different things
- The tree of life and the tree of the knowledge of good and evil are all spiritually symbolic
- The animals, birds, and fishes are all representative of other things in the earthly and heavenly dimensions
- All numbers—years, days, etc.—have a deeper meaning

Now let's examine a few of the categories of symbolism in the Bible. The following items were extracted randomly from literally hundreds, even thousands of examples.[1]

- **Symbolic creatures**

Serpent, calf, goats, sheep, camels, fox, wolf, bear, horse, lamb, lion, clean animals, unclean animals, all types of birds, fishes, all types of insects, worms.

- **Symbolic directions**

Up, down, north, south, east, west, straight, crooked, narrow.

- **Symbolic actions**

Baptism, anointing, being awake, bathing, circumcision, clapping, dancing, running, sitting, sleeping, sweating, banqueting, standing, sitting, committing adultery, marrying.

- **Symbolic colors**

Amber, black, white, blue, crimson, purple, red, scarlet.

- **Symbolic objects**

Altar, armor, bread, closet, door, eye salve, harps, iron, lamp, linen, net, ointment, pillar, sickle, staff, tent, tower, wheel. Human objects such as body, bosom, eyes, ears, feet, hand, heel, offspring, shoulder. Natural objects like brimstone, jewels, emerald, sand, salt, pearls, smoke, vapor. Objects in the sky including clouds, rain, stars, sun, moon, wind. Vegetation such as barley, cedar, field, flower, olive tree, tares, seed, vineyard.

The Tabernacle In the Wilderness

One of the most obvious examples of symbolism is the Old Testament tabernacle and temple. All the dimensions, the furniture, the rituals and blood sacrifices, the garments the priests wore—all are intended to be symbolic and representative. Though it was an earthly structure, everything about the temple was intended by God to represent things which are heavenly, spiritual and eternal.

In the New Testament, Christians *themselves* are called the temple of God.

> Know ye not that ye are the temple of God, and that the Spirit of God dwelleth in you? (1 Cor. 3:16)

Everything that took place in the earthly temple is symbolic and representative of the work God ultimately wants to do in our spirit, soul, mind, and body.

The Garden of Eden Is the Original Temple

A major theomatic study I have just completed (while this book was preparing to go to press), clearly establishes that the garden of Eden represents the temple. The earthly garden when physically laid out is a foundational model for the temple. The word "Eden" has a numeric value of 124, and all things to do with the temple of God, the temple of heaven in the paradise of God, fit this 124 pattern.

Everything about the garden and the temple has to do with the relationship that God has with man. The environment He created within the Garden (the place) of Eden (the space) was specifically designed so as to promote and enhance that encounter. In essence, the Garden of Eden was, in fact, the "First Temple." It was the place that God and man could dwell together. In the most basic form, the Garden of Eden was a *model* intended to express God's fundamental plan and basis of communion and relationship.

In the Book of Revelation, objects are seen in heaven that were once on this earth—the tabernacle (13:6), the temple (14:17), the ark of the covenant (11:19), the tree of life (22:2,14), the manna the Israelites ate in the wilderness (2:17), and so forth. This proves that the earthly things only *represent* that which is heavenly in nature.

It is through theomatics that these kinds of truths and relationships can be discovered and clearly seen.

Old Testament Promises

We now come to Abraham and the Promised Land. Everything to do with the promises given to him by God is to be understood as representative of the eternal Promised Land, which is heavenly (there is an entire theomatic structure that demonstrates this). Even though God used earthly geography and biological Jews to act the whole thing out, all of it was intended to ultimately bring forth truth concerning His true chosen people—all those who have put their trust in Jesus by faith. Abraham looked for a permanent city with *foundations*, a city whose origin was heaven and whose builder and maker was God, i.e., the "New Jerusalem" (Heb. 11:10, Rev. 21:2). All of the Old Testament patriarchs dwelt in tents; they were "sojourners" on the earth. What is significant about that? Tents are not permanent structures; they have no foundations. The apostle Paul was a tentmaker.

All of these things in Scripture are spiritually symbolic and carry a tremendous depth of meaning—matters that no one has even thought of yet. Theomatics is starting to bring much of it to light. Everything to do with the physical city of Jerusalem is only representative of things that are eternal and in the heavens (Gal. 4:26 and Heb. 12:22).

Another Fallacy

Theomatics completely destroys a major fallacy and interpretive rule that exists in present-day evangelical thought. According to those who adhere strictly to the grammatical-historical method, we are to understand the meaning of Scripture *by observing to whom the words were originally addressed.* Accordingly, when God made His promises to Abraham, He addressed biological Jews and described earthly geography. *The purpose of the Bible is not the original addressees.* God simply *used* those people, places, and events, to carry out a higher and more permanent solution. As chapter 11 on Bible prophecy will show, theomatics completely destroys current evangelical thinking in this area.

Types

In addition to symbolism, there are types. A type is something that represents or reveals information about something different. Isaac was a type of Christ (the true child of promise and obedient sacrifice). So were Joseph (the redeemer) and David (the king). In the book of Isaiah, chapter 14, the "King of Babylon" is a type of Lucifer who fell from heaven; Pharaoh the king of Egypt is a type of Satan, who kept the children of Israel in the house of bondage. Egypt is also a type of the world. Throughout the Old Testament, there are hundreds of people, offices, institutions, and events which are types of something else and represent things in the future and things that are heavenly in nature.

Theomatics Will Underscore the Language of the Symbol

Theomatics will show the *extent* of all of this. The more we learn and understand about theomatics, the more we will learn about the network of symbolism that God has established. We will come to the point of more fully understanding the manner in which God thinks. *We will simply learn what something means and represents from God's viewpoint*, instead of trying to figure it out according to our own strength and limited reasoning abilities.

The Most Inductive Process

In helping Christians understand the true and exact meaning of Scripture, theomatics is in a whole different league than any method heretofore seen. The reason is that the procedure, when properly used, is a highly inductive process. We are just now learning how to use this tool.

Everything humans believe is based upon two things: *premises* and *conclusions*. In order to establish premises and arrive at conclusions, we use both *deductive* and *inductive* logic. I will not take the time here to explain definitions (see *Theomatics II*, pp. 132, 133), except to say that inductive logic is generally much more objective. It is the form of logic that science uses by following a method of making observations, testing results, and *then* drawing conclusions.

Generally, people start out with fundamental premises and then try to shape everything to fit those premises. Unfortunately, this approach is applied to much of what Christians believe. Most Christians believe something not because they researched the matter in the Bible for themselves, but because someone they respected and had confidence in (usually their parents or theology professor) told them it was true. From that point on, they tend to read and see everything in the Bible through those rose-colored glasses.

Someone who has established which persuasion to follow will also tend to ignore any evidence that seems to disagree with his or her fundamental premise (or try to find a way to explain away "those other annoying passages" in the Bible).

Theomatics operates on an entirely different principle. With the theomatic method, we watch the flower unfold itself. Then we stand back and ask, Why is this working out to these numbers, and why are all those numbers coming up over there? From these sorts of observations, we start seeing where various things connect and tie together. Proceeding onward, our knowledge is improved as the flower continues to unfold itself. This is the correct inductive procedure—first observe and then draw conclusions based upon the evidence. We must be willing to change our position or ideas on many things as the truth brings in more light on a particular subject. That requires humility.

Numbers Are the Only Objective Thing

What is the most objective thing possible in the entire universe? Here is what I stated in *Theomatics II*.

Why did God put theomatics in the Bible? If you stop and think about it, numbers are really the only thing in the universe that are absolute and determinate. Of all the sciences known to man, mathematics and logic are *the only exact and pure science.* Every branch of science uses and depends upon math. Words and their meanings are interpretive in nature—they are relative to so many different contributing factors: various cultures, ideas, feelings, emotions, viewpoints, and interpretations. Scholars who attempt to deal with the Bible based solely upon the grammatical-historical system— words and their meaning (hermeneutics), must forever be working with some degree of uncertainty. (If not, then why are there so many viewpoints about God and the Bible?) Numbers are absolute and inflexible. Mathematical laws and principles never change, and since God is the Unchangeable One, it only makes sense that He would boil down the meanings in His Word to mathematical exactness and precision.

I went on to further state,

Once all the rules and principles are discovered according to which the theomatic structure operates, all the meanings in scripture will be cast in stone. Every meaning in the Bible (God's original intent) will be crystal clear as a bell. There will be no conflicting "schools of theology" or "religious denominations" in heaven. There will be complete unity within the Body of Christ for all eternity.

It would be impossible to communicate or function as an intelligent society without numbers. Imagine trying to call someone on the phone and not use any numbers, just words (how could the telephone switching equipment work without numbers?) How about your address? How about your car? In order to engineer it and manufacture the parts, everything had to be explained numerically and broken down to numbers. The drawings all had to express dimensions with numbers. You could never know whether you were going the right speed limit with just words. Obviously, we express mph in numbers. And the policeman who writes a speeding ticket will give you the date and time to appear in court, with numbers, and the amount of the bail you will have to post will also be expressed in numbers.

Recently when some NASA engineers set up a broadcast antenna and focused it on distant stars, trying to communicate with any "intelligent life" out there, they decided that the only possible language they could use that would make sense to other civilizations was based solely upon numbers.

In our society, numbers are necessary in order to explain anything and everything. Why should the eternal Word of God, the Holy Bible, be any different? Everything else in God's creation is numerically based.

And yet it never ceases to amaze me how various evangelical Bible scholars try to accuse theomatics of being either "mystical nonsense" or some sort of "loony theory." Most biblical scholars would rather sit and haggle over the historical definition of words and semantics. *The truth of the matter is, if God put theomatics in the Bible, then the numerist who is investigating this—and applying the scientific method to the process—is really the true objectivist,* not some scholar who knows only historical church doctrine, which is both relative and susceptible to many errors in reasoning.

Words will never be definite until they can be expressed with mathematical precision. Cultures change through time. There are many words in the Bible that have historical meanings that we do not fully understand (we only think we do based upon the best available history). This is especially true of the Hebrew Old Testament. Couple that fact with all the theological connotations in Scripture, and you have a smorgasbord of meanings and shades of meaning. And if we can't always settle the definition historically, *then what was God's original intended and spiritualized meaning?* At this time I could easily list a hundred areas of dispute and issues over which Christians are thoroughly perplexed and divided. Any reader should be aware of this fact.

So the conclusion must be that words and their meanings are not always a reliable means of receiving and understanding information—no matter how much various scholars would like to protest. That is why God ultimately put theomatics in the Bible. In heaven we will all be of one mind and spirit with the Lord (1 Cor. 6:17).

The Pearl of Great Price

Let me give just one example that will show the perfect manner in which theomatics opens up the meaning of scripture, and helps us see things that would never be apparent otherwise.

A number of years ago I corresponded with a seminary president who is one of the most reputed evangelical leaders in the United States. He had written an entire book intended to discredit any approach such as theomatics. He stated the following in a letter.

> I have studied your work *Theomatics* and appreciate the enormous amount of effort that went into the research. I do have abiding suspicions about that and other approaches to mystical numerology. When all the work is done on numerological analysis of the text, the question still remains as to what it tells us that is not already apparent from the direct statements of scripture.

In Matthew 13 Jesus spoke concerning the pearl of great price. There are no doubt many things this pearl could represent, as well as many applications. Thousands of sermons have been preached on this Bible passage.

The pearl is a type of the kingdom of heaven. It could represent Jesus or even God Himself. It could mean our salvation when we find it. The pearl could apply to anything that has great spiritual value. Yet we find through theomatics what the pearl *really* represents.

> Again, the kingdom of heaven is like unto a merchant man, seeking goodly pearls: Who, when he had found one pearl of great price, went and sold all that he had, and bought it. (Mat. 13:45,46)

ONE PEARL OF GREAT PRICE   1720
Mat. 13:46 ενα πολυτιμον μαργαριτην'

Here is number 15, the number of power and strength.

AND BOUGHT IT   86 x 15
και ηγορασεν αυτον'

When the number 1720 presented itself, the significance did not seem obvious at first. Then it dawned on me; of course! Previously I had seen that the 86/172 pattern had to do not only with separating and dividing in general, but it also had to do with spiritual discernment—being able to rightly divide and understand truth.

> Strong meat belongeth to them that are of full age, even those who by reason of use have their senses exercised to discern good and evil (Heb. 5:14).

TO DISCERN GOOD   172 x 8
Heb. 5:14 προς διακρισιν καλου

> For God doth know that in the day ye eat thereof, then your eyes shall be opened, and ye shall be like God, knowing good and evil (Gen. 3:5).

YE SHALL BE LIKE GOD, KNOWING GOOD   172 x 4
Gen 3:5 והייתם כאלהים ידעי טוב

So what the pearl represents is the ability to know the difference between good and evil, to be able to discern all spiritual things. Here are three Greek words.

HE THAT IS SPIRITUAL DISCERNS ALL THINGS   172 x 13
(mt) 1 Cor 2:15 ο δε πνευματικος ανακρινει τα παντα'

A man who finds this pearl, realizing that it is the key to discernment, will give every penny he has in order to buy it. What could be more valuable than the ability to discern every issue and every matter in the universe? Through His eternal Word, God is ultimately going to give all His saints in heaven the ability to do just that. Once we see that fact, we will be willing to let loose and give up everything we possess in this world.

> Give not that which is holy unto the dogs, neither cast the pearls of me before swine, lest they trample them under their feet, and turn again and rend you (Mat. 7:6).

THE PEARLS OF ME   172 x 13
(vn) Mat. 7:6 τους μαργαριτας μου

New Wine and Old Bottles

Let's talk now about the future of theomatics. Here are the words of Jesus:

> No one puts a piece of unshrunk cloth on an old garment; for the patch pulls away from the garment, and the tear is made worse. Neither do men put new wine into old bottles: else the bottles break, and the wine runneth out, and the bottles perish: but they put new wine into new bottles, and both are preserved. (Mat. 16,17)

In the days of the Bible, wine was fermented in leather bottles. When the fermentation process took place, the bottles expanded. This would work well for a number of seasons. But after the wineskins had seen their better days, they would get old and brittle and eventually split apart. So the new wine had to be placed into new bottles.

Our minds are like wine bottles. God cannot place His new wine of truth easily into old, fermented bottles. This is why I have given up trying to impress various Christian leaders and skeptics with the findings of theomatics. They just don't think that way. There are a lot of old wineskins out there.

To properly come to an understanding of truth, we need to constantly erase and clean the hard disk of our minds. Then we need to build the right file structure in which to place the new data or code so we are able to sort the truth objectively and untangle the knots.

About a year ago, a gentleman flew from New York City to Oregon, in order to discuss theomatics with my wife and me. He had just retired from being the number-one architect for Merrill Lynch—hiring the other architects and being in command of their new forty million dollar world headquarters—a brilliant man. He stated the following to me in a letter.

> Few people, particularly scientists and scholars change their minds about fundamental issues. And the more firmly they have based their professional lives, writings, and teaching on those ideas, the less likely they are to do so—unless, of course, they are touched and compelled to do so by the Holy Spirit. The uncommitted—mostly the young—pick up new ideas and carry them forward. The people with old ideas die out.

Nowhere will this be more evident than with theomatics. The whole subject is so far removed from "normal" and conventional thinking patterns that it will require a whole generation of progressive new thinkers to become established and take hold. Yet God is capable of making that happen when the time is right.

10   A Man with Two Sons

And the Prodigal Hits the Road

This chapter will pave the way for the one to follow, which will discuss the scientific method and how theomatics is unequivocally proven "in the laboratory."

Part I: Luke 15:11-32

11 And he said, A certain man had two sons:

12 And said the younger of them to his father, Father, give me the portion of goods that falleth to me. And he divided to them his living.

13 And after not many days the younger son gathered all together, and departed into a far country, and scattered his property living prodigally.

14 And when he had spent all, there arose a mighty famine in that land; and he began to be in want.

15 And went and he joined himself to a citizen of that country; and he sent him into his fields to feed swine.

16 And he longed to fill his belly with the husks that the swine did eat: and no man gave unto him.

17 And when he came to himself, he said, How many hired servants of the father of me have bread enough and to spare, and I perish with hunger!

18 And rising I will go to my father and say unto him, Father, I sinned against heaven, and before thee,

19 No longer am I worthy to be called thy son: make me as one of thy hired servants.

20 And rising he came to his father. But when he was yet a great way off, his father saw him, and had compassion, and ran, and fell on his neck, and kissed him.

21 And the son said unto him, Father, I sinned against heaven, and in thy sight, no longer am I worthy to be called thy son.

22 But the father said to his servants, Bring forth the best robe, and put it on him; and put a ring on his hand, and shoes on the feet:

23 And bring hither the fatted calf, and kill it; and let us eat, and be merry:

24 For this my son was dead, and is alive again; he was lost, and is found. And they began to be merry.

25 Now was the son of him the older [one] in the field: and as he came and drew nigh to the house, he heard music and dancing.

26 And he called one of the servants, and asked what these things meant.

27 And he said unto him, For the brother of thee is come; and thy father hath killed the fatted calf, because he hath received him back in health.

28 And he was angry, and would not go in: therefore the father of him came out and besought him.

29 And he answering said to his father, Lo, these many years do I serve thee, neither transgressed I at any time thy commandment: and yet thou never gavest me a kid, that I might make merry with my friends:

30 But as soon as this thy son was come, which hath devoured thy living with harlots, thou hast killed for him the fatted calf.

31 And he said unto him, Child, thou art ever with me, and all that I have is thine.

32 It was meet that we should make merry, and be glad: for this thy brother was dead, and is alive again; and was lost, and is found.

This story contains some very deep mysteries. Based upon extensive research in theomatics, and numerous patterns that have been found, it relates to the angelic realm and the original rebellion that took place sometime in the past ages. I plan to discuss this in great detail in a forthcoming book (see p. 225 chapter 14). For now I will simply state a few things and then go directly to the theomatics presentation.

The Number 90

The numbers 90 and 900 in theomatics are two of the key numbers associated with all the angels or host of heaven. It speaks of vast quantities of living beings—innumerable numbers. The two brothers in this story represent all the angels of heaven—those who rebelled and left their original habitation (Jude 6) vs. the "good guys" who stayed home and were faithful to the Father.

The expression "angels" (τοις αγγελοις") in Greek, has a value of 900, and the expression "angels in heaven," from Matthew 22:30, is 900 x 3.

In Genesis, God separated the waters from the waters, which were all in the heavens. The Hebrew word in Genesis for waters (מים) has a value of 90, and the word "heavens" in Greek (ουρανοις') has a similar value of 900. This language of creation not only involves the making of the material universe, but also contains parallel symbolic language describing the angelic rebellion and fall that took place. When the text states that God "separated the waters from the waters"—those above the expanse and those below (Gen. 1:6,7)—it is referring to vast quantities of living beings. (Again, all of this will be discussed in great length in my next book.)

Waters and the sea in Scripture always speak of vast numbers of people or living beings (see Rev. 17:15). The Book of Isaiah says, "Woe to the multitude of many people, which make a noise like the noise of the seas; and to the rushing of people, that make a rushing like the rushing of mighty waters." Here, the word "people" (אמים) has the same value of 90, and so does the word for "waters." The Book of Hebrews talks about "an innumerable company of angels." The one Greek word meaning "innumerable company" is actually "myriads," and the word "myriads" (μυριασιν') has a value of 810, which is 90 x 9. The Greek word for "stars" (αστερες') also has the same value of 810, or 90 x 9. Stars throughout Scripture have always been representative of angelic beings (see Rev. 12:4). It is significant that both "myriads" and "stars" come out to the same value.

Most interesting is the story of the Gadarene demoniac, where Jesus cast the demons out of the man who was crying and cutting himself in the tombs. In this story the demons stated, "Our name is legion, for we are many." The word "legion" (λεγιων") has a value of 900.

All the above examples are just a small sampling. Again, this particular topic would require an entire chapter to even begin an adequate discussion—many dozens of passages would have to be analyzed. Regardless of all the above, in this story of the prodigal son, virtually every clear cut and specific reference to the two sons, the two brothers, is saturated with 90s. I discovered this pattern about four months ago and felt that it would be a good one to show in this book— simply because it is so scientifically provable. Let us begin with the first verse of this story.

And he said, A certain man had two sons.

SONS   90 x 12
Luke 15:11   υιους

And said the younger of them to his father, Father, give me the portion of goods that falleth to me. And he divided to them his living.

AND SAID THE YOUNGER   90 x 19
Luke 15:12   και ειπεν νεωτερος'

THE YOUNGER OF THEM   90 x 35
ο νεωτερος αυτων'

THE YOUNGER   90 x 17
νεωτερος

The second portion of this verse, "Father, give me the portion of goods that falleth to me," more accurately translated from the Greek would be, "Father, give me the falling upon share of the property."

FATHER, GIVE ME THE FALLING UPON 90 x 17
πατερ δος μοι το επιβαλλον"

This passage then states that the father divided the living to both of His sons.

AND HE DIVIDED TO THEM HIS LIVING 90 x 14
(mt) και διειλεν αυτοις βιον"

And after not many days having gathered all things, the younger son departed into a far country, and scattered his property living prodigally.

THE YOUNGER SON DEPARTED 90 x 19
Luke 15:13 νεωτερος υιος απεδημησεν'

THE SON DEPARTED 90 x 12
υιος απεδημησεν'

And when he had spent all, there arose a mighty famine in that land; and he began to be in want.

HE 90 x 13
Luke 15:14 αυτου'

And went and he joined himself to a citizen of that country; and he sent him into his fields to feed swine.

HE JOINED HIMSELF 90 x 2
Luke 15:15 εκολληθη

And he longed to fill his belly with the husks that the swine did eat; and no man gave unto him.

TO FILL HIS 90 x 16
Luke 15:16 γεμισαι αυτου

And when he came to himself, he said, How many hired servants of the father of me have bread enough and to spare, and I perish with hunger!

OF THE FATHER OF ME 90 x 14
Luke 15:17 πατρος μου'

The above is in reference to the son himself because it contains the genitive pronoun. Here is another direct pronoun; "And I perish with hunger."

I   90 x 9
εγω"

And rising I will go to the father of me and say unto him, Father, I sinned against heaven, and before thee.

I WILL GO TO THE FATHER OF ME AND SAY   90 x 42
Luke 15:18 πορευσομαι προς τον πατερα μου και ερω'

Earlier we showed that the word "heavens" was 900 and that this story involved the angelic rebellion. The following value is 90 x 9.

FATHER, I SINNED AGAINST HEAVEN   90 x 9 x 3
Πατερ ημαρτον εις τον ουρανον'

And in Jude 6, it speaks of the angels that left their original home or habitation.

And the angels who did not keep their first estate, but left their own habitation, he hath reserved in everlasting chains under darkness unto the judgment of the great day.

THE ANGELS   900
τοις αγγελοις"

WHO DID NOT KEEP THEIR FIRST ESTATE   900 x 5
Jude 1:6 τους μη τηρησαντας εαυτων αρχην'

KEEP   90 x 13
τηρησαντας"

Let us return to our story in Luke.

No longer am I worthy to be called thy son: make me as one of thy hired servants.

AM I WORTHY TO BE CALLED THY SON   90 x 21
Luke 15:19 ειμι αξιος κληθηναι υιος σου"

AM I WORTHY TO BE CALLED   90 x 6
ειμι αξιος κληθηναι"

Now look at this!

THY SON 90 x 15
υιος σου

The next phrase says, "Make me as one of thy hired servants."

MAKE ME AS 90 x 17
ποιησον με ως'''

And rising he came to the father of him. But when he was yet a great way off, his father saw him, and had compassion, and ran, and fell on his neck, and kissed him.

HE CAME TO THE FATHER 90 x 11
(mt) Luke 15:20 ηλθε προς πατερα'

The last part reads, "and ran, and fell on his neck, and kissed him."

AND KISSED HIM 90 x 22
Luke 15:20 και κατεφιλησεν αυτον'

And said the son unto him, Father, I have sinned against heaven, and in thy sight, No longer am I worthy to be called thy son.

AND SAID THE SON 900
Luke 15:21 ειπεν ο υιος

THE SON UNTO HIM 90 x 25
ο υιος αυτω'

Earlier, we saw how the phrase "Father, I have sinned against heaven" was 90 x 9, and the words "no longer am I worthy to be called thy son" also worked out to three features (above).

But the father said to his servants, Bring forth the best robe, and put it on him; and put a ring on his hand, and shoes on the feet.

Again, the word "his" works out to 90 x 13.

And bring hither the fatted calf, and kill it; and let us eat, and be merry: For this my son was dead, and is alive again; he was lost, and is found. And they began to be merry.

FOR THIS MY SON 90 x 29
Luke 15:24 οτι ουτος υιος μου

MY SON 90 x 14
ο υιος μου

All who belong to the Father (not just the younger son) have a value of 90.

Now was the son of him the older [one] in the field: and as he came and drew nigh to the house, he heard music and dancing.

WAS THE SON OF HIM THE OLDER   90 x 39
Luke 15:25 ην ο υιος αυτου ο πρεσβυτερος·

WAS THE SON OF HIM   90 x 22
ην ο υιος αυτου·

WAS THE SON   90 x 9
ην ο υιος"

The above states that the older brother heard music and dancing when "he came and drew nigh to the house." The following is translated from three Greek words.

HE CAME AND DREW NIGH TO THE HOUSE   90 x 17
ερχομενος ηγγισεν οικια

Now we come to the most significant part of all this. We saw earlier that the word "younger" had a value of 1530. So does the "older" brother.

THE YOUNGER   1530 (90 x 17)
Luke 15:12 νεωτερος

THE OLDER   1530 (90 x 17)
ο πρεσβυτερος"

This phrase also equals 1530:

HOW MANY HIRED SERVANTS OF   1530 (90 x 17)
THE FATHER
Luke 15:17 ποσοι μισθιοι πατρος

The temptation at this point is to take off and start showing examples from all over the Bible, that relate to the above concept—multiples of 153 and 1530. The one Hebrew expression that appears five times in the Old Testament, "sons of God," (בני האלהים), *and is only referring to angelic beings*, has a numerical value of 153. The number 153 is 9 x 17, and we saw in the last chapter on the 153 fishes how 17 speaks of great multitudes, and so does number 9.

The above examples verify again that Jesus in this parable is speaking of the angels of heaven during the original rebellion.

And he called one of the servants, and asked what these things meant. And he said unto him, For the brother of thee is come; and thy father hath killed the fatted calf, because he hath received him back in health.

FOR THE BROTHER   90 x 14
Luke 15:27 οτι ο αδελφος

Nothing could be more direct than the following. The word *brother* all by itself is 90 x 9.

THE BROTHER   90 x 9
αδελφος

The phrase reads "because he hath received him back in health."

RECEIVED HIM BACK IN HEALTH   90 x 21
υγιαινοντα αυτον απελαβεν

There is one other specific reference (or pronoun) to the older son.

And killed the father of thee calf fatted.

THE FATHER OF THEE CALF   90 x 29
πατερ σου τον μοσχον'

And he was angry, and would not go in.

AND HE WAS ANGRY   90 x 9
Luke 15:28 ωργισθη δε και

Therefore the father of him came out and besought him.

THE FATHER OF HIM CAME OUT AND   90 x 41
BESOUGHT HIM
Luke 15:28 πατηρ αυτου εξελθων παρεκαλει αυτον"

THE FATHER OF HIM CAME OUT   900 x 3
ο δε πατηρ αυτου εξελθων"

OF HIM   90 x 13
αυτου

And he answering said to his father, Lo, these many years I served thee, neither transgressed I at any time thy commandment: and yet thou never gavest me a kid, that I might make merry with my friends.

LO, THESE MANY YEARS I SERVED   90 x 42
Luke 15:29 ιδου τοσαυτα ετη δουλευω"

I SERVED   90 x 19
δουλευω'

The last part says, "that I might make merry with my friends."

I MIGHT MAKE MERRY   90 x 9 x 3
(nv) αριστησω'

But as soon as this thy son was come, which hath devoured thy living with harlots, thou hast killed for him the fatted calf.

THY SON   90 x 15
Luke 15:30 υιος σου

KILLED FOR HIM THE FATTED CALF   90 x 52
εθυσας αυτω σιτευτον μοσχον'

And he said unto him, Child, thou art ever with me, and all that I have is thine.

THAT I HAVE IS THINE   90 x 9
Luke 15:31 εμα σα εστιν"

The first portion of the above verse is the only major phrase of this entire story that did not contain a 90 pattern.

It was meet that we should make merry, and be glad: for this thy brother was dead, and is alive; and was lost, and is found.

FOR THIS THY BROTHER   90 x 33
Luke 15:32 οτι ο αδελφος σου ουτος

THIS THY BROTHER   90 x 28
αδελφος σου ουτος

THIS THY   90 x 19   BROTHER   90 x 9
σου ουτος   αδελφος

WAS DEAD AND IS ALIVE   90 x 9
νεκρος ην και εζησεν'

Conclusion

We have now examined every single possibility that exists in all twenty two verses from this account. Our examination was limited to those references that spoke *explicitly* of the two sons who were brothers. In chapter 11 on the scientific method, we will give a statistical probability analysis of all this and demonstrate how "impossible" it would be for anyone to debunk the above with random numerical values. The most significant statistic is that all the phrases average only 2.36 words in length. These are very short and explicit phrases.

The Pattern of Separation, 172

While I was compiling the above examples lo and behold an entire 172 pattern opened up in this chapter at the locations where the passage spoke of both separation and coming together. You will be impressed by the following, especially after all that was shown in chapter 6 on the topic of separation and the 86/172 pattern.

> And said the younger of them to his father, Father, give me the portion of goods that falleth to me. And he divided to them his living.

AND HE DIVIDED   172 x 2
Luke 15:13 ο δε διειλες'

DIVIDED TO THEM HIS LIVING   172 x 8
διειλες αυτοις βιον'

> And after not many days the younger son gathered all together, and departed into a far country.

AFTER   172 x 2
Luke 15:13 μετ'

The reason the pattern shows up here is that the word "after" is pointing to the time of action when the prodigal son gathered his belongings and headed out—separating himself from the father. He separated when he "departed into a far country."

INTO A FAR COUNTRY   86 x 23
εις χωραν μακραν'

In this phrase a host of recognizable patterns with other number structures appears that I would love to comment on. I will discuss only one of them.

The above comes to 86 x 23. I immediately recognized, of course, the 86 (half of 172) as having to do with separation. But the 23 was also very obvious. This number has always been linked to fornication and immorality relative to this world. There is a whole pattern to do with fornication based on 23. The expression "fornicators of the world" in 1 Corinthians 5:10 is 230 x 6. But I noticed that the Greek word for "prodigally"—the word that is the *descriptive basis for this story*—had this value.

> And departed into a far country, and scattered his property living prodigally.

PRODIGALLY 2300
ασωτως'

Look at 1 Corinthians 10:8:

Neither let us commit fornication, as some committed fornication, and fell in one day twenty-three thousand.

SOME COMMITTED FORNICATION, AND FELL 230 x 15
1 Cor. 10:8 τινες αυτων επορνευσαν και επεσαν'

The text states in this story from Luke that the prodigal son "devoured thy living with harlots."

THY LIVING WITH HARLOTS 2300
Luke 15:30 σου βιον μετα πορνων"

HARLOTS 230 x 5
πορνων

There you have it! Another key number in theomatics—mentioned in the text and right out in the open.

FORNICATION 172 x 3
Mat. 5:32 πορνειας

Fornication resulted when the prodigal son separated himself from his father.

We have, of course, seen much in this book concerning separation and the number 172. I happened to notice in the above verse from Matthew, where Jesus talked about fornication, that He also stated that "whoever marries a divorced woman, commits adultery." Obviously, both fornication and adultery involve separation. The following is the translation of one Greek word.

COMMITS ADULTERY 172 x 8
μοιχαται

Now back to the 172 pattern in Luke 15. The prodigal son divided and separated his father's property by scattering it.

SCATTERED THE PROPERTY LIVING PRODIGALLY 172 x 27
διεσκορπισεν ουσιαν ζων ασωτως'

And when he came to himself, he said, How many hired servants of the father of me have bread enough and to spare, and I perish with hunger!

The next example is significant. After having scattered all and finding himself in the pigsty, the young man came to his senses. In the Greek, the passage reads "and unto himself coming, he said." His senses came back, and he mentally came together.

HIMSELF COMING   1720
Luke 15:17 εαυτον ελθων'

> And rising [he] came to his father. But when he was yet a great way off, his father saw him, and had compassion, and ran, and fell on his neck, and kissed him.

In the Greek, it reads, "But when he was afar being away, saw him the father." This is the best example of the 172/separation concept.

BEING AWAY   172 x 8
Luke 15:20 απεχοντος

> And said the son unto him, Father, I have sinned against heaven, and in thy sight, No longer am I worthy to be called thy son.

AGAINST HEAVEN   172 x 8
Luke 15:21 εις τον ουρανον'

It was the original rebellion that brought about a separation in heaven. That is why we see the 172 pattern here.

Now we will see the 172 pattern manifest itself as the Father brings back together his son who was separated from him.

> And bring hither the fatted calf, and kill it; and let us eat, and be merry: For this the son of me was dead, and lived again; he was lost, and is found. And they began to be merry.

THIS THE SON   1720
Luke 15:24 ουτος υιος

Now look at this!

WAS DEAD, AND LIVED AGAIN   860 (172 x 5)
νεκρος ην και ανεζησεν

> And he called one of the servants, and asked what these things meant. And he said unto him, For the brother of thee is come; and thy father hath killed the fatted calf, because he hath received him back in health.

The following is one Greek word. It states, "and him received back."

RECEIVED BACK   172
Luke 15:27 απελαβεν"

And he said unto him, Child, thou art ever with me, and all that I have is thine.

WITH ME   860 (172 x 5)
Luke 15:31 μετ εμου

WITH   172 x 2
μετ'

The above simply shows how the 172 pattern fits itself into the structure—along with the entire host of other numerical structures—also running parallel throughout the passage. We see here the magic square principle at work.

An Important Comment

Earlier I stated that these two sons represent the angels of heaven. No doubt many readers will ask themselves, "Does that mean that God is going to accept back [with open arms] and forgive some of the angels who rebelled and left heaven?"

There is a clear answer to this question, but it will require an extensive explanation. (Again that will be covered in my next book, entitled *The Luciferian Rebellion,* p. 225).

Part II: The Fatted Calf and the Golden Calf Idol

In the second part of this presentation, we are going to explore some truly profound concepts. The interesting part of this prodigal son's story is the portion concerning the fatted calf. When the rebellious son returned the big event relative to his homecoming was the killing of the fatted calf. What could this possibly represent? The calf was fatted, fully developed, ripened, and prepared. It was now ready to be killed, eaten, and digested. It was a time of great rejoicing.

What is most fascinating here is that throughout the Bible worshipping a calf (which is an idol) is related to worshipping the stars or angelic host of heaven. Here again, we see the angelic connection— the deeper symbolism that someone just reading the story would never understand. *We will look at numerous verses that clearly state openly that link in the Bible..* There are eternal mysteries tied to this story from the Book of Luke.

The number 103

Everything relating to calves in the Bible is connected to the number 103. 103 is a prime number. There are five instances in which the word "calf" is used in the New Testament. Three of the occurrences are in Luke 15.

And bring hither the calf fatted, and kill it; and eat it, and be merry.

BRING HITHER THE CALF FATTED   1030 x 4
Luke 15:23 φερετε τον μοσχον τον σιτευτον

EAT IT AND BE MERRY   1030 x 3
φαγοντες ευφρανθωμεν'

He said unto him, For the brother of thee is come; and thy father hath killed the calf fatted.

AND THY FATHER HATH KILLED THE CALF FATTED   103 x 41
Luke 15:27 και εθυσεν πατηρ σου μοσχον αιτευτον'

FATHER HATH KILLED THE CALF   103 x 26
εθυσεν ο πατηρ τον μοσχον

But as soon as this thy son was come, which hath devoured thy living with harlots, thou hast killed for him the calf fatted.

KILLED THE CALF   103 x 22
(mt) Luke 15:30 εθυσας τον μοσχον'

And from all of these accounts, here is the numerical value for just the word "calf."

CALF   1030
μοσχον

There are only two other mentions of a calf in the New Testament. We shall examine one of them later. But here are the words from the Book of Revelation. This is the only time that the spelling of calf does not equal 1030.

And the second living creature was like a calf.

LIVING CREATURE WAS LIKE   103 x 12
Rev. 4:7 ζωον ομοιον'

LIVING CREATURE   103 x 9
ζωον

WAS LIKE   103 x 3
ομοιον'

The Hebrew Old Testament

To begin, I want to show a pattern that is scientifically consistent. It links every single reference in Exodus 32 that refers in any way to the golden calf. Nearly all of these related references have a short explicit multiple of 103—a very consistent pattern.

If you are not familiar with the well-known story of the golden calf, you may wish to read that story in its entirety before proceeding.

> And when the people saw that Moses delayed to come down out of the mount, the people gathered themselves together unto Aaron, and said unto him, Come make for us gods who will go before us.

MAKE FOR US GODS WHO 103 x 13
WILL GO BEFORE US
Exo. 32:1 עשה לנו אלהים אשר ילכו לפנינו׳

From the above Hebrew phrase of six words come the following three and very distinct words. The number 1030 sets the pace for this entire structure. 103 is a prime number. A numerical value of 103 or 1030 is the most clear-cut feature possible. As we shall see, everything relating to the false god and the golden calf is based upon this structure.

MAKE GODS WHO WILL GO 1030
עשה אלהים אשר ילכו״

> And he received what they handed him, fashioning it with an engraving tool, and made a molten calf. Then he said, These are your gods, O Israel, who brought thee up out of the land of Egypt.

A simpler translation of the above would be: "and he fashioned with the tool, and made a molten calf."

HE FASHIONED WITH THE TOOL 103 x 9
Exo. 32:4 יצר אתו בחרט׳

MADE A MOLTEN CALF 103 x 6
יעשהו עגל מסכה׳

Here now are both the Hebrew and Greek words for "calf"—side-by-side. It would be hard for anyone to believe that the following is just a coincidence.

CALF 103
עגל

CALF 1030
μοσχον

The mathematical probability that all of these short, distinct phrases could exhibit this phenomena is positively overwhelming. If all of the world's greatest mathematical minds understood what God has done and comprehended the significance of theomatics, it would change the entire world and all religious philosophy forever. In other words, if God did not put theomatics in the Bible, what we are witnessing would be as impossible as the unabridged dictionary resulting from an explosion in a printing shop. If God (or anyone else) did not place this 103 pattern in the text, nothing would be apparent except random numbers (just like numbers in a phone book).

> And he made a molten calf. Then he said, These are your gods, O Israel, who brought thee up out of the land of Egypt.

THESE ARE YOUR GODS   103
Exo. 32:4   אלה אלהיד'

WHO BROUGHT YOU UP OUT OF   103 x 13
THE LAND OF EGYPT
אשר עלוד מארץ מצרים'

> The next mention of the calf, or worshipping the calf, is in verse 7.

> And the LORD said unto Moses, Go, get thee down; for became corrupt your people whom you brought from land of Egypt.

BECAME CORRUPT YOUR PEOPLE WHOM   103 x 13
Exo. 32:7   שחת עמד אשר

I would like to leap ahead to verse 9, which specifically talks about the people who corrupted themselves with the idol.

> And the LORD said unto Moses, I have seen the people this, and behold, they are a people stiff of neck.

THE PEOPLE   103 x 5
Exo. 32:9   את העם'

THEY ARE A PEOPLE STIFF OF NECK   103 x 9
הנה עם קשה ערף''

A PEOPLE STIFF   103 x 5
עם קשה

Now we will back up to verse 8.

They have turned aside quickly out of the way which I commanded them: they have made for themselves a molten calf, and bowed down to it, and have sacrificed thereunto, and said, These be thy gods, O Israel, which have brought thee up out of the land of Egypt.

THEY TURNED QUICKLY FROM THE WAY   103 x 8
Exo. 32:8 'סרו מהר מן דרד

They have made for themselves a molten calf, and bowed down to it.

THEY HAVE MADE A MOLTEN CALF,   103 x 13
AND BOWED DOWN
Exo 32:8 'עשו עגל מסכה וישתחוו

MADE A MOLTEN CALF   103 x 6
Exo. 32:4 'יעשהו עגל מסכה

CALF   103
עגל

Verse 10 does not mention the calf at all, but the following pattern was just too obvious to ignore. The next series of features will show that a 103 goes through other aspects of this topic. They are not direct references to the actual worshipping of the golden calf, but they show the almost unbelievable consistency that emanates from this pattern. The following words were spoken to Moses by God.

Now therefore let me alone, that my anger may burn against them, and that I may destroy them: and I will make of thee a great nation.

MY ANGER MAY BURN   103 x 3
Exo. 32:10 יחר אפי

And Moses besought the LORD his God, and said, LORD, why does your anger burn hot against thy people, which thou hast brought forth out of the land of Egypt with great power, and with a mighty hand?
Therefore should the Egyptians speak, and say, It was for an evil intent he did bring them out, to slay them in the mountains, and to consume them from the face of the earth? Turn from thy fierce anger, and repent of this evil against thy people.

YOUR ANGER   103
Exo. 32:11 "אפד

The two verses above are full of 103s. For the sake of interest I would like to show side by side two examples that are parallel in meaning. We saw how the words "my anger may burn" have a value of 103 x 3 and the word translated as "your anger" equalled 103. Now look at this outstanding result.

"Turn from thy fierce anger, and relent of this evil against thy people.

TURN   103 x 3
Exo. 32:12 שׁוּב׳

RELENT   103
הנחם

And the LORD relented from the evil which he threatened to do unto his people.

RELENTED FROM   103 x 2
Exo. 32:14 ינחם עלׁ"

HE THREATENED   103 x 2
דבר

Verses 16 and 17 describe how Moses went down from the mountain holding the tablets of stone.

And when Joshua heard the noise of the people as they shouted, he said unto Moses, There is a noise of war in the camp.

Now look at the following. The term *camp* describes all those who were worshipping the calf.

THE CAMP   103
Exo. 32:17 מחנה

And it came to pass, as soon as he came nigh unto the camp, that he saw the calf, and the dancing: and Moses' anger burned.

SAW THE CALF   103 x 7
Exo. 32:19 ירא את העגל

And he took the calf which they had made, and burnt [it] in the fire, and ground [it] to powder.

TOOK THE CALF WHICH   103 x 7
Exo. 32:20 יקח עגל אשר׳

The text states that he ground the golden calf to "powder."

POWDER   103
Exo. 32:20 'דק

And scattered it upon the water, and made the children of Israel drink of it.

DRINK OF IT   103 x 4
"ישק

And Moses said unto Aaron, What did this people do unto you, that you led them into such great sin.

LED THEM INTO SUCH GREAT SIN   103 x 6
Exo. 32:21 'כי הבאת עליו חטאה גדלה

And Aaron said, Let not the anger of my lord burn hot: thou knowest the people, how inclined to evil they are.

THE PEOPLE, HOW INCLINED TO EVIL   103 x 4
Exo. 32:22 עם כי ברע

THE PEOPLE   103 x 5
'את העם

HOW INCLINED TO EVIL THEY ARE   103 x 3
כי ברע זה

The first and last features are six word English translations, but the originals consisted of only three Hebrew words.

For they said unto me, Make us gods, which shall go before us: for as for this Moses, the man that brought us up out of the land of Egypt, we don't know what is become of him (Exo. 32:23).

We previously saw above that the phrase "make us gods, which shall go before us" had two distinct features of 103.

And I said unto them, Whosoever hath any gold, let them take it off. So they gave it to me: then I cast it into the fire, and there came out the calf this.

CAME OUT THE CALF   103 x 2
Exo. 32:24 "יצא עגל

And Moses returned unto the LORD, and said, Oh, this people sinned a great sin, and have made for themselves gods of gold.

THIS PEOPLE SINNED A GREAT SIN   103 x 2
Exo. 32:31 'חטא עם זה חטאה גדלה

MADE FOR THEMSELVES GODS   103 x 5
ויעשו להם אלהי"

> And the LORD struck the people with a plague, because of what they did with the calf that Aaron made.

THE CALF THAT AARON MADE   103 x 12
Exo. 32:35 'עגל אשר עשה אהרן

All the References to the Calf Itself

The number 103 touches on many themes that relate in one way or another to the golden calf and the abomination that the children of Israel conjured in making "other gods." In the pockets where 103 appears, there are very distinct patterns as the thread weaves its way though the tapestry of this theme and its many related side topics.

MADE A MOLTEN CALF   103 x 6 [3]
Exo. 32:4 'יעשהו עגל מסכה

CALF   103 [1]
Exo. 32:8 עגל

SAW THE CALF   103 x 7 [2]
Exo. 32:19 ירא את העגל

TOOK THE CALF WHICH   103 x 7 [3]
Exo. 32:20 'יקח עגל אשר

CAME OUT THE CALF   103 x 2 [2]
Exo. 32:24 '"יצא עגל

THE CALF THAT AARON MADE   103 x 12 [4]
Exo. 32:35 'עגל אשר עשה אהרן

All six phrases that contained the word "calf" fit this pattern. The word "calf" is included in all the above phrases. And the average length for each phrase is only 2.5 words.

There are a few other Old Testament passages where the word is used.

> And Abraham ran unto the herd, and fetched a calf of the herd, tender and good, and gave it unto a young man; and he hasted to dress it.

AND FETCHED A CALF OF THE HERD,   103 x 7
TENDER AND GOOD
Gen. 18:7 ויקח בן בקר רך וטוב

THE HERD   103 x 3
הבקר"'

FETCHED A CALF, TENDER AND GOOD   103 x 4
יקח בן רך וטוב'

Here is the next verse.

And he took butter, and milk, and the calf of the herd which he prepared, and set it before them.

THE CALF OF THE HERD WHICH HE PREPARED   103 x 12
Gen. 18:8 בן הבקר אשר עשה'

THE CALF WHICH HE PREPARED   103 x 9
Gen. 18:8 בן אשר עשה'

We are focusing our attention on specific references to the word "calf"; however, there is one other mention of calves that will leave an indelible imprint on this design. Let's go right to the beginning of Genesis. We saw that the word "herd" above was 103. Look at this next example.

And the LORD God said unto the serpent, Because thou hast done this, thou art cursed above all cattle, and above every beast of the field; upon thy belly shalt thou go, and dust shalt thou eat all the days of thy life.

ALL CATTLE   103
Gen. 3:14 כל בהמה'

The next mention of a calf takes place in Leviticus.

And he said unto Aaron, Take for thee a young calf for a sin offering, and a ram for a burnt offering, without blemish, and offer them before the LORD.

TAKE A YOUNG CALF   103 x 2
Lev. 9:2 קח עגל בן'

Aaron therefore went unto the altar, and slew the calf of the sin offering, which was for himself.

THE CALF OF THE SIN OFFERING   103 x 9
Lev. 9:8   את עגל החטאת

Now we come to a specific mention of the golden calf incident outside Exodus, in Deuteronomy. Here the Lord is found speaking.

> The calf which you made, I took and burned it with fire, and crushed it and ground it very small, even until it was as fine as dust.

THE CALF WHICH YOU MADE ,   1030 x 2
I TOOK AND BURNED
Deu. 9:21   "עשיתם שת עגל לקחתי ואשרף

THE CALF WHICH YOU MADE   103 x 9
'עשיתם העגל

Look now at the following series of 103 to do with dust.

CRUSHED IT AND GROUND IT VERY SMALL   103 x 9
'אכת אתו טחון היטב

It was ground until it was "fine as dust."

FINE   103
'דק

In the past, I have done considerable research on the subject of dust in the Bible (see *Theomatics II*, pp. 102-105). And I just happened to remember the story of the ten plagues in Egypt, where God speaks to Moses and Aaron.

> And the LORD said unto Moses and unto Aaron, Take to you handfuls of ashes of the furnace, and let Moses sprinkle it toward the heaven in the sight of Pharaoh. And it shall become fine dust in all the land of Egypt.

FINE DUST   103
Exo. 9:9   אבק

In Genesis God pronounced judgment on the serpent. "thou art cursed above all cattle; upon thy belly shalt thou go, and dust shalt thou eat all the days of thy life." When Moses destroyed the calf he turned it into dust. When God cursed the serpent, He pronounced that dust was to become his food.

From the Book of Acts in the New Testament, an unusual Greek verb is used meaning "they made a calf." The following example consists of only three Greek words (and the conjunction).

> And they made a calf in the days those, and offered a sacrifice to the idol, and rejoiced in the works of their hands.

AND THEY MADE A CALF IN THE DAYS 103 x 18
Act. 7:41 και εμοσχοποιησαν εν ημεραις

IN THE DAYS THOSE 103 x 7
εν ημεραις εκειναις'

Here is the outstanding result. The last half of the above verse states: "and offered a sacrifice to the idol."

OFFERED A SACRIFICE TO THE IDOL 103 x 7 x 5
Act. 7:41 ανηγαγον θυσιαν τω ειδωλω

THE IDOL 103 x 16
ειδωλω'

And after they offered a sacrifice to the idol, the text states that "they rejoiced in the works of their hands." Interestingly, the number 34 is the major number to do with Babylon, the city of man.

THE WORKS OF THEIR HANDS 103 x 34
εργοις χειρων αυτων"

When we go to the Book of Isaiah, we find the expression "idols of gold."

> In that day a man shall cast his idols of silver, and his idols of gold, which they made each one for himself to worship, to the moles and to the bats.

IDOLS OF GOLD 103
Isa. 2:20 אלילי זהבו"

This Could Go On and On

I went through the Old Testament looking at all the times the word "calf" or "calves" was used. I put together an entire page of outstanding 103 hits, all distinct short phrases. If I were to list these, this study would multiply, particularly in examining specific references to idol worship in the Old Testament. I compiled pages and pages of incredible examples—well over one hundred of them. However, I will only discuss in general terms what the calf really represents.

The Stars and Host of Heaven

Worshipping the golden calf actually represents the worship of the host of heaven, or angelic beings.

The term "stars" in the Bible represents all sorts of angelic beings. I have observed that the word in Hebrew has a value of 103.

STARS   103
הכוכבים

CALF   103
עגל

And when we come to the Book of Hebrews, in the New Testament, God said the following concerning the seed of Abraham. The word "stars" from the following clusters by three of 900. Of course, the word "angels" has a similar value of 900 in Greek.

> As the stars of heaven in multitude, and as the sand which is by the sea shore innumerable.

AS   1030
Heb. 11:12   καθος

In Luke Jesus tells of the time when there will be "signs in the stars." There is a whole pattern of 103 in Greek, to do with the stars.

SIGNS IN   103 x 3
Luke 21:25   σημεια εν'

It would seem that a calf (or a cow), which is a relatively dumb animal, would be the furthest thing from stars (angelic beings) one could possibly imagine. But there is verse after verse in the Bible that unmistakably links idolatry, or the worship of the calf, with the host of heaven and demons. Look at this example where Jehovah is speaking to the children of Israel.

> And when you look up to heaven, and you see the sun and the moon and the stars all the host of heaven, and you are enticed, and you bow down to them, and you worship [them].

AND YOU SEE   103 x 6
Deu. 4:19   וראית

THE STARS ALL THE HOST OF HEAVEN 1030
את כוכבים כל צבא שמים"

STARS 103
הכוכבים

AND YOU BOW DOWN 103 x 11
ושתחוית"

YOU WORSHIP 103 x 5
עבדתם'

Zephaniah tells of worshipping the host of heaven on the roofs of the houses.

And them that worship upon the housetops to the host of heaven.

UPON THE HOUSETOPS TO THE HOST OF HEAVEN 1030
Zep. 1:5 על גגות לצבא השמים

THE HOUSETOPS 103 x 4
גגות

TO THE HOST OF HEAVEN 103 x 5
לצבא השמים"

In the New Testament there is only one mention of the host of heaven being worshipped. This particular verse connects the worship of the golden calf with the worship of the host of heaven.

And they made a calf in those days, and offered a sacrifice to the idol, and rejoiced in the work of their own hands. And God turned them over and gave them up to worship the host of heaven as it has been written in the roll of the prophets.

GOD TURNED THEM OVER 103 x 16
Act. 7:42 εστρεψεν θεος'

In the portion of the phrase that concerns worshipping the host of heaven, I could find no pattern of 103. There were other absolutely unmistakable patterns with every possible phrase combination; the word "worship" had a value of 900. But then this amazing feature manifested itself. It will show us how God has *embedded* these structures within all of the numerical values—the manner in which the symbolism is brought forth.

> And God turned them over and gave them up to worship the host of heaven AS it has been written in the roll of the prophets.

AS   1030
καθως

This is very important, and its significance is confirmed by the following result. In the words that follow the number 1030 appears twice in reference to making various false gods.

> Did you not offer me slain beasts and sacrifices, forty years in the wilderness, O house of Israel? And you took up the tent of Moloch, and the star of the god Remphan, the models which you made to worship; and I will remove you beyond Babylon.

There are numerous other 103s here. I show a few of the more clear-cut examples.

TOOK UP THE TENT OF MOLOCH   103 x 15
Act. 7:43 ανελαβετε σκηνην Μολοχ

AND THE STAR OF THE GOD REMPHAN   1030 x 3
και το αστραν του θεου Ρομφα'''

THE STAR   103 x 7 (also 90 x 8)
αστρον

THE MODELS WHICH   1030 x 3
τους τυπους ους

So the number 103 speaks of more than just the golden calf—it ties into all idolatry and models, and worship of false gods in general.

Probably the most famous false God in the entire Old Testament is Baal.

> And they bowed down to all the hosts of heaven, and worshipped Baal.

AND WORSHIPPED BAAL   103 x 2
2 Ki. 17:16 ויעבדו הבעל'

BAAL   103
בעל'

Throughout the Old Testament, whenever Baal worship is mentioned, an "Asherah pole" is also set up.

ASHERAH POLE   103 x 5
2 Ki. 17:16 'אשירה

> And he erected altars to Baal, and made an Asherah pole, as Ahab king of Israel had done. And he bowed to all the host of heaven, and worshipped them. And he built altars to all the host of heaven in both courts of the temple of Jehovah.

BUILT ALTARS   103 x 5
2 Ki. 21:4 'בנה מזבחת

ALTARS TO ALL THE HOST OF HEAVEN 1030
2 Ki. 21:5 'מזבחות לכל צבא השמים

I have shown only a fraction of the design that exists with this theme.

11 Theomatics and the Scientific Method

Putting the Skeptics to Bed

This is the chapter where theomatics either lives or dies. This is where this subject must stand naked before the death rays of the scientific method and confront reality honestly and objectively.

If there is one department where theomatics has done its homework, this is it.

A number of very capable and brilliant individuals have tried their best over the years to debunk (disprove) theomatics. For whatever reasons, they refused to believe even the possibility that something like this could exist. They tried to poke holes from every angle. When they were appropriately confronted with hard facts and impenetrable data, without exception all gave up and limped off into the shadows. No one has successfully challenged this subject, and no one ever will. In fact, no one will even come close to it. Why? The answer is simple. *It is impossible to disprove something that simply exists!* If you don't like the Great Pyramid or the Golden Gate Bridge, you cannot deny their existence or make them vanish.

> NOTE: There are three chapters in *Theomatics II* that cover this more thoroughly. The following will only be a synopsis. Here we shall simply discuss the essential facts of importance. In addition, there is a 300-page manuscript, *Theomatics and the Scientific Method*, which presents the computerized testing and data.

The Scientific Method

The most simple definition of the word science is *the state of knowing—knowledge of fact—as opposed to intuition or belief.*

Science deals with real facts in a real world. It deals with that which can be tested through a process that is repeatable and produces an outcome that is determinate and predictable. The *World Book Encyclopedia* would define science or the scientific method, as follows.

> Science covers the broad field of human knowledge concerned with facts held together by principles (rules). Scientists discover and test these facts and principles by the scientific method, which is an orderly system of solving problems. Scientists obtain data by performing experiments and observing the results. The information collected has to be interpreted; science has therefore an intellectual as well as a practical side and it is at least partly rational. The sciences include: (1) mathematics and logic; (2) the physical sciences (such as physics, chemistry, astronomy); (3) the biological sciences, (such as botany and zoology); and (4) social sciences (sociology and anthropology).[1]

The Purest of All Sciences

The one branch of science that concerns us is *mathematics and logic.* It is the purest of all the sciences. It is also the most objective and absolute. The state of development of any science is indicated by the use it makes of mathematics. A science begins with simple mathematics to measure then works toward more complex mathematics in order to explain. Known or established mathematical laws are without question the most undisputed and universally provable facts in all the universe, for they are eternal in nature. The fact that $2 + 2 = 4$ is something that was never created; therefore, it is impossible to destroy it. The fact $2 + 2 = 4$ never had a beginning (only the discovery of it had a beginning). Every similar mathematical formula or equation is also eternal and absolute truth.

Science versus Theology

Over the centuries, there has been a great canyon or divide between scientists and theologians. Both live on almost completely different planets. It has been said that science deals with the realm of facts, and religion deals with the realm of faith and anticipation. Science concerns itself with things seen, and religion with things that are invisible; the former is material and the latter spiritual.

The scientist is always in search of strictly universal laws. This is necessary in order for him to find comprehensive explanations for all that exists. The theologian can rarely, if ever, test his beliefs by any such method(s). For that reason, the scientist can usually be more confident that his knowledge and beliefs lie at a higher level of objectivity and certainty.

Yet as wonderful as science is, we need to also understand that it has its own limitations.

Although scientists can study many objects and events, there are many things they cannot test. For example, a scientist cannot measure a mother's love for her children. He cannot measure the difference between good and evil. There is no way to tell scientifically what feeling an artist expresses in a painting. Such information cannot be scientifically observed and measured.[2]

Virtually no Biblical teaching or doctrine can be scientifically proven in a laboratory. Theologians must use entirely different methods, or tools of logic (hermeneutic principles and exegesis), in order to arrive at their conclusions. These methods, while valid in their own realm, do not necessarily produce conclusive results. One man's heresy may end up being another man's orthodoxy. For instance, there is no way to scientifically prove or disprove the doctrine of eternal security (once saved always saved). There is no way to scientifically prove or disprove that Sunday is the proper day of worship (and the Seventh-Day Adventists are all wrong). There is no way to scientifically prove in a laboratory whether or not there is going to be a future millennial reign of Christ on earth (or as many people believe, that the "1000 years" is symbolic). None of these teachings are provable in any way that would be acceptable to science. This brings us to a critical statement.

The Validity of Theomatics

The validity of theomatics has nothing to do with theology. The methods of theology are not applicable in attempting to either prove or disprove theomatics. Whether the entire concept makes sense to a person or agrees with their belief system about God and the Bible—how they think God should operate—none of this is relevant. We don't accept the validity of theomatics based upon any theological standards, confessions, or creeds. Whether or not theomatics exists must be based solely on pure science. In the end, if theomatics is proven to be true, then our theology must conform to fit the facts. We must bow to it (and to the God who placed it in the Bible). It does not have to bend to us and our own way of thinking.

Does Theomatics Exist?

This is the critical question. All other concerns and arguments fall into the secondary category of the "implications of theomatics." And in that department, there are certainly many theological considerations.

The implications have been discussed in past chapters of this book. Here, however, our concern is not "why" or "what," but "if."

Numerous people have clearly seen the fact that theomatics either exists or it does not. There is no gray area. It is either present in its entirety, or not at all. There is no such thing as a woman being 50 percent or partially pregnant. We can safely assume that if God did place an inherent structure—based upon the number-to-letter allocations—then it probably saturates everything from top to bottom.

Time to "Round 'em Up"

Before proceeding to show the reader the method and manner in which all of this is unequivocally proven (and subsequently put the skeptics to bed), it is important to pin down any possible or potential criticism of the validity of this subject. In other words, at the outset, we are going to corral the skeptics and box them into a corner from which there will be no escape.

Many individuals will ultimately reject the reality of the existence of theomatics for a host of philosophical or theological reasons. However, no matter what the reason or logic may be, there is one highway that all of them must eventually travel.

All Roads Lead to This

For any destructive critic, the only valid assumption is that no matter how impressive the theomatic features, no matter how logical and conclusive the data, no matter what the statistical odds, the one inevitable position he must essentially and irrevocably maintain, as a matter of necessity to his position, is that these so-called results are only coincidence and nothing more than the product of random chance. All data that theomatics has ever discovered was found by arbitrarily picking and choosing from a base of numbers that is strictly random; it is selective data. The researcher in some careful and subtle manner has "cooked the results" of the inquiry—he is the reason, not "God." In the end, there must be nothing unique or special—no special characteristics or supernatural element—relative to the assignment of numerical values to the Hebrew and Greek texts of the Bible.

For the skeptic, this is the only possible conclusion. *To admit otherwise is to admit that theomatics may actually be true.* The only other alternative is to provide a natural cause that would explain the positive results (if there are any). There are only two possibilities.

- The whole thing is the product of lost ancient knowledge, handed down. It was then introduced into the Bible according to a conspiracy that lasted sixteen hundred years, in which all forty Bible writers secretly participated (and for which there is not even the slightest historical evidence). This idea is, of course, ridiculous (see *Theomatics II*, p. 185).

- It is a product or aberration of the Hebrew and Greek languages. When examined, this argument completely falls apart as well (see *Theomatics II*, p. 186). Whoever put the patterns there had to engineer the words. The patterns only appear in the Bible. And they only appear when related words or theological meanings are examined. And they only appear with the standard numerical values.

Finding the Fatal Flaw

I have had occasion to observe many skeptics over the years. What I have learned is that various individuals who are skeptical about claims of this nature (those who enjoy playing the role of devil's advocate) will immediately seek to pounce on a weakness or fatal flaw, in either the scientific logic or the statistical procedure.

Most dudes out there who are cynical will only give the subject a perfunctory examination. If they think they have found the fatal flaw, like a predator they will tend to pursue. However, if they eventually find themselves in quicksand and cannot produce a substantial and provable weakness, at that point they will usually make some snide remarks and you never hear from them again (the Internet is loaded with thousands of these types of arrogant smart alecks, especially in the newsgroups.)

Or they will resort to an approach called *deflection.* If theomatics has as its established defense scientific data that is irrefutable, then the critic will ignore that evidence—refusing to admit to it—and in lieu of challenging the facts, focus on other more trivial issues that are non-fatal. Or they will try to find one silly mistake, or lack of sophistication in a certain discipline, and from that "build a man of straw," knocking him down.

Quite honestly, no skeptic will waste a lot of time with something like this, unless there is a personal "reward" at the other end. What is most unfair is the fact that if someone ever does make a serious attempt to debunk theomatics, and the attempt fails, we are unlikely to be told.

The Science of Statistics and Probability

Professional statisticians and probability experts have been consulted and a great deal of work has been done to calculate the actual mathematical probabilities for various design structures in theomatics. It has been shown that the mathematical odds of many theomatic patterns occurring by chance (assuming a valid null hypothesis that numbers must occur at random unless someone with intelligence arranges things differently) is only one in so many millions, billions, trillions, quadrillions, etc.

Presenting this type of data can become quite technical and takes great effort to explain to the average person. In this chapter, I will bypass that sort of evidence and simply focus on "the Method." This discussion here will be conclusive and mathematically unimpeachable.

The scientific method according to which theomatics is effectively proven (or disproven) is simple. In fact, it is so simple and straightforward that those who want to build a big, complicated thesis to try to debunk the subject will find that, when confronted with "the method," their trail ends abruptly at the edge of the Grand Canyon. Unless they can find a way to build a bridge over this one, all philosophical or theological arguments they will seek to set forth, *or any deflective arguments*, will be completely nullified by "the method."

How Many Permutations Are There?

To demonstrate how impossible it would be for there to exist any divine or supernatural element in the Bible—based on the numerical values of the Hebrew and Greek alphabets—*unless someone with intelligence deliberately put it there,* I now present the explanation that forms the backbone of theomatics validity. We have already seen that there are twenty-two letters in the Hebrew alphabet and twenty-six letters in the Greek alphabet. *There is a mind-boggling number of other possibilities present for the numerical values that theomatics uses.*

GREEK ALPHABET RANDOM COMBINATIONS

```
 1 ......... 1
 2 ......... 2
 3 ......... 6
 4 ......... 24
 5 ......... 120
 6 ......... 720
 7 ......... 5,040
 8 ......... 40,320
 9 ......... 362,880
10 ......... 3,628,800
11 ......... 39,916,800
12 ......... 479,001,600
13 ......... 6,227,020,800
14 ......... 87,178,291,200
15 ......... 1,307,674,368,000
16 ......... 20,922,789,888,000
17 ......... 355,687,428,096,000
18 ......... 6,402,373,705,728,000
19 ......... 121,645,100,408,832,000
20 ......... 2,432,902,008,176,640,000
21 ......... 51,090,942,171,709,400,000
22 ......... 1,240,007,277,776,000,000,000
23 ......... 25,852,016,738,884,900,000,000
24 ......... 620,448,401,733,239,000,000,000
25 ......... 15,511,210,043,330,900,000,000,000
26 ......... 403,291,461,126,605,000,000,000,000
```

To illustrate, let us suppose that we were to create a language that had an alphabet that consisted of only two letters, *a* and *b,* each having a specific numerical value. *a* could equal a value of 1, and *b* could equal a value of 2. From a mathematical standpoint, there are two different possibilities, or ways that these numerical values could be assigned.

```
a = 1    or    a = 2
b = 2          b = 1
```

If we had a three-letter alphabet, *a*, *b*, and *c*, each with a respective numerical value, there would be six different combinations or permutations possible.

a = 1	a = 1	a = 2	a = 2	a = 3	a = 3
b = 2	b = 3	b = 1	b = 3	b = 1	b = 2
c = 3	c = 2	c = 3	c = 1	c = 2	c = 1

To find the combinations for a particular number, one simply multiplies that number times the total combinations for the previous number.

For two letters, it would be 2 x 1 = 2 combinations. For three letters it would be 3 x 2 = 6 combinations. For four letters it would by 4 x 6 = 24 combinations. For five letters it would be 5 x 24 = 120 combinations.

That is 403 septillion, 291 sextillion, 461 quintillion, 126 quadrillion, 605 trillion combinations! And that is considering only the *standard numerical value sequence* of 1 to 9, 10 to 90, 100 to 800. If other numerical arrangements were used, the number of possible random combinations would be infinite.

Here Is the Crux of the Whole Matter

What is important to note is that each one of these 403 septillion possibilities would produce a completely *different* set or mix of numerical values for all the words in the Bible. Two inescapable requirements are necessary in order for theomatics to be a valid discovery. It must be proven beyond any reasonable doubt that

- The *only* number-letter arrangement that can possibly work to produce "theomatic features" that go consistently beyond the laws of chance is the one that theomatics uses—the one that has been traditionally known for thousands of years and can be found in *Webster's Dictionary* and the earliest New Testament papyrus fragments, and that

- The only manuscripts in history that can produce any consistency that can be demonstrated according to the scientific method, i.e., that goes beyond the laws of chance, are the original sixty-six books of the Bible—Genesis through Revelation.

None of the other 403 septillion alphabetical number-letter arrangements can work. *If even one of them could produce the same average side-by-side results that theomatics has been able to produce, theomatics would be null.* This would prove, or at the very least indicate, that there was nothing unique or special about the features that theomatics has found.

You see, if God (or anyone else) did not place the theomatic structure in the Bible, then the numerical values theomatics uses would produce nothing more than random numbers when applied to the Hebrew and Greek words. Therefore, any other random number-letter equivalencies would have just as good a chance of producing "features" as theomatics has. Why not? If the theomatic number-letter equivalencies are random, they are *only one out of 403 septillion possibilities.*

Let's Ask an Expert

For the record, here is the professional statistician's report that appeared in my original book.

Mr. Del Washburn:

I have considered the material you sent me concerning your approach to proof of "theomatic" design in the Bible. In considering your material, I addressed myself in particular to your proposal of the construction of "random interlinears." I am in complete agreement with you in the idea that if there is nothing inherently "special" or "non-random" about the interlinear resulting from the assignment of number values to Greek letters as given in Webster's dictionary, then one should be able to substantially duplicate your findings with *any random assignment* of number-letter equivalencies. More precisely, if one examines an interlinear resulting from random assignment of equivalencies in the same manner as you examined the interlinear resulting from the assignment appearing in Webster's, and if there are no special characteristics of the latter assignment, then one should be able to produce results, i.e., theomatic features with the same general probability (or improbability) as those you have been able to produce. In comparing the results of both efforts one should then expect: (1) As many features from the one as from the other. (2) The features produced from the one would have the same clear significance as those of the other. By this I mean one should be able to find groups of phrases with the same theological theme, i.e., Jesus, Satan, the flesh, etc., rather than phrases consisting of odd collections of words with no clear theological significance and chosen only for the similarity of numerical equivalents. (3) The features would exhibit the same general "clustering" characteristics. In particular, the clustering from the random interlinear should be around multiples of numbers of the same general magnitude as those of Webster's, not smaller numbers. It should be noted that numbers of the same general magnitude would be necessary to produce comparable probabilities of occurrence. Pursuant to the idea discussed above, I have constructed a table of random numbers, two random assignments of number-letter equivalencies which may be used to construct random interlinears. In closing I would like to wish you good luck with the forthcoming publication of your book. Please keep me informed.

Sincerely,
LaVerne W. Stanton,
Ph.D., Associate Professor and Chair,
Department of Quantitative Methods,
California State University, Fullerton

With his letter, Dr. Stanton provided two sets of random number-letter equivalencies, which I used in the statistics chapter of the original *Theomatics*. Using them now is completely unnecessary because the computer programs that I currently use can mix up to one million random seed numbers and number-letter equivalencies.

Standard Allocations		Random Allocations	
α	1	α	6
β	2	β	5
γ	3	γ	3
δ	4	δ	9
ε	5	ε	8
ϛ'	6	ϛ'	2
ζ	7	ζ	1
η	8	η	4
θ	9	θ	7
ι	10	ι	30
κ	20	κ	70
λ	30	λ	50
μ	40	μ	80
ν	50	ν	10
ξ	60	ξ	20
ο	70	ο	40
π	80	π	90
ο	90	ο	60
ρ	100	ρ	700
σ - ϛ	200	σ - ϛ	200
τ	300	τ	400
υ	400	υ	500
φ	500	φ	800
χ	600	χ	100
ψ	700	ψ	300
ω	800	ω	600

Shown above is an example of a random assignment. In order to make it as objective as possible the letters have been mixed up within their respective groups: the single digits (1 to 9), the double digits (10 to 90), and the triple digits (100 to 800).

Any time I run theomatic tests of phrases by computer, I can simultaneously call up *one million random assignments* of number-letter equivalencies. The computer then duplicates the exact same calculations in searching for features with the random values as it does with the theomatic values. If a theomatic word comes out a multiple of 10, so will the random word. This removes any argument that the theomatic values may have certain characteristics that produce the "results," or that the outcome results from some mathematical artifact.

Shown below is a Greek phrase from John 3:16: "For thus loved God the world so as the Son the only begotten He gave." The first example shows the theomatic numerical values. The second example is random. Only the values in the first line would be able to produce meaningful results. The words with the random values would only yield results according to what mathematicians call "the null hypothesis."

1770	104	355	70	284	420	450	1305	420	530	420	296	884
ουτος	γαρ	ηγαπησεν	ο	θεος	τον	κοσμον	ωστε	τον	υιον	τον	μονογενη	εδωκεν

1740	709	325	40	255	450	440	1208	450	580	450	195	705
ουτος	γαρ	ηγαπησεν	ο	θεος	τον	κοσμον	ωστε	τον	υιον	τον	μονογενη	εδωκεν

"Tit for Tat"

It is clear that in comparing both efforts, theomatic versus random, the following similarities should and would in all probability occur (if theomatics was not valid.)

- On the average, both efforts should produce the *same number* of features or examples of phenomena.
- On the average, both efforts should produce features or multiples of numbers of the *same size* or magnitude or of equal probability.
- On the average, both efforts should produce features of the *same general distinction* relative to meaning or theological theme.
- On the average, both efforts should produce features of phrases of the *same length.*

In any scientific test that is performed, there must be no advantage given to either the theomatic or the random values. Each side must stand on an equal footing.

What About the Phone Book?

Let the following illustration show how ridiculous all of this would be if theomatics was not true.

Suppose that someone came along and tried to publish a scientific paper in which they claimed to have had an amazing revelation concerning the Greater Chicago telephone directory. He has discovered that the vast majority of phone numbers for people with the last name of *Smith* clustered around multiples of 93. Furthermore, he has discovered that phone numbers of people with the last name of *Jones* were structured primarily on multiples of 153.

In publishing this discovery (even if it were true), the most difficult problem our investigator would have would be getting another scientist to even take the time to test such a hypothesis. Everyone knows that numbers in a phone book are simply random numbers. In fact, even to consider the possibility of anything else would be incomprehensible, a total absurdity. A Jones number has just as good a probability or chance of producing a 93 as a Smith number does. In looking for multiples of 93 from any random number, one would only be able to find an exact hit every 93 numbers. (To find a hit within a cluster of 93 would be only 1 chance in 18.6, i.e., 93/5 = 18.60.)

So why should the Bible, or any other work of literature, be any different when one tries to apply numerical values to words and theological themes? I must constantly remind myself to be somewhat sympathetic to those who are skeptical of the validity of theomatics. Certainly, by all human or secular logic, applying this sort of a method could not be expected to produce any consistent numerical patterns (like theomatics) in any work of literature, any more than in a local phone directory. It would be no more likely.

Putting the Big Argument to Sleep

At this point I will briefly interrupt the progression of thought to discuss the major argument skeptics try to throw at both Bible codes and theomatics.

Many evangelical leaders opposed to the entire concept of a hidden numerical structure in the Bible have asserted that the phenomenon can be found anywhere outside the Bible. In other words, the methods employed by the proponents will exhibit the same identical results when applied to any work of literature. Of course, the conclusion they are trying to draw from that argument is that since the methods are suspect and not valid to begin with, they can work just as easily anywhere.

Unfortunately, this conclusion will fall flat on its face when it comes to theomatics. One is no more likely to find theomatic patterns in other works of literature than to find provable patterns in the Chicago phone book.

No one could ever demonstrate that any other work of literature contains words and topics that produce number patterns that go beyond the laws of random chance. Let us suppose that someone takes any number of references from a Hebrew or Greek literary work, tries all the various phrase combinations, and eventually produces a string of hits that contain a common denominator. This could never be done in such a manner that another person, adhering to the same ground rules, could not take a random or different set of allocations to the letters and words, and following the same procedure, achieve similar average results. It would be a "piece of cake" to prove and demonstrate that fact.

The Final Conclusion

If theomatics is untrue, then everything that has been shown thus far in this book (as well as everything else that has been discovered) could be easily duplicated by *any one random assignment.* A person could take any one random assignment and produce as many short phrases on *agape* love all with values of multiples of 93 (or any number of the same general magnitude). In reference to fishing, the net, fishers of men, etc., he could produce as many multiples of 153, 170, and 289 (or any other relational numbers), and he could also produce as many 86 and 172 examples related to separation, from both the Hebrew and Greek.

Testing the Hypothesis

If a person wishes to investigate all this thoroughly, there is material available for in-depth analysis.[3] The computer software currently used is very sophisticated and absolutely mathematically thorough.

Here now is an explanation of both the ground rules and the testing procedure.

- To begin the experiment, *every single passage or possibility* that exists within a distinct category must be clearly identified in *advance* of performing any tests (No human bias factor or selective use of data is allowed; see *Theomatics II*, pp. 170,171.)

- Only *one Hebrew or Greek text* can be used, with no variant readings. If variant readings are looked at, then all variants need to be calculated into the program.

- Every possible phrase combination that exists, i.e., all mathematical possibilities, are taken into account and extracted by computer.

- Each phrase used from all the feature references must *contain a specific Hebrew or Greek word.* Without doing it this way there is no objective way of defining what constitutes a feature.

- The computer program goes through every single phrase combination from every reference and looks for theomatic results. These results are then recorded.

- Then the program does a parallel analysis, recalculating the value of every word according to a random seed number, reassigning all the allocations of numbers to letters. The entire base is shuffled and changed so it is unquestionably random.

- Finally, the computer looks for features with the best possible number that is similar in size to the theomatic multiple and tries just as hard to find hits with the random values, as it did with the theomatic values.

The computer programs are also able to search through a whole string of references and find the one random number that produces the best results common to the greatest number of references.

Theomatics is confined to the use of one set of allocations of numbers to letters. The skeptic trying to debunk theomatics is allowed use of literally thousands of random/alphabet allocations (trying the same experiment over and over again) in trying to find *just one* of them that will come close to matching the results.

This investigation and comparison of theomatics versus random numbers is absolutely conclusive. There is not a mathematical scientist on the face of the earth who will find any fault with it. Again, if the theomatic base is random (and there is no supernatural or Divine element present), then any other random assignment should produce similar average results.

Right now there are several hundred studies in my files that can apply the above analysis in an absolutely thorough and objective manner; random numbers cannot even come close to producing the same results.

Back to the Prodigal Son

The pattern that was shown in the previous chapter relative to the prodigal son will now be analyzed. It will show how ridiculous and impossible it would be to try and mathematically debunk theomatics. Anyone who is skeptical after a careful study and analysis of the following will have no choice but to simply pack their bags and go home.

Shown below are all of the hits that specifically refer to the two sons who were brothers. The only examples that qualify are those that (1) use a word that specifically refers to the brothers, (2) use a pronoun in the phrase, or (3) imply a pronoun in the verb. In every example shown, the specific English and corresponding Greek word that speaks of the brothers is underlined.

Also following the feature is a number in brackets [ ]. This is the number of Greek words that exist in the phrase (not counting variables such as articles and conjunctions). You will also notice that in a few cases, examples that should be underlined are not. This is because the particular word or phrase is underlined from another verse and each example must be non-redundant. *You can only use an original hit one time.* Obviously, if the same word appears over and over again, you cannot count each instance as an original hit. That fact should be obvious.

Verse #11: And he said, A certain man had two sons.

SONS 90 x 12 [1]
Luke 15:11 υιους

Verse #12: And said the younger of them to his father, Father, give me the portion of goods that falleth to me. And he divided to them his living.

AND SAID THE YOUNGER 90 x 19 [2]
Luke 15:12 και ειπεν νεωτερος'

THE YOUNGER OF THEM 90 x 35 [2]
ο νεωτερος αυτων'

THE YOUNGER 90 x 17 [1]
νεωτερος

FATHER, GIVE ME THE FALLING UPON 90 x 17 [4]
Πατερ δος μοι το επιβαλλον"

AND <u>HE</u> DIVIDED TO THEM THE LIVING 90 x 14 [3]

(mt) και <u>διειλεν</u> αυτοις βιον"

Verse #13:   And after not many days having gathered all together, the younger son departed into a far country, and scattered the property of him living prodigally.

THE YOUNGER <u>SON</u> DEPARTED 90 x 19 [3]

Luke 15:13 νεωτερος <u>υιος</u> απεδημησεν'

THE <u>SON</u> DEPARTED 90 x 12 [2]

<u>υιος</u> απεδημησεν'

<u>HE</u> SCATTERED PROPERTY OF HIM LIVING 90 x 43 [4]

<u>διεσκορπιωεν</u> την ουσιον αυτου ζων'

Verse #14:   And when he had spent all, there arose a mighty famine in that land; and he began to be in want.

<u>HE</u> 90 x 13 [1]

Luke 15:14 <u>αυτου</u>'

Verse #15:   And went and he joined himself to a citizen of that country; and he sent him into his fields to feed swine.

<u>HE</u> JOINED HIMSELF 90 x 2 [1]

Luke 15:15 <u>εκολληθη</u>

Verse #16:   And he longed to fill his stomach with the husks which ate the pigs.

TO FILL <u>HIS</u> 90 x 16 [2]

Luke 15:16 γεμισαι <u>αυτου</u>

Verse #17:   And when he came to himself, he said, How many hired servants of the father of me have bread enough and to spare, and I perish with hunger!

HE CAME TO HIMSELF, <u>HE</u> SAID, HOW MANY 90 x 25 [4]

(mt) Luke 15:17 εαυτον ελθων <u>ειπε</u> ποσοι

THE FATHER OF <u>ME</u> 90 x 14 [2]

πατρος <u>μου</u>'

<u>I</u> 90 x 9 [1]

εγω"

Verse #18:   And rising up I will go to the Father of me, and I will say to Him, Father, I sinned against heaven and before thee.

FATHER, <u>I</u> SINNED AGAINST HEAVEN 90 x 9 x 3 [4]

Luke 15:18 πατερ <u>ημαρτον</u> εις τον ουρανον'

Verse #19: No longer am I worthy to be called thy son: make me as one of thy hired servants.

AM I WORTHY TO BE CALLED 90 x 6 [3]
Luke 15:19 ειμι αξιος κληθηναι"

THY SON 90 x 15 [2]
υιος σου

Verse #20: And rising [he] came to the father of him. But when he was yet a great way off, his father saw him, and had compassion, and ran, and fell on his neck, and fervently kissed him.

HE CAME TO THE FATHER 90 x 11 [3]
(mt) Luke 15:20 ηλθε προς πατερα'

AND FERVENTLY KISSED HIM 90 x 22 [2]
και κατεφιλησεν αυτον'

Verse #21: And said the son unto him, Father, I have sinned against heaven, and in thy sight, No longer am I worthy to be called thy son.

SAID THE SON 90 x 10 [2]
Luke 15:21 ειπεν ο υιος

THE SON UNTO HIM 90 x 25 [2]
ο υιος αυτω'

Verse #23, 24: And bring hither the fatted calf, and kill it; and let us eat, and be merry: For this my son was dead, and is alive again; he was lost, and is found. And they began to be merry.

FOR THIS MY SON 90 x 29 [3]
Luke 15:24 οτι ουτος υιος μου

MY SON 90 x 14 [2]
ο υιος μου

HE WAS LOST 90 x 23 [2]
ην απολωλως'

Verse #25: Now was the son of him the older [one] in the field: and as he came and drew nigh to the house, he heard music and dancing.

WAS THE SON OF HIM 90 x 22 [3]
Luke 15:25 ην ο υιος αυτου'

WAS THE SON 90 x 9 [2]
ην ο υιος"

THE OLDER 1530 (90 x 17) [1]
ο πρεσβυτερος"

HE CAME AND DREW NIGH TO THE HOUSE   90 x 17 [3]
ερχομενος ηγγισεν οικια

Verse #26, 27: And he called one of the servants, and asked what these things meant. And he said unto him, For the brother of thee is come; and hath killed the father of thee calf fatted, because he hath received him back in health.

FOR THE BROTHER   90 x 14 [1]
Luke 15:27 οτι ο αδελφος

THE BROTHER   90 x 9   [1]
αδελφος

FATHER OF THEE CALF   90 x 29 [3]
πατηρ σου τον μοσχον

RECEIVED HIM BACK IN HEALTH   90 x 21   [3]
υγιαινοντα αυτον απελαβεν

Verse #28: And he was angry, and would not go in. Therefore the father of him came out and besought him.

AND HE WAS ANGRY   90 x 9 [1]
Luke 15:28 ωργισθη δε και

THE FATHER OF HIM CAME OUT   90 x 30 [3]
ο δε πατηρ αυτου εξελθων"

Verse #29: And he answering said to his father, Lo, these many years I served thee. And never a command of thee I transgressed. And yet thou never gavest me a kid, that I might make merry with my friends.

I SERVED   90 x 19   [1]
Luke 15:29 δουλευω'

A COMMAND OF THEE I TRANSGRESSED   90 x 17 [3]
εντολην σου παρηλθον'

I MIGHT MAKE MERRY   90 x 9 x 3 [1]
(vn) αριστησω'

Verse #30: But as soon as this the son of thee this was come, which hath devoured thy living with harlots, thou hast killest for him the fatted calf.

THE SON OF THEE   90 x 15
Luke 15:30 υιος σου

OF THEE THIS   90 x 19 [2]
σου ουτος

KILLEST FOR HIM THE FATTED CALF   90 x 52 [4]
εθυσας αυτω σιτευτον μοσχον'

Verse #31: And he said unto him, Child, thou art ever with me, and all mine are thine.

MINE ARE <u>THINE</u>   90 x 9 [3]
Luke 15:31 εμα <u>σα</u> εστιν"

Verse #32: It was meet that we should make merry, and be glad: for this thy brother dead he was and came to life; and was lost, and came to life.

FOR THIS <u>THY</u> BROTHER   90 x 33   [3]
Luke 15:32 οτι ο αδελφος <u>σου</u> ουτος

THIS <u>THY</u> BROTHER   90 x 28 [3]
αδελφος <u>σου</u> ουτος

THIS THY   90 x 19   BROTHER   90 x 9
σου ουτος   αδελφος

DEAD <u>HE</u> WAS AND CAME TO LIFE   90 x 9 [4]
νεκρος <u>ην</u> και αζησεν'

Statistical Data

(1) The above forty-four hits are all *unique* and *different*.

(2) All but four of the above *came from the straight Nestle Text* (25th edition). Four of forty-four features used variant readings from either Nestle or the Majority Text.

(3) Every hit included *a key word* that was a direct reference to either of the two sons who were brothers (see words underlined).

(4) The word length average (WLA) for all the above is *only 2.36 words*; the total number of words divided by the occurrences (104/44 = 2.36 WLA).

(5) No phrases were considered over *four words in length* (including the key word that was a direct reference). A number of occurrences that missed above did contain five and six-word phrases that contained a 90 pattern.

(6) All hits were *within −1, +1 and −2, +2* of the multiples of 90.

(7) None of these results were arbitrarily selected. Every *possible occurrence* in these twenty-two verses from Luke 15 was carefully analyzed. The complete statistical analysis and breakdown are available upon request for $5.00 from the Institute for Theomatics Research, P.O. Box 507, Dundee, Oregon 97115.

(8) Almost every major possibility—all the key words and phrases—within this passage fit the 90 pattern. The ones that missed were for the most part from minor or secondary references. Only one major instance (verse 31, the word "child") was a miss.

Statistical Analysis

The analysis in this book is going to be simple, straightforward, and very brief. I will effectively show the reader how completely "impossible" it would be for anyone—by any method or procedure—to even come close to reproducing the above results with random allocations to the Greek alphabet.

In order for a skeptic to debunk the above results, i.e., demonstrate that they are nothing more than the product of random chance, he would have to take this entire passage from Luke 15:11-32, completely randomize the values for the letters and words, take *any* number the size of 90 (say a number in the range of 80-95), and *demonstrate* that he can produce any of forty-four examples meeting all the above criteria—that includes a direct reference to either of the two brothers. Four of the hits may come from any variant textual reading that exists. All others must be taken from the straight Nestle Text. Of critical consequence is the fact that all forty-four hits must be original; examples cannot be redundant.

The most intimidating statistic is that the random features cannot average more than 2.36 words. This fact is very important. If a person goes on a "feature hunt" and stretches out a phrase longer and longer, eventually he could find any number. Such gymnastics would prove nothing. Short phrases, on the other hand, allow a limited number of possibilities. A one-word phrase has only one possibility. A two-word phrase, three possibilities. A three word phrase, six possibilities (less than that if the phrase must include a specific key word).

How Difficult Is It?

One simple mathematical calculation will overwhelmingly demonstrate how difficult and formidable this would be.

The odds of finding a multiple within the cluster of 90 is 1 chance in 18, i.e., 90/5 = 18. For every 18 phrase combinations looked at, one of them (on the average) will produce a hit. Probability experts, however, don't quite figure it that way. Instead, they work with percentages. For example, if you looked at just 18 phrase combinations, your chance of finding at least one hit would be $85/90^{18}$ = .3574, i.e., $1 - .3574 = 64.26\%$ probability of finding at least one successful hit. There is of course the chance that you might actually find more than one hit, or you might obtain none. However, the more times the experiment is done, the closer to the *null hypothesis* (expected result that is statistically meaningless) one will be. Example: if you were to take 180 random numbers, looking for multiples of 18, the result should be that ten of those 180 would produce hits, and 170 would be non-hits.

Here is the critical statistic. The above twenty-two verses from Luke 15 produced forty-four hits. Each successful hit should have required eighteen tries to achieve the positive result. If the above examples were derived from random numbers, then for every successful hit there should be seventeen non-hits (phrase combinations that did not work out). For all forty-four successful hits, this would equal 44 x 17 = 748.

The Balance Hypothesis

In order to balance everything out, there must be 748 equally impressive phrase combinations—that *do not* fit the pattern of 90. That is what would have to be produced to *negate* the theomatic hits and prove that theomatics derived its results out of sheer randomness.

- None of the 748 non-hits can include any phrase combination that did fit the 90 pattern. Those examples have already been used up by the positive theomatic results.

- Each non-hit phrase used must include a word that specifically points to one of the two brothers.

- All 748 non-hit phrase combinations can average no more than 2.36 words in length.

- The overall quality of the non-hits must be as concise and explicit as the theomatic phrases.

It will be immediately apparent to even the most casual observer that the preceding analysis had far fewer non-hits. There is nowhere near the amount of 748, that even exists. I seriously doubt if anyone could find much more than 75 to 100 short and explicit non-hit phrases. Most of those would be from phrases considered sub-standard in comparison to the most explicit examples that worked for theomatics.

Matching the Results

Of course if anybody does not believe (or dislikes) the reality of the above analysis, they are perfectly welcome to start from scratch by taking any random assignment of allocations, take any number near the size of 90, and find forty-four random features within these twenty-two verses that specifically refer to the two brothers and do not average over 2.36 words in length.

It would not take very long for any investigators to throw up their arms in total despair. They would immediately fail with the vast majority of critical key words and phrases, words such as "sons," "the older," "the younger," "his son," "thy son," "brother," etc., as well as all the other examples that consisted of just one or two words.

Even a supercomputer crunching millions of different alphabet arrangements and simultaneously looking through all the references to find the best random number possible would find matching the results a formidable task.

If some computer wizard did use that sort of automated method to try to duplicate the findings, what would such gymnastics prove? When the skeptic got done using that technique, then he would have to *stick and adhere* to that one random assignment and further demonstrate that he can successfully go head to head with other patterns that theomatics has found, and match those as well.

Theomatics did not find its results by any such method or technique—it is limited to the historical alphabet-to-number arrangement. Yet the skeptic is allowed the "pick of the litter" of infinite random possibilities.

My Own Tests

Just for fun, I took the word "sons," and using the random allocations on page 167, the value worked out to 1270. The largest factor (less than 90) divisible into the cluster of 1270 was the number 53, i.e., 53 x 24 = 1272. This was a number much smaller than the required 90. Then I went through all the short, explicit phrases from this passage in Luke, looking for examples of 53. I immediately failed with most of them. I was able to produce only two short, explicit examples before I had to start looking at the longer phrases. Then I went to the value of the word "the younger," (which had failed on 53) and found a random 82. But when I want back and checked all the references with the number 82, it did not work on a single one.

This is the type of uphill approach any skeptic will face when working with random numbers. It is like squeezing air out of an air mattress. If you get the bulge out of one area, it pops up somewhere else. When you find one number common to two or three or four references, then you have to make it work on all the others. As any statistician knows, it is virtually impossible to maintain a viable consistency with random numbers.

Various Reactions

The vast majority of individuals who carefully look at the mountain of evidence will be convinced that something valid is happening with theomatics. At the very least, it should warrant a more serious and careful investigation. Yet there will always be those who have a deep-rooted bias and will remain skeptical—they don't want theomatics to be true. How will these individuals react?

1) The most common course of attack is that various individuals will seek to formulate their own tests and experiments, and perform them in their own ways, according to their own styles and method of logic. In that process, they will select their own words, topics, and numbers for analysis. Or in the process of claiming to verify the theomatic evidence, they may end up distorting it. Many people using this approach will be sincere and honest seekers with no bias or bone to pick. They just want to get to the truth and see it for themselves. That is perfectly legitimate. However, other individuals will start out with a negative bias, looking to find any way the system does not work (subsequently ignoring the places where it *does* work). After a perfunctory test, they will successfully locate one snippet or limited example that produces a null/random result. "See! Look! It doesn't work! It's all a hoax!" In their analysis, they will most likely commit one or more of the common statistical fallacies: (1) data limited in quantity, (2) data of an unrepresentative

quantity, or (3) data compiled from false precision. (See *Theomatics II*, pp. 200-204.)

2) The second approach will be speculative, hypothetical, mathematical theorizing. This is the sort of logic that tries to prove that aeronautically, it is impossible for bumblebees to fly. The person using this approach will formulate various hypotheses— mathematical models and simulations that theoretically seek to get the point across that theomatics does not work and is therefore not valid. This approach has already been attempted by a man from Virginia, a brilliant mathematician, and another individual who did various randomized simulations, none of which applied to or had any effect on the method(s) of theomatics. Those using this approach will offer these models and simulations as an explanation for the theomatic results (most of this written in language and notation that only a theoretical Einstein can understand). In theory, this approach may sound good, but in practice, it cannot be demonstrated to work. None of these individuals will take the time to *match* the theomatic results with random allocations, or duplicate the clustering phenomena with random allocations (see next chapter).

3) The third method will be to attack the logic of the whole system. This mostly philosophical approach will seek to demonstrate that the method of logic in interpreting numbers and associating theological meaning and concepts to words and numbers can only bring conclusions that are ridiculous and bizarre. Therefore, the argument will be made that the message theomatics seeks to set forth cannot be trusted. This approach is not scientific but is based upon the assumption that a system of numbers cannot carry objective meaning from God to man, i.e., only words can contain a meaningful message. The person using this argument will take "theomatic" examples, and then seek to find comparisons of words to numbers where the most absurd and ridiculous conclusions are possible. Or they will argue that the many factors or multiples divisible into all of the phrase combinations of a particular passage could not possibly contain precise theological meaning. In reply, we don't know that they can't. *All of the divisional factors are part of a vast network that even now we are only beginning to understand.* As the examples in this book have shown, much in theomatics *does* make incredibly good sense. Yet there is a great deal waiting to be learned. All the facts concerning how it was designed by God have not been fully discovered yet, and just like the universe, there is much out there no one fully understands. That's why we build space telescopes. You obviously don't tell an astronomer that he does not know *anything* about the universe, and that the universe itself is not valid unless he can provide a crisp answer to every mystery and every objection. No arguments challenging the logic of the method(s) of theomatics can

have any effect on the irrefutable and statistical evidence thus far discovered. The person using this approach will probably concede none of it.

4) The last approach goes hand in hand with number 3 above. It is hardly worth mentioning because it is thoroughly unscientific. It is the main approach used by fundamentalist-evangelical scholars opposed to the existence of any sort of hidden code in the Bible related to meaning (for a complete refutation see chapter 6, *Theomatics II.*) The argument is made that it is not in God's character to do something like this. Since the Bible is a simple and open revelation from God, and He is not trying to hide His truth from us, we have no reason to believe that there is any message in Scripture beyond the simple grammatical-historical meaning of the words. Therefore, it is probably a waste of time to even consider hidden codes in the Bible. According to this viewpoint, the Bible was meant by God to be understood, not deciphered. *The knowledge of truth is not limited to a select few who use esoteric methods in order to have an inside track to the Divinity.* Such methods cannot bring forth any coherent knowledge. This kind of approach is nothing more than mysticism and a modern-day revival of Gnosticism—even occultic in nature. Of course, those offering these arguments will have no explanation for the statistical results that have been achieved. Nor will they want to take the time to consider the scientific aspect of the issue. This is the same approach currently being propagated in the new book attacking ELS and the Bible Code—as well as the entire concept of hidden codes in the Bible.[4]

Conclusion

Again, the vast majority of people who carefully look into all this will be overwhelmingly convinced that "something" is going on in there. Yet there will always be those individuals out there—most of them in positions of influence and leadership—who will refuse to accept even the possibility that something like this exists in the Bible. Jealousy may also be a factor. They will insist that the investigator, not God, is behind the results. None of these individuals will ever take the time to sufficiently challenge the data in a direct and forceful manner. If someone does eventually go public with any "evidence"—whether it is true or not—those who are opposed *will simply quote* that person(s) as their excuse.

This is currently the case with the ELS and Bible code evidence (see discussion in appendix). Those who want to believe the discovery spend their time quoting the proponents and their findings. Those who don't want to believe it spend their time quoting those who claim to have debunked the findings. People tend to base their conclusions on what other people say, and whether or not they *want* something to be true. Few individuals truly know how to think for themselves. In any scientific discipline, there will always be individuals who can produce *some* negative evidence.

When I was twenty, I worked one summer at a sales job. My sales manager told me something I never forgot.

> When you are in the home demonstrating the product, just remember one thing. People do not buy what they need. They do not buy what they can afford. They buy what they want.

This entire issue will eventually boil down to just five things: open-mindedness, not rushing quickly to judgment, a careful examination of the facts, intellectual honesty, and humility.

12 The Clustering Phenomenon

Nailing the Coffin Lid Shut

The previous chapter laid out in very general yet explicit terms the method by which theomatics must be either validated or disproved. In order to debunk this discovery in a competent way, it must be *demonstrated* that it is *possible* for a random assigning of numerical values to the letters and words to produce the same average results. There are literally hundreds of patterns in the research files where this is "impossible" in any sort of practical manner. This is true not just for each individual study; if the larger portions of the theomatic population are looked at en masse, the weight of evidence becomes insurmountable.

Any individual who wants to take the time either to verify or challenge the findings will find himself buried under an avalanche of data.

Nevertheless, if for any reason a skeptic objects and tries to raise any issues with what was presented in the last chapter, he will be completely devastated by what is going to be shown next.

It's time to open the door to the armory and roll out the big gun.

The Big Artillery

Suppose we were to summon one hundred of the world's greatest mathematicians, statisticians, and probability experts and line them up in a row on a stage, subsequently giving them a verifiable presentation of what you are about to see here in this chapter; when it was all said and done, their knees would buckle and they would quite literally fall to the ground.

Never before in the history of the world has the type of objective evidence that you are about to see demonstrated been discovered—an outright mathematical miracle that defies all known logic. (Any viable statistical evidence supporting the Bible Code, or ELS phenomena, could perhaps compare.) *The clustering phenomenon is even more miraculous than if somebody was resurrected physically from the dead.*

It can be guaranteed that any secular mathematical objectivist (who *cannot* accept the idea that any of this is of supernatural or extra-terrestrial origin) will go crazy—right out of his mind—trying to find an explanation for the following. Never has there existed a more baffling mathematical anomaly, for there is no natural explanation.

The clustering phenomenon is no more likely to happen by sheer coincidence than flipping a coin a thousand times and obtaining an outcome of 800 heads and 200 tails, and then being able to repeat the spectacular outcome a second time and a third time. Every mathematician who has examined the clustering has been completely befuddled.

The clustering phenomenon—all by itself—scientifically validates the existence of theomatics.

Many people who are not sophisticated mathematically will fail to see the earth-shattering significance of what this is all about. Please pay attention. History is being made at this very moment. We are standing on absolutely holy ground, witnessing a supernatural miracle that could literally turn the scientific world upside down and change forever the entire scope of religion for the remainder of this world's history.

What About the Prodigal Son?

In the last chapter, it was shown how ridiculously "impossible" it would be to take all the direct references in Luke 15 to the two sons of the Father and find forty-four distinct features with any number at least as large as 90, none of which can be over four words in length and all of them averaging no more than 2.36 words in length. After theomatics carefully and faithfully recorded every possible result, here is the clustering.

	Actual Results	Expected Results
Direct Hits: 18	40.90%	20% or 8.8 hits
−1 or +1: 18	40.90%	40% or 17.6 hits
−2 or +2: 8	18.20%	40% or 17.6 hits
Total Hits: 44		

What Are the Odds?

The odds of the above happening by chance have been calculated by professional statisticians (shown on page 191). If you were to try finding forty-four features that deviated from the null hypothesis (expected result that is statistically meaningless) according to the above percentages, you would be successful only six times in ten thousand tries. The probability is 1 chance in 1,689. This number, statistically speaking, is very significant; in fact, it is astounding.

If someone were to try and debunk this pattern, they would not only have to match the forty-four references according to the statistical criteria shown in the last chapter, but the resultant clustering would also have to match the above percentage distribution. And they would have to achieve this clustering result on their first attempt.

That is why we can safely say that theomatics is "disprove-proof."

Clustering Defined

Here is the definition of clustering.

When theomatics discovers a pattern, either by observation or by computer, and faithfully records every hit that occurs, there will invariably be far more direct hits and –1, +1 hits than the laws of chance will allow. Subsequently, the –2, +2 hits are well below the expected number. The structure is heavily weighted toward the center of the cluster. This cannot occur naturally. By all probability expectations, there should be an even balance and distribution, the same way a coin has an equal chance of landing on heads as tails, i.e., 50% - 50%.

The following will eliminate any possible statistical alibi.

- The clustering phenomenon occurs only with the standard numerical allocations to the Hebrew and Greek alphabets.

- It occurs only in the Bible and nowhere else.

- It occurs only when related theological words and meanings are looked at.

  NOTE: If a person takes phrases selected at random from the Bible and looks for examples with any multiple factor, the prevailing results will be predictably random (similar to test shown on the next page). *This proves that the languages themselves, and/or the standard numerical values for the alphabets, are not producing the phenomenon.* Only when there is a clear theological connection of related meaning, does the miracle occur.

Whenever any other occasion is looked at and tested—different from the above—the results will be predictably random, the same as flipping a coin or rolling a pair of dice.

The clustering phenomenon has happened with at least thirty to forty thousand examples, and virtually never fails to occur.

Performing a Random Cluster Test

Let us look at a random example of clustering. The following exercise is really academic, but I show it to simply make a point of what is already known to be true. I'll explain a little later on.

Taking three chapters from the New Testament, Luke 15 on the prodigal son and two more selected at random (1 Thessalonians 5, and Hebrews 11), I performed a random test by computer with the following five multiple factors: 93, 122, 133, 153, and 165. For this particular test, the random seed entered was 666, and this caused the computer to mix up all the values for the letters and words, as shown on page 167. Then I programmed the computer to look in sequence through every verse in each chapter (the phrases did not have a common word or theological connection like the theomatic results) and find all random multiples of 93, 122, 133, 153, and 165 from all existing phrases of four words or less. Here are those results. The numbers in each column are the total results from all three chapters.

	93	122	133	153	165	total	%
Direct Hits	64	55	42	32	32	225	19.7 %
-1, +1 Hits	127	86	85	76	75	449	39.3 %
-2, +2 Hits	126	96	96	67	81	466	40.0 %
Total Hits	317	237	223	175	188	1140	100 %

A Further Explanation

If we were to take any cluster that exists around a target number, we would discover that there are five numbers in any given cluster. Take for example the number 100 (or any multiple of 100):

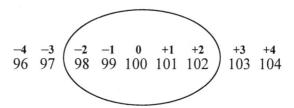

Based upon a presumption of randomness, if a person were to go on a "feature hunt," looking to find any specific words or phrases that fall within the boundaries of the cluster of a certain target multiple, there would be an *equal chance* that the value of the word or phrase would land on any one of the following five numbers.

–2	1 chance in 5, or 20%
–1	1 chance in 5, or 20%
0	1 chance in 5, or 20%
+1	1 chance in 5, or 20%
+2	1 chance in 5, or 20%

Another way of putting it, if one were to examine a hundred features or numerical values, 20 percent of them would be direct hits, 40 percent would be –1, +1 hits, and 40 percent would be –2, +2 hits. Again, this would be every bit as predictable as flipping a coin or rolling a pair of dice.

The random cluster test on page 186 proves that this happens not only theoretically. When we test the hypothesis on actual words and phrases from the Bible, it comes out "perfectly" as expected (provided enough examples are looked at, of course). There were 20 percent (19.7 actual) direct hits, 40 percent (39.3 actual) –1, +1 hits, and 40% –2, +2 hits.

This Is an Axiom

The above principle is an *axiom*. In logic and mathematics, an axiom is a statement that needs no proof because its truth is obvious and assumed. It is an established principle of science that no one has the right to question or challenge.

Before showing the reader the statistics that objectively substantiate all this, let us briefly digress and talk about the history of how this phenomenon was discovered. A somewhat lengthy section in *Theomatics II* (pp. 87-97) discusses this, as well as the subjective criticism that numerous evangelical leaders have thrown at the cluster concept, i.e., why God would use a plus or minus "fudge factor" system.

Paul Ackerman

Over the years I have been asked by a number of people if anybody has ever performed any scientific tests intended to challenge the findings of theomatics. Yes! Only one man has.

Paul Ackerman is a psychology professor at Wichita State University in Kansas and also a scientific creationist who has written a number of books dealing with the evolution/creation controversy. In the early 1980s, he published a lengthy scientific investigation of theomatics in the *Bible Science Newsletter*.[1] The article headline read "A Computer Test of Theomatics." In it, he performed three computerized tests that attempted to prove that several Bible topics produced results that were strictly "random." In his conclusive argument, he states: "I believe that this author's research refutes theomatics in all its aspects. The result was clear. Theomatics does not work! Theomatics is not true!" A few months later the *Bible Science Newsletter* published my lengthy rebuttal. Paul Ackerman had misunderstood theomatics. His calculations were totally flawed and spurious. Two more exchanges followed my initial rebuttal.

In the summer of 1989, I completed my three hundred page manuscript entitled *Theomatics and the Scientific Method*. I mailed a copy to Ackerman, and we had two or three rather amicable exchanges. What is most interesting about this encounter is that in the final analysis, God used Paul Ackerman to help substantiate the validity of theomatics.

Before I tell you how this happened, let me backtrack. In my original *Theomatics* book, I stated this concerning the concept of clusters:

> The greatest percentage of the features to be presented in this book are exact multiples of the key numbers. A smaller number of the features are within plus 1 or minus 1 of the multiples, and fewer still are within the range of plus 2 or minus 2 (*Theomatics*, p. 36).

What is remarkable is that after I made that initial observation, for almost eleven years I completely forgot about the idea of clusters. *I never once gave it any thought whatsoever!* It never occurred to me that clustering was a phenomenon that would help prove the theomatic concept.

In the entire first edition of *Theomatics*, 1002 features were given. Here were the results that occurred when I made this initial discovery. These results were not even checked until recently.

	Actual Results	Expected Results
Direct Hits: 348	34.73%	20% or 200.4 hits
+1 or -1: 423	42.22%	40% or 400.8 hits
+2 or -2: 231	23.05%	40% or 400.8 hits
Total Hits: 1002		

For years after I wrote the first book, my files swelled to many thousands of theomatic features within numerous studies. My research goal was always to look for the most distinct words and shortest phrases that had clear objective and spiritual significance. To me, where the hit fell within the cluster was insignificant. I was looking for quality words and phrases, not for any clustering characteristics.

The basic method for proving the existence of theomatics does not consider clustering at all (that aspect was presented in the last chapter). In my original way of thinking, as a very young man starting out, my only concern and major fear was that it might be possible for some skeptic to match the theomatic results with random allocations. If that could be easily achieved, all of my supposed findings would have been laughed out of town.

Clustering Discovered

The evidence presented in *Theomatics and the Scientific Method* is overwhelming from a scientific perspective. After I sent it to Paul Ackerman, he replied with a cordial letter. Based upon his short response, it appeared that he hardly took the time to seriously evaluate the core of scientific evidence and calculations that I presented. But he did have this to say:

> Regarding theomatics, I have studied the material you sent me. It appears that you have developed an excellent computer set-up along with some sophisticated software. I will rely on you and your system to answer my questions. I prefer to keep matters simple and tackle one issue at a time. The first one I would like to probe is the matter of clustering. Your program makes it extremely easy to test this concept, and so it constitutes a good test for me. *I will put it on the line. If the verses presented in Section 4 of your manuscript show clustering in the manner described in your first book, then I will have to completely re-examine my position* [italics mine]. On the other

hand, if no clustering is present in those verses then my position [that theomatics is not valid] must be correct and the question of why you got significant results on the scientific test of Section 6 examined.

When Paul wrote to me, the above paragraph took me totally by surprise. At first I did not even know what he meant by "clustering." I finally figured it out just before I was about to call him to ask what he meant.

Up to this point I had never thought of this concept as being significant. But when I checked it out, the data was more than a little impressive. It completely blew me away. I had not expected to see the results that were staring back at me.

What Paul Ackerman was in essence probing was that no matter what other basis of evidence I had discovered, if the conclusion to the premise was wrong and theomatics were not true, then clustering definitely should not occur. In light of that fact, I would like to state the following:

> The absence of clustering would not in essence disprove the existence of theomatics (if other scientific evidence supported it). The presence of clustering, however, would unequivocally substantiate and prove the existence of theomatics.

Here Are the Numbers

I wrote a lengthy reply to Paul Ackerman in which I went through *Theomatics and the Scientific Method* and tabulated the clustering for all the features from various categories. In my manuscript, I had done a computerized test on every single reference to Jesus as "the Son," both in the Gospel of John and in 1 John, 2 John, and 3 John. All fifty-five independent references were examined and tested by computer. Many other occurrences in the New Testament were also examined (but were not part of the scientific tests). Virtually every single reference to this topic contained a multiple of 150, and almost all the references contained a multiple of 250 as well (from the straight Nestle Greek Text). Each phrase used to establish the feature (i.e., the specified pattern) was required to be short and include the word "son" in the phrase. There was no possibility of any arbitrary picking and choosing. The statistical odds were staggering! In my reply to Ackerman, I stated this:

> My basic assumption has always been that since the structure was put together on the cluster principle, a -2 or +2 is just as significant as a -1 or +1, etc. If the ball goes "swish," the basket still counts the same two points as if the ball bounced around on the rim before dropping. A score is a score. I have never felt that for any clustering hypothesis to be true, that this was an essential ingredient for the validity of theomatics. In all my calculations and computer tests, I have been *conservative* and have not tried to use any advantage that may have existed with favorable clustering. So that is why I never took the time to look into it.

Here is the data. From each passage the computer tallied the *shortest possible phrase* that fit the specified pattern. Looking at the seventy-three total hits for multiples of 150 and 250 from John's Gospel and the Epistles of John, here are the results. All redundant hits (those that appear more than once) were removed from the tally.

	Actual Results	Expected Results
Direct Hits: 19	26.00%	20% or 14.6 hits
−1 or +1: 36	49.30%	40% or 29.2 hits
−2 or +2: 18	24.70%	40% or 29.2 hits
Total Hits: 73		

What is significant about these results is the fact that all the hits are the mathematically shortest phrases *possible* from seventy-three separate references (or occurrences) to Jesus' being the Son. They were not found by poking numbers into a calculator by hand. The computer found and printed out *every single shortest possible hit* from each passage.

If the numerical values were random, these results would be less likely than flipping a coin seventy-three times (or fifty-four times) and get twice as many heads as tails. There were twice as many −1, +1 hits, as −2, +2 hits.

In going through my computer printouts and listing every feature shown, including long phrases, short phrases, and all phrases possible, I found these results.

	Actual Results	Expected Results
Direct Hits: 55	23.40%	20% or 47 hits
−1 or +1: 119	50.64%	40% or 94 hits
−1 or +1: 61	25.96%	40% or 94 hits
Total Hits: 235		

Getting back to the mathematical principle of flipping a coin, the more flips that are tallied, the closer to the *null hypothesis* (the expected yield according to the presumption of randomness) the results will be. But this is not true of theomatics. In the above example, there were 180 features that were within −1, +1 and −2, +2. Regardless of how many direct hits there are, the ratio of −1, +1 hits to −2, +2 hits should have been 50/50. There were twice as many of the closer hits.

Paul Ackerman's Response

Paul Ackerman's response was most revealing.

I concede round one. The features presented in Section 4 show clustering and, furthermore, they show clustering in precisely the same manner as the features presented in your book. They do so either because of the "scientific validity of theomatics" or some human, intelligence factor biasing their selection. There is, of course, the possibility of some unrecognized mathematical artifact relating to the issue, but I have no idea what it could be. I have considered this possibility and do not think that is the explanation. I believe the explanation lies in a human factor, and you believe the explanation lies in a Divine factor.

In stating that the explanation "lies in a human factor," Ackerman is now asserting that I arbitrarily and deliberately *selected* the features that were direct and –1, +1 hits, over the hits that were –2, +2. In my next response to him, I pointed out the fact that I did not come up with these results, the unbiased computer did! The computer calculated every possibility and simply printed out the results. When presented with that fact, along with a great deal of additional evidence (Round 2), he gave no reply and did not even answer my letter. And so the dialogue ended.

The Chi-Square Formula

The formula that accurately calculates the clustering odds is well known and established among mathematicians. It is called the "Chi-Square Goodness of Fit." It will take all the occurrences and, by comparing actual results to expected results, calculate the "p" factor, or probability.

$$\chi^2 = \sum \frac{(o-e)^2}{e}$$

I personally consulted with two mathematics professors at Portland State University stats lab (fifteen thousand students). We created a spreadsheet in Microsoft Excel. The first thing it did was calculate the value for the cluster distribution (x), and it uses the "chidist" statistical formula in Excel "=CHIDIST(x,df)," to compute the actual probabilities according to the degrees of freedom (df). Here is a sample of the calculation for the forty-four prodigal son features.

CLUSTERING CALCULATIONS --- 3 Instances, 2 Degrees of Freedom					
	Observed	Expected		% distribution	
0 HITS	18	8.8	9.618182	0.409091	
-1, +1	18	17.6	0.009091	0.409091	
-2, +2	8	17.6	5.236364	0.181818	
Total	44	44	14.86364		
		Probability =	0.000592		
		1 CHANCE IN	1688.875		

The probability of taking any forty-four features and getting the above cluster distribution is 1 expected occurrence every 1,689 attempts. This is amazingly significant.

Now let's look at the above examples where the computer found all the results. Here is the probability or chance that the seventy-three shortest hits could distribute the way they did.

CLUSTERING CALCULATIONS --- 3 Instances, 2 Degrees of Freedom					
		Observed	Expected		% distribution
0 HITS		19	14.6	1.326027	0.260274
-1, +1		36	29.2	1.583562	0.493151
-2, +2		18	29.2	4.29589	0.246575
Total		73	73	7.205479	
			Probability =	0.027249	
		1 CHANCE IN	36.69864		

The probability here is 1 chance in every 36 tries. This is significant. If a person tried this experiment over and over, his chance of this degree of success would only be 2.7 percent of the time. 1 chance in 36 may not seem that impressive, but it is actually more significant than most people realize. A probability of 1 chance in 50 to 100 is considered to be extremely significant by statisticians. In the above, only seventy-three examples occurred, and the zero hits were close to the expected number. For seventy-three numbers, there is likely to be some fluctuation, so that is the reason for the .027 figure.

In this experiment, the computer found a total of 235 hits. Here the p factor is staggering—only one occurrence every 18,000 attempts.

CLUSTERING CALCULATIONS --- 3 Instances, 2 Degrees of Freedom					
		Observed	Expected		% distribution
0 HITS		55	47	1.361702	0.234043
-1, +1		119	94	6.648936	0.506383
-2, +2		61	94	11.58511	0.259574
Total		235	235	19.59574	
			Probability =	5.56E-05	
		1 CHANCE IN ...	17995.42		

What About This Book?

Every pattern here in this book exhibited outstanding clustering beyond the laws of chance. There were a total of 473 features shown. The probability for all of the clustering, according to professional statisticians, is zero.

CLUSTERING CALCULATIONS --- 3 Instances, 2 Degrees of Freedom					
	Observed	Expected		% distribution	
0 HITS	139	94.6	20.8389	0.293869	
-1, +1	229	189.2	8.372304	0.484144	
-2, +2	105	189.2	37.47167	0.221987	
Total	473	473	66.68288		
	Probability =		3.31E-15		
	1 CHANCE IN ...		3.02E+14		

The "p factor" here is .00000000000000331. The above was calculated by professional statisticians at the Portland State University math department as being zero probability. There is *no chance* that the above could ever even happen.

What Are the Overall Statistics?

The example of clustering shown at the beginning of this chapter, surrounding the prodigal son, is just one very small pattern that exists in only one chapter of the Bible. What about the tens of thousands of features that have been found thus far, all of which exhibit this same clustering curve?

A general estimate has been made. From the numerous distinct patterns that have been catalogued, the overall clustering curve falls somewhere between the following percentages. (This is a conservative estimate.)

	Actual Results
Direct Hits:	28% to 32% (average 30%)
+1 or -1:	42% to 50% (average 46%)
+2 or -2:	22% to 26% (average 24%)

Total Hits: 30,000 to 40,000

It should be pointed out that this does not apply to taking any portion of Biblical text, sticking any number into the computer, and getting this kind of a result. In fact, if one goes through contiguous theomatic text with any multiple factor—the result will be no different than the above test where we first randomized the values on page 186.

It must first be determined which factor is key to a specific topic or theological concept (such as the 93 agape/love example shown in chapter 4.) And then when the related passages are examined with the right key factor, or multiples, two things will happen:

- There will be many more hits than expected.
- The hits that do result will exhibit clustering.

This fact is the one that the skeptics are going to have a hard time explaining. If a Divine or intelligent factor is not involved in all this, then how did the phenomena get into the Bible? There exist only two possible explanations.

Explanation #1: A Human Factor

In his reply, Paul Ackerman came up with the following conclusion:

I believe the explanation lies in a human factor.

What he is evidently implying by his statement is that the theomatics researcher *selected* the results—showing all of the direct hits and most of the −1, +1, but deliberately ignored a large quantity of lesser −2, +2 results—in order to make the clustering look favorable. This accusation is simply not true.

In all of the examples sent to Ackerman, it *was the computer* that discovered the features, and computers do not have any sort of theological bone to pick or other bias. This fact destroys Ackerman's allegation (and subsequent excuse).

Is there ever any sort of bias factor involved? In *Theomatics II* (p. 96) three extremely minor instances where a human/selective factor is perhaps involved are noted. All of them are rare and have a virtually negligible effect on the overall outcome.

- The very first feature or key leadoff example in some patterns (like *agape* being an exact multiple of 93).
- Instances where two redundant phrases occur (these are very rare instances).
- Small numerical values less than 100, or numerical values in the teens. In double-digit numbers (such as 93) I look only at −1, +1, and in the teens the hits must be exact.

Note: In all the above tables and calculations, redundant hits and words with small numerical values were eliminated.

Where Are They?

Now comes the critical question. If there is a human factor involved—which there positively is not—*then where are the needed hits to balance out the null hypothesis?* Take, for example, the prodigal son.

Assuming a presumption of randomness, what the above shows us (page 184), is that if the direct hits are the actual results from sheer randomness, then there must be forty-six additional hits hiding somewhere (18 x 5 = 90 – 44 = 46), for *equally impressive* words and phrases—that the theomatics researcher deliberately ignored—in order to make the clustering look favorable here in this book.

A quick check will clearly show that *all* possible hits were carefully and faithfully tabulated and that the number of hits necessary to bring us back to the null hypothesis *does not even exist*! *That is the startling fact about the clustering phenomenon every place it occurs, with every single pattern that theomatics has ever discovered.* If for some reason I did inadvertently miss one or two examples, there is a better than even chance that *they too* will be direct hits and –1, +1 hits, further strengthening the argument. The important fact is that *any time* any hit within the range of –2, or +2 is discovered, it must be faithfully recorded and written down.

In the final analysis, to present this subject in a way that honors God, the investigation and the results collected must be done fairly and honestly. That does not necessarily mean that every statistical analysis is going to be impeccably flawless, and without some subjective cut-off point. However, anyone is welcome to check these findings for any major discrepancies. I have been very careful to let the chips fall as they will fall. There is nothing to be gained in deceiving or deluding oneself.

Another Critical Fact

Let us imagine for a moment that some of these wild clustering distributions are the product of random chance. This of course is out of the question, as we can accurately calculate what the actual probability or chance is of these events occurring. But let us suppose that some strange thing produces it. *Why is it that the distribution always goes in favor of the direct hits and the –1, +1 hits?* If some mathematical quirk is the explanation, would it not be reasonable to presume that in half the instances there should be twice as many –2, +2 hits as –1, +1 hits? The quirk should just as easily go the other direction!

I could probably count on one hand the number of times in all my research that the –2, +2 hits won out significantly over the –1, +1 results. The only time it has occurred is in a few short stretches. Yes, it is feasible to flip a coin fifteen times and get thirteen heads. That sort of thing can and does happen with randomness.

Virtually always the –1, +1 hits are twice (or at least a third more), as the –2, +2 hits.

Explanation #2: Mathematical Artifacts

One of the first questions any statistician will ask is whether there is some sort of anomaly or mathematical artifact present that could possibly explain the results. Conclusive testing has proven that there is a complete random mix to everything. However, there is one place that an anomaly does occur, but it is of minor consequence.

A careful examination of the text will show that the numerical values for the words are *not* spread evenly over the numerical spectrum. There are more words that are direct multiples of 10 than just 1 in 10. A random test of fifteen hundred words from the New Testament yielded a little less than 20 percent, or 1 in 5 words, directly divisible by 10. Most all of these are extremely short words consisting of four letters or less, and they appear much more frequently than other words. The reason for this higher yield is that practically all of these short words do not use any of the first nine letters of the Greek alphabet, numbered 1 to 9.

However, when you add their numerical values to the words in juxtaposition, the entire thing goes very quickly into complete randomness, just like shuffling a deck of cards.

Extensive testing has shown that in looking for any factor that is a multiple of 10, on phrases four words or less, approximately 23 percent of the random features will be direct hits. The −1, +1 versus the −2, +2 distribution, will be a perfect 50 - 50.

However, if in the test the redundant hits are shaved back and counted only one time (which is done in all theomatics instances), the direct hit percentage drops to around 21 to 22 percent of the total yield.

Of major importance is the fact that in all random tests done—the numerical values are mixed within their respective groups. If the numerical value of a word in theomatics comes out to a multiple of 10 (and does not contain any of the first nine Greek letters), then the random value for the same word will also be a multiple of 10. This places both sets of numbers on an equal footing relative to this anomaly; that way an objective comparison can be safely made.

Clustering in **Theomatics II**

Here is the clustering from all of the patterns and studies that were presented in *Theomatics II*. Any one of the major studies presented, consisting of 200 examples or more, would have a zero probability, or some figure very close to that amount.

		Actual Results	Expected Results
Direct Hits:	887	33.00%	20% or 537 hits
+1 or -1:	1154	43.00%	40% or 1074 hits
+2 or −2:	644	24.00%	40% or 1074 hits
Total Hits:	2685		

Clustering in the Hebrew

The Hebrew clustering is consistently better than that in the Greek of the New Testament—not by a large margin, but it usually is always more predictable. This is no doubt due to the fact that the Hebrew text is more pure than the Greek text. (Appendix D of *Theomatics II* discusses the entire issue of the New Testament text at length.) For example, in *Theomatics II*, I discovered a pattern concerning man created in the image of God. All the features came out as multiples of the number 425, a huge number by probability standards. Here was the clustering; the chance is 1 in 704,225,352.

	Actual Results	Expected Results
Direct Hits: 31	50.00%	20% or 12.40 hits
+1 or -1: 25	40.30%	40% or 24.80 hits
+2 or -2: 6	9.70%	40% or 24.80 hits
Total Hits: 62		

The clustering for the golden calf pattern in chapter 10 of this book exhibited the following clustering. (75 percent of the examples were from the Hebrew Old Testament.) The chance here is 1 in 1,797,715.

	Actual Results	Expected Results
Direct Hits: 27	36.50%	20% or 12.40 hits
+1 or -1: 39	52.70%	40% or 24.80 hits
+2 or -2: 8	10.80%	40% or 24.80 hits
Total Hits: 74		

Conclusion

The question some may ask is "What does clustering prove? What is it telling us?"

For one thing, it proves that theomatics exists. Secondly, it provides an impenetrable defense against anyone who thinks he can easily take on "codes in the Bible" and "put the lights out" on the issue, i.e., debunk it. Like the well-known story of Daniel in the lion's den, it seals shut the mouths of the lions. Many evangelical leaders and others will try to argue that it is not in God's character to use a plus or minus system (is not God supposed to be mathematically precise?) and that clustering is nothing more than a "fudge factor" being used by the researcher in order to come up with many more examples of the supposed phenomenon.

The fact that the clustering phenomenon occurs at all completely squashes these objections.

The deliberate clustering structure validates the principle of plus and minus as being part of a network operating upon laws of mathematics— which are completely heavenly in origin and which only now are we just beginning to see and understand.

13 The Great Bible Prophecy Debacle

Predictions Gone Sour, and Nobody Yet Knows the Day or the Hour

W ithout a doubt, the number-one subject of interest to Christians the world over is the second coming of Jesus Christ. When is Jesus going to return to planet Earth? What is going to happen after He gets here?

No subject has elicited more questions and interest relative to theomatics than this one. People everywhere want to know if the discoveries made in theomatics shed any new light on the subject of eschatology (the end of the world.) The answer is a resounding—Yes!

The Greek word *eschatos*, from which eschatology is derived, means "the last or final things." There are two hundred pages in *Theomatics II* that discuss this area extensively (pp. 375-573) and show a large number of theomatic patterns. In this condensed version, I shall simply give the reader a synopsis and general overview—explaining in simple terms the conclusions I have arrived at based upon the research.

I sincerely believe, in all humility, that the following will be the most objective explanation ever given to the Christian Church relative to the book of Revelation. However, be forewarned. What you are about to read may not be what many people expect or anything close to it!

Right now there is mass confusion and utter frustration among Christians when it comes to the subject of Bible prophecy. People have heard so many different things—all kinds of predictions, date setting, and loony theories. As we approach and surpass the year 2000, the hype and hysteria surrounding this subject are likely to increase dramatically.

The Fun Stuff

When compared to other aspects of Bible study, the subject of Bible prophecy has been appropriately called the "fun stuff." It seems to titillate and excite people as nothing else can. Over the years, and even now, the Christian media is saturated with various radio and television ministries, hundreds upon hundreds of books and video programs—all focused on Bible prophecy and the end times. The Seventh-Day Adventist Church has spread its weeks-long prophetic seminars into nearly every city and neighborhood in the country. Numerous individuals are caught up in the idea of trying to fit modern-day events and all the events happening in the world and associating them to the things mentioned in the Bible.

So much has been said, particularly since the 1970s. Books such as the *Late Great Planet Earth,* by Hal Lindsey, have sold upward of fifteen million copies. From this has come a prophetic pop culture, which has almost reduced the Bible to a *National Enquirer* level of spirituality.

Most Christians today seem apathetic toward the subject, and many don't seem to know what to believe anymore, given the many failed predictions about when the rapture was supposed to have taken place. Even though confusion has settled in, many Christians are still hopeful and expectant.

Theomatics will bring a whole new focus of understanding to this entire subject. After reading the following, your heart should breathe a sigh of relief. We may not have the answer to every question, but there will finally be a crisp solution to the whole dilemma.

There Are Major Cracks in the Foundation

Almost everything being taught today in the Christian Church, the media, books, etc. about Bible prophecy and the end times *is operating under a delusion of false premises* (and conclusions that are even worse). Bible students have grossly misunderstood the Word of God. Few, if any, scholars have ever comprehended the correct method of understanding the Books of Daniel and Revelation and other significant passages.

The basic premise that people are trying to go on today is that God gave us Daniel and Revelation so that we could figure out and understand future world events. In other words, embedded inside the Bible is a prophetic blueprint describing the major world events to come—up until the return of Jesus. We just have to be clever enough to figure it all out.

Section 1 of this chapter will examine the various persuasions, or schools of thought, that are currently prominent. In section 2, the correct premise and method of investigation will be discussed in light of theomatics.

Section 1: Pick Your Persuasion

The issue of Bible prophecy—the entire debate—is centered on just one passage of scripture, Revelation chapter 20, verses 1-8. This passage talks about a period of time consisting of "the thousand years."

And I saw an angel come down from heaven, having the key of the bottomless pit and a great chain in his hand.

2 And he laid hold on the dragon, that old serpent, which is the Devil, and Satan, and bound him the thousand years,

3 And cast him into the bottomless pit, and shut him up, and set a seal upon him, that he should deceive the nations no more, till the thousand years should be fulfilled: and after that he must be loosed a little season.

4 And I saw thrones, and they sat upon them, and judgment was given unto them: and I saw the souls of them that were beheaded for the witness of Jesus, and for the word of God, and which had not worshipped the beast, neither his image, neither had received his mark upon their foreheads, or in their hands; and they lived and reigned with Christ the thousand years.

5 But the rest of the dead lived not again until the thousand years were finished. This is the first resurrection.

6 Blessed and holy is he that hath part in the first resurrection: on such the second death hath no power, but they shall be priests of God and of Christ, and shall reign with him the thousand years.

7 And when the thousand years are expired, Satan shall be loosed out of his prison,

8 And shall go out to deceive the nations which are·in the four quarters of the earth, Gog and Magog, to gather them together to battle: the number of whom is as the sand of the sea.

This is a watershed passage. The manner in which you understand and interpret it will determine how everything else in the Bible *must* be interpreted.

In the Rocky Mountains of the United States there is an invisible line called the Continental Divide. All the little streams that start on one side of the line eventually form rivers that flow toward the Atlantic Ocean. The streams on the other side of the line will eventually make their way to the Pacific Ocean. When a drop of rain falls, only a few inches determine which ocean the drop will eventually end up in. The same is true here. Christians today are totally divided on how the above passage is supposed to be interpreted.

Right now there are five camps or schools of thought. Virtually everyone out there will fall into one of these five categories, in one form or another. The following may seem a little academic but is very important to understand before proceeding. You will find the following interesting and helpful.

- *Historic premillennialism* — This teaching believes there will be a *literal* and *future* one-thousand-year reign of Christ on earth after Jesus returns. It also believes that the church is going to go through what is called "the great tribulation," a period lasting either three-and-one-half or seven years preceding the second return of Christ. During the thousand-year period that follows the great tribulation and the Antichrist, the world will experience peace and tranquillity as Christ rules over the earth and the Church administers his kingdom. According to this view, there is no future hope for the nation of Israel or Jewish people outside the Church and faith in Jesus Christ. This belief system is adhered to by many Christians, especially those who have seen the errors of the next group below.

- *Premillennial dispensationalism* — A future one-thousand-year reign of Christ on earth will occur, but in a whole different context. Today this is the dominant belief among 85 to 90 percent of all evangelical Christians. If you attend a Bible-believing evangelical, fundamentalist, Charismatic, or Pentecostal church, you are most likely a dispensationalist (but you probably don't know it).

  Everything in this belief system revolves around the nation of Israel. At its foundation, premillennial dispensationalism teaches that God has two separate and distinct bodies of people—Israel and the Church. There is a separate plan and different eternal destiny for each of these two peoples. The Church's hope is eternal bliss in heaven (the kingdom of heaven). Israel's hope is an earthly kingdom (the kingdom of God). The proponents of this system are the ones who teach that Israel returning to Palestine in 1948 is the fulfillment of Bible prophecy.

  Essentially, this persuasion teaches that when Christ came the first time, he did so as the Messiah with the objective of offering the Jewish people an earthly political kingdom. When the Jews rejected the Lord's offer, as dispensationalism teaches, God was forced to go with "Plan B," and that is where the whole idea of the cross and the Church first came into being. According to dispensational teachings, the Church was never foreseen or prophesied in the Old Testament. It came about only because the Jews rejected Christ's supposed offer.

  As Christians today, we are now living in "the 2,000 year" gap period, running from the cross to the present, called the "dispensation of the gospel of grace." The kingdom that Jesus supposedly offered to Israel has been temporarily postponed and "placed on the back burner." *Before it can finally be realized, the Church must be taken out of this world and raptured to heaven.* When the Church departs this earth, so will the Holy Spirit. That will then bring to a close the Church age and usher in the next dispensation, or the millennium.

Dispensationalists are vehemently opposed to the concept that the Church is going to go through the great tribulation. The doctrine of the "pre-tribulation rapture" is of major and critical importance to the dispensationalist. This event *must* take place *before* the tribulation, also known by dispensationalists as "Daniel's seventieth week."

Then all hell breaks loose as the nation of Israel must face the wrath of the Antichrist. At the end of the great tribulation, Israel will be purged, and Jesus will return in the clouds, land on the Mount of Olives, and finally restore the Old Testament Jewish kingdom, which had to be abandoned at Christ's first coming. At that point, Jesus will march into Jerusalem, sit on David's throne, and along with all the Jewish people, rule the world for a thousand years. The temple in Jerusalem will be rebuilt, lambs will again be sacrificed on the altar, and a revised version of the Old Testament religious and sacrificial system will become the new world religion. However, the people of Israel, for the most part, will become believers only *after* they physically see Jesus landing on the Mount of Olives. When Christ shows them the nail prints in His hands, they will all repent, fall down, and finally accept Him as their Messiah.

Most evangelical Christians today follow this persuasion, whether they fully comprehend it or not. Just about every ministry that focuses on Bible prophecy and the end times—every book out there on the subject of Bible prophecy—is founded on these ideas and notions. Yet not one in a thousand Christians has ever investigated the history behind this supposed enlightenment, nor have they done an in-depth analysis to see how thoroughly it contradicts the clear teachings of the Bible. Premillennial dispensationalism completely destroys (mixes up and confuses) the eternal plan and purpose of God.

For example, if the Jews had accepted Christ's original "kingdom offer," they would have been saved by legal obedience instead of faith, and the cross of Christ would not have been necessary as a means to salvation. As the Bible so clearly contradicts, Jesus was the Lamb of God slain from the foundation of the world (Rev. 13:8). The truth is, the Bible nowhere states that Jesus ever offered the Jews an earthly kingdom. In fact, what is absurd about this argument is that in John 6:15, the Jews tried to take Jesus by force and *make* him a king! But the Bible says that the Lord left them and went up in a mountain to pray. *It was Christ Himself who rejected the Jews' offer of an earthly kingdom.*

The other major problem with this theory is why God would ever allow the Jews to be saved by sight (instead of by faith), after they physically see Jesus, and not give the same opportunity to the billions of other people living on earth at the time Jesus returns. The dispensationalist teaches that all of this is possible because the Jews are from a different dispensation and under a different covenant,

204 / *The Original Code in the Bible*

where salvation can come by legal obedience. This thoroughly contradicts all scripture that clearly teaches that it is only through faith in Christ's shed blood that anyone ever has or ever will be saved, regardless of time. All of the animal sacrifices in the Old Testament pointed to just one thing—God's ultimate sacrifice of His Son on the cross.

The dispensationalist tries to get around all this by saying that God simply knew ahead of time the Jews would reject Christ. When fully examined, this argument comes apart at the seams. As the existence of theomatics clearly proves, God never had any plan different from what actually took place. The Church and the New Testament were in God's mind from the very beginning of creation. That is why in Acts 7:38, Old Testament Israel is called "the church in the wilderness." The old covenant failed because it was based upon a legalized system. Jesus came to bring all humanity—Jews and gentiles—a new covenant along with a "fresh and living way" (Heb. 10:20). In the end, it is those who are of faith who are the true children and descendants of Abraham (Gal. 3:7).

God has a very special love for the Jewish people, but they must come to Him on the same terms as everybody else (Rom. 11:7-33).

There are three complete chapters in *Theomatics II* (chapters 14, 15, and 16) that thoroughly discuss these issues and document everything. What is most interesting is that very few of these teachings existed before the year 1830. They began in England with a group of Christians called the Plymouth Brethren and from there spread to America.

Premillennial dispensationalism is a horrible deception that has infiltrated the Christian church without Christians being aware of its false premises and conclusions. Once its errors are exposed, just about everything being taught today in the Christian media about Bible prophecy and the end times will completely collapse.

- *Amillennialism* — Theomatics generally confirms this teaching. *It is the historical teaching of the Christian Church.* For over eighteen hundred years, the Church taught, for the most part, that the expression "thousand years" was simply symbolic of a complete period of time (there are many symbolic numbers throughout Revelation). It is the time running from the cross until the second advent of Christ. The "resurrection" or coming to life that takes place is of the souls of Christians who have died and they come to life in heaven and reign there with Christ. There is no proof that this passage indicates a physical or bodily resurrection.

The millennium is therefore a period when God's heavenly kingdom and Satan's evil kingdom run parallel with each other. The binding of Satan took place at the cross of Calvary, and that is why the gospel can now go forth to the nations and Satan is no longer able to deceive them.

The Catholic, Lutheran, and Presbyterian churches have always followed amillennialism. A number of other evangelical Christian denominations are also amillennial in their eschatology. The amillennialist does not believe that there will be any future kingdom of God upon earth (in the earth's present sinful state). When Jesus returns, everything will be wrapped up in one major event. We will enter into eternity, and there will be both a new heaven and a newly re-created earth that will last for all eternity.

- *Postmillennialism* — The postmillennial viewpoint believes there is going to be a future period of time upon earth of a thousand years, but it will take place *before* Jesus returns. It will be a time when the Church rules upon earth and essentially dominates every aspect of society. The basic premise of this teaching is that suddenly and dramatically the world will experience a massive revival and conversion, as evil will be supernaturally ripped out of the world. Inexplicably, mankind will make a U-turn and begin following righteousness and the principles of God. This will usher in the golden age of the millennium, a thousand years of utopia and peace.

  The implications of this belief is that the church, through "anointed apostles," will rule the world politically. This also infers both military and police powers. This teaching is founded on the premise that God created Adam to have dominion. This dominion was lost because of sin. So if Christians and the church get right with God, then God will give them back the reigns of rulership, and the lost dominion can be reclaimed.

  This theory has had many followers through the centuries. In recent years it has experienced a modern-day resurgence, cloaked in "neo" teachings that have been referred to as "Christian recontructionism," "dominion theology," or "kingdom now theology." Whenever a great revival and outpouring of love for God take place, people tend to take another look at postmillennialism as being an attractive idea.

- *Preterism* — This is the fastest-growing eschatology theory. Numerous ministries are springing up promoting books and seminars, and being very vocal about it. Preterism is a complete backlash to everything else currently being taught.

  The other four persuasions are known as *futurist*. Preterism is the exact opposite. It considers everything in the Books of Daniel and Revelation fulfilled between the time of Christ's ascension and the destruction of Jerusalem in 70 A.D. when Titus the Roman invaded the holy city and slaughtered millions of Jews (this was evidently the fulfillment of Matthew, chapter 24). Preterists believe that there is very little, if any, future prophecy present in the Bible. Everything must be interpreted historically. Preterists have gone to great lengths to find a historical explanation for just about everything mentioned in Scripture and the Book of Revelation.

Preterists are divided over whether Christ will someday return to this earth. The world could continue indefinitely, or God could suddenly end it all. However, the Bible does not tell us anything about how that may happen.

Many well-known and highly educated evangelical and Christian leaders are turning to preterism as the answer to the whole Bible prophecy debacle. This no doubt has a great deal to do with the fact that so many dispensationalist predictions about the future have gone sour and failed to materialize.

A Most Perplexing Dilemma

What is difficult to understand is: how is it even possible for so many people who claim to love God and study the Word objectively to come up with five completely different and diverse views? Each persuasion claims to base its position squarely on the Word of God. Probably the most tormenting question is how any honest and sincere Christian is supposed to know which of these premises is correct.

We know for sure that God is not the author of confusion, yet every direction we look, we see Christians greatly divided over the subject of eschatology.

Heresy Is Hereditary

Dallas Theological Seminary is universally recognized as the unofficial world headquarters for premillennial dispensationalism. It is probably the most influential evangelical institute in the United States. Also, its adherents do not believe in the baptism of the Holy Spirit or gifts of the Spirit, as taught by modern-day Pentecostal and Charismatic Christians. A number of years ago, one professor changed his viewpoint on a number of issues, and upon leaving Dallas Seminary wrote a best-selling book entitled *Surprised by the Power of the Spirit*. I would like to quote a portion of Dr. Jack Deere's chapter entitled "The Myth of Pure Biblical Objectivity."

> The idea that fallen humanity, even redeemed fallen humanity, can arrive at pure biblical objectivity in determining all their practices and beliefs is an illusion.
>
> Let me illustrate this for you. It is common for professors of theology to protest that Scripture, not their experience, determines their doctrine. If you ask a Dallas Seminary professor his view of the millennium (the thousand year reign of Christ described in Rev. 20:4-6), he will tell you that he is premillennial. That means that when Christ comes back to the earth, he is going to set up a kingdom on earth and will reign here a thousand years before the creation of the new heavens and new earth. If you ask him why he believes this, he will declare to you that it is the plain teaching of the Scriptures.

If you ask a professor from Westminster Seminary [in Philadelphia] the same question, he will probably tell you that he is amillennial. That means there will be no literal thousand-year reign of Jesus on earth between his second coming and the creation of the new heavens and new earth. If you ask him why he believes this, he will tell you it is the plain teaching of the Scriptures.

Both cannot be right, in fact, neither may be right. The truth is that both Westminster Seminary and Dallas Seminary have godly, intelligent, and skillful interpreters of Scripture who disagree on quite a few doctrines of Scripture. Yet both sides will claim that the reason they hold their position is because it is the plain teaching of the Scripture! I suspect that this is not the whole truth.

The truth is, if you take a student who has no position on the millennium and send him to Westminster Seminary, he will probably come out an amillennialist. If you take that same student and send him to Dallas Seminary, he is even more likely to come out a premillennialist. There will be few exceptions to this rule. Our environment, our theological traditions, and our teachers have much more to do with what we believe than we realize. In some cases they have much more influence over what we believe than the Bible itself.

Consider the preceding example. Either the amillennialist or the premillennialist is definitely wrong. If the premillennialist is wrong, then no matter how much he protests, his doctrine could not have been derived from the teaching of Scripture because Scripture would not have taught that, assuming the doctrine of premillennialism is an error.

Over the years, I have observed that the majority of what Christians believe is not derived from their own patient and careful study of Scriptures. The majority of Christians believe what they believe because godly and respected teachers told them it was correct. I have seen this illustrated in hundreds of ways.[1]

It's Time for a New Direction

The conclusion that theomatics research has led me to over the past twenty years is that the above interpretations of Bible prophecy are essentially false and erroneous. In all honesty, no one yet has accurately interpreted Scriptures that pertain to future events. What is there to make us believe that just around the corner, someone is going to finally strike gold, put all the events and dates together in correct chronological order, and pull the prophetic rabbit out of the hat?

God's word emphatically teaches that we are not to divinate by trying to figure out what the future is going to be. Yes, it is indeed true that in the Old Testament there are many prophecies concerning the coming of Christ, all of which had a literal historical fulfillment. Many people have drawn the inference that God just kept right on predicting in the same manner—all the way out to the end.

Jesus told us in plain words, "But of that day and that hour knoweth no man, no, not the angels which are in heaven, neither the Son, but the

Father" (Mark 13:32). Jesus also stated, just before His ascension to heaven, "It is not for you to know the times or the seasons, which the Father hath put in his own power" (Acts 1:7).

Throughout the ages, God the Father has reserved totally for Himself all knowledge and control of the future. Even Jesus, the only begotten Son of God, had to submit to that. He stated that even He Himself did not know many of these things. Why should it be different for any of us? We too must walk by faith.

The simple reason why there is so much confusion on this issue is because no one has ever gotten the premises right. The amillennial position generally comes close to being correct. Amillennialism admits that there are certain aspects that God has not yet revealed to us. All the other persuasions are probably light-years from the truth.

The old car cannot be fixed—too many parts are worn out. It is ready for the junk heap. We need to buy a brand-new car. This whole subject needs a fresh start, a new beginning.

This book is going to present an entirely new premise, one that will ultimately provide some conclusive answers and finally place the train on the right track.

Two Completely False Premises

Dispensationalists have taken almost the entire Book of Revelation and crammed it into a little time slot called "The Great Tribulation," making it applicable mostly to the Jewish people. They have taken the passage from Revelation 4:1, where John goes up into heaven, and in order to make everything fit their premise, contrived the fantastic interpretation that this event of John going up is talking about the rapture of the Church to heaven. What this enables the dispensationalist to do, is take everything from chapter 4 onward, and make it apply to Israel and the Jews, essentially stuffing eighteen chapters of the Bible into a three and one-half or seven year period of time. Something, obviously, about God taking a huge section of the Bible just to tell us about what happens during three years of time (after the Church has left this world), does not sound right.

Then you have the preterist viewpoint, which teaches that none of it is future, but the whole thing took place in the first century.

Both of these premises prove unequivocally that someone has probably missed the whole point of what Revelation is all about. Recently I received a letter from an American schoolteacher who currently lives and teaches in Japan. She gave the following analogy after reading the prophetic section of *Theomatics II*.

> It's kind of like if someone gave you a map of Rochester, Minnesota, in order to help you navigate around Rochester, New York. You might just glance at the city name without realizing it's the wrong reference completely. Then, when you try to navigate you get really frustrated because nothing adds up. There's a City Hall, and hospitals, and churches, and a

"Main Street," etc. But somehow you just can't seem to find your way around. There's just enough similarity in content that you don't notice what the problem is for quite some time. Then, one day it dawns on you that you aren't just confused on some minor points; the problem is that THE WHOLE MAP IS THE WRONG MAP! In other words, as you say in *Theomatics II*, the whole BASIS is the wrong one. No wonder we're all confused.

Section II: Establishing the Right Basis and Premise

Let us begin by asking ourselves a very simple question. What is the major purpose of the Bible? Why did God give us His Word? The answer is simple. It was to reveal to us His eternal plan and purpose. In essence, the Bible is the eternal Word of God, and in those very words we have the key to understanding everything.

The purpose of the Bible is to reveal eternal truth. It is not primarily to reveal future times and events.

The purpose of Daniel and Revelation is not to satisfy our intellectual curiosity in attempting to know the future world events.

Times and events are not important to God—He simply uses those things to illustrate a higher meaning. *What is important are the spiritual and eternal truths that are imbedded in symbolical language.* All times and events will someday be history. If all God gave us Revelation and Daniel for was to predict a future world history, then when everything was over with, the Bible would have no more meaning than a newspaper 150 years old. Eternal truth is all that God cares about. That is why, when it comes to the subject of Bible prophecy, everybody today is caught up in the wrong thought pattern.

What we are about to discover—and it will be painfully clear—is that *the overall subject of Bible prophecy, as it is commonly believed and taught, is something that does not even exist in the Bible.* Christians are waiting for times and events that will probably never take place: things such as an Antichrist, a coming time called "the Great Tribulation," a computerized mark on the right hand or forehead, the battle of Armageddon, a certain kind of rapture, and a restored kingdom lasting for one thousand years.

The Bible Is Relevant

Does the Bible still relate to this earth and all of its times and events? Most certainly! But as it will be shown, *it will do so in a whole different context.* It will relate to the events in a spiritual or symbolic context, rather than a direct material or physical manner. It will relate everything that is happening in the world according to the overall eternal plan and purpose of God. In a few moments I'll be more specific.

As humans, we tend to view everything according to place and time, because that is our nature. We want to deal with real facts in a real world. It makes us feel comfortable and more secure when we are able to understand and relate times and events to the dimension we are living.

But that is the view from the human/carnal perspective. God looks at things completely differently. He is above all of us. He sees everything in the context of eternity. That is why to understand these things one needs to see them from God's perspective, through His eyes instead of physical eyes. Let us not forget that we are just the creature; He is the Creator. What we think, how we believe, is not important. How God thinks *is* all-important.

Everything that people are trying to apply to specific times and events is actually talking about something much more significant! *We must first understand how all the things specifically mentioned in Revelation relate to the spiritual, heavenly realm. Then we will be able to connect to the physical realm.* John could not be shown the things in Revelation until he was taken up into heaven (Rev. 4:1). It was only from that vantage point that all of it could be visualized.

Theomatics shows us that the Bible is intended to reveal the big picture, the overall plan that God has for the entirety of His creation, including the angelic realm. He has embedded eternal truth in His Word with an elaborate system of symbols and types, all intended to bring forth that eternal truth (refer to chapter 9 on understanding the implications).

Theomatics Crushes Literalism

All schools of prophecy, both futurist and preterist, follow the predisposed premise of *literalism.* As a rule, you interpret all prophetic passages in a grammatical-historical literal manner, as much as is reasonably possible. Everything is to be understood in a specific earth-time sequential manner. This principle is especially true for premillennial dispensationalism; it is the very cornerstone of the system. Such a method of interpretation will send Christians away from the truth—in the exact opposite direction.

Dispensationalism detests the idea that God might use numbers symbolically in the Bible. Most evangelical scholars won't touch the subject. It is an area of biblical interpretation that few dispensationalists (or futurists) know how to deal with, so it is basically ignored. Dispensationalists would much prefer to debate other issues. Their standard position is that since everything is to be taken literally, numbers are no exception. According to them, "We have no reason to believe that there is any significance to the numbers mentioned in the Bible, other than their quantitative value" (pp. 139-142, *Theomatics II*).

To admit that God may have imparted a symbolic principle to numbers in the Bible would in effect destroy their system. The very fact that theomatics exists—the very fact that God has put a hidden and symbolical system of this nature in the Bible—is going to knock the pilings out from underneath the entire grammatical-historical-literal premise.

There are hundreds of specific things mentioned in the Bible that could be analyzed in making this refutation. This is an enormous subject that implicates hundreds of Bible passages. Trying to cram this entire discussion into one brief chapter would be the equivalent of trying to eat an entire elephant in one sitting. The only possible way to eat an elephant is one bite at a time So I'm going to begin by discussing three very specific items.

The Big Three

At times I have had the opportunity to debate various proponents of the pre-millennial position. Recently, I had a private discussion with an individual based in Washington, D.C., who is recognized as one of the world's major proponents and defenders of the pre-mil/pre-trib dispensational persuasion. Like all others, he admitted that *if numbers are used in Revelation in a symbolic sense (instead of literal), the entire futurist system of premillennial dispensationalism would collapse.* This admission is exceedingly significant, for it admittedly shows what a thin presumptuous thread everything is hanging by.

Here are three major items, any one of which if it is not literal, and does not mean *exactly* what the dispensationalist says that it means, the entire system will topple.

Item 1: The 144 Thousands

In my previous two books, I have had entire chapters that deal with this number from Revelation. Both in Revelation 7 and 14, the discussion concerns the "144,000." Actually, in the original Greek the number 144 appears in the papyrus with the three Greek letters ρμδ, which add up to 144. It is followed by the word *thousands* in the plural (ρμδ χειλιαδες), meaning "144 thousands."

This number is highly symbolic. Scores of Bible scholars have seen this fact, apart from any knowledge of theomatics. *The number 144 is one of the major symbolic numbers in theomatics for all of God's people from all ages.* It stands for all Christians who comprise spiritual Israel, or the Church. It is the "great multitude, which no man could number, from all nations, and kindreds, and people, and tongues," which "stood before the throne, and before the Lamb, clothed with white robes, and palms in their hands" (Rev. 7:9).

Dispensationalism takes this passage literally. It teaches that this is a literal number of 144,000 Jews (Scofield's Jewish evangelists), who are saved during the tribulation period after the church has been raptured to heaven. Then they start evangelizing the nation of Israel just before Jesus returns to set up the millennium.

It should be noted this passage also states that these 144,000 are celibate virgins, and that they have never told a lie (Rev. 14:4,5). The problematic question is this. Where are you going to find 144,000 male

Jewish virgins in Israel (or anywhere for that matter), who have never had sex or ever told a lie? Obviously, those qualifications are spiritually symbolic of purity and honesty.

If dispensationalism is going to be consistent in its method, it must also take these words at face value.

Also, the Book of Revelation names the twelve tribes that these 144 thousands come out from. However, the list in Revelation chapter 7 includes the names of tribes that never existed in the Old Testament—and tribes that existed in the Old Testament are eliminated elsewhere in Revelation. This too destroys the literal principle. All of the Jewish bloodlines would have to have been kept intact—over a period of three thousand years—within their respective tribes, if all of this were to be taken literally.

Here again, theomatics overwhelmingly confirms that this number 144 is symbolic. The value of 144 is 12 x 12, and twelve always represents God's chosen people in Scripture. God's chosen people from the Old Testament consisted of twelve tribes. Jesus had twelve disciples. After all the multitudes were fed, there were twelve basketfuls gathered up and saved.

Item 2: The Great Tribulation

How many times have you heard a Christian brother or sister ask this question: "Do you believe the rapture is going to take place before the great tribulation, or at the end of the great tribulation?" In reality, this may be the wrong question, because what if there is no such thing as a literal three and one-half or seven year "great tribulation"? *No one seems to even question that idea.* It is a foregone conclusion for 99 percent of all born-again Christians.

Theomatics completely destroys the idea that there is going to be a future period on earth called "The Great Tribulation"—a specific period lasting three and one-half or seven years. Chapter 17 of *Theomatics II* is devoted to a complete discussion of this.

The "Great Tribulation" theory is based upon four passages that discuss a time frame of forty-two months (Rev. 11:2, 13:5) and the time of 1,260 days (Rev. 11:3, 12:4). Both forty-two months and 1,260 days equal three and one-half years. This number is also referred to twice in the Book of Daniel, as "time, times, and half a time" (and also in Rev. 12:14).

Theomatics clearly indicates that all of these expressions are used in a symbolic sense. They apparently have nothing to do with future, earthly, time. *These expressions represent the entire period of this world or age—the time that the woman in Revelation 12 was in the wilderness.* There is an entire theomatic structure for the topics of wilderness, desolation, and time—all based upon patterns of 1,260 and 420.

In theomatics, both the words "the woman" (της γυναικος") from Revelation 12 and the word "wilderness," (τη ερημω') have a numerical value of 1,260, and the text states "the woman was in the wilderness 1,260 days" (Rev. 12:6). (That's a small coincidence, of course.)

This world is a spiritual wilderness. John the Baptist, who was the last Old Testament prophet, came crying as a voice in the wilderness. Jesus began His ministry in the wilderness. Again, all of this is to be interpreted symbolically. Theomatics unequivocally links this woman in Revelation 12 to Eve, "mother of all the living," who represents fallen humanity as a whole. Again, it represents the entire age of this world. If this understanding is correct, it will most likely overturn the one assumption most sacred to dispensationalism, the idea of Daniel's seventieth week, which is also discussed extensively in *Theomatics II* (pp. 429-432).

Here again, we have misread the city map because we simply assumed that God meant a literal and future time period. There is no valid basis for giving these passages only a literal interpretation.

The Bible does, however, teach that there will be persecution and great tribulation in general. Christians from all ages have undergone great tribulation. Their troubles will undoubtedly increase before the end.

Item 3: The Millennium

This subject has already been discussed briefly. There are two chapters in *Theomatics II* that cover this aspect (chapters 22 and 23).

A host of powerful and dramatic theomatic patterns point to the fact that the expression "thousand years" is highly symbolic. It concerns ruling and reigning with Christ in general. For that reason, I am not convinced that this passage may have any sort of an earth/time sequential interpretation. Right now we just can't say for sure. The best approach is to study the meaning in light of the numbers, performing a symbolic comparative analysis with similar passages. When the time comes, God's light will shine through.

A Table with Two Legs Cannot Stand

If a three-legged table has one leg knocked out from under it, the entire thing will collapse. To presume that all three of the above can have only a very explicit, futuristic, and literal interpretation, and hang your entire eschatology on that clothesline, is recklessly presumptuous. It's like walking a tightrope between two skyscrapers before making sure the cable has been securely attached. But that is what dispensationalism and thousands of books on Bible prophecy have done. They have skipped merrily down the garden path, and never once stopped and pondered the above passages to see if maybe, perhaps, God has placed a symbolic meaning there. Again, if any one of the above is not literal, man's entire "prophetic system" falls from the sky.

Theomatics establishes that not just one but *all three* are highly symbolic. It makes me cry to even think about so many who have devoted their entire lives to lecturing and writing on the subject of Bible prophecy, the thousands of people who have attended prophetic conferences and listened to speaker after speaker eloquently and confidently talk of how all the things in Revelation and Daniel are "lining up." And yet in certain aspects, these folks are a million light years away from the truth. They are trapped in an erroneous thought pattern.

We should bow down in humility before God, pleading for His mercy, lest we ourselves fall into the same delusion.

> NOTE: It should be stressed that erroneous thinking in this area has nothing to do with whether or not an individual is saved or a Christian. The subject of Bible prophecy is simply a diversion. For the most part it does not affect the essentials of the Christian faith.

A Wide-Angle View

There is one very important and major fact concerning the Book of Revelation (and various portions of Daniel). Very little of it is to be understood primarily in a futuristic context (trying to understand everything in a past historical, or preterist way, is equally erroneous.)

The Book of Revelation covers the entire span of the world's history— bumper to bumper—from the creation of Adam to the new heavens and new earth.

Everything that is mentioned carries deeper symbolic meaning. It comprises an enormous network—all of it operating on the language of the symbol. Things relate to one another in ways that we have never imagined, which would be virtually impossible to comprehend with just a "simple" reading of the text, i.e., the grammatical-historical method. Chapter 9 of this book discussed this.

There are so many things that could be shown to illustrate this. Here, we will have time only to take a few more bites out of the elephant.

Genesis and Revelation Are Linked

One of the major keys to putting the entire puzzle together is understanding the fact that the Book of Genesis is directly linked to Revelation. You cannot understand Revelation without Genesis. Genesis gives us only part of the picture, and when that is connected with Revelation, we can start to see how all of it comes together.

The Woman of Revelation, Chapter 12

> And there appeared a great sign in heaven; a woman clothed with the sun, and the moon under her feet, and upon her head a crown of twelve stars:
>
> 2 And being pregnant with child, she cried out in labor and pain to give birth.
>
> 3 And there appeared another sign in heaven; and behold a great red dragon, having seven heads and ten horns, and seven crowns upon his heads.

4 And his tail drew the third part of the stars of heaven, and did cast them to the earth: and the dragon stood before the woman who was ready to give birth, for to devour her child as soon as soon as it was born.
5 And she brought forth a man child, who was to rule all nations with a rod of iron: and her child was caught up unto God, and to his throne.
6 And the woman fled into the wilderness, where she hath a place prepared of God, that they should nourish her there for 1,260 days.
7 And there was war in heaven: Michael and his angels fought against the dragon; and the dragon fought and his angels,
8 And prevailed not; neither was their place found any more in heaven.

Many people have wondered who this woman might possibly be? Virtually all dispensationalists teach that she represents Israel. The primary question is this. Where else in Scripture do you find statements made concerning a woman and a serpent, and the seed or offspring of the woman? The answer is obvious—in Genesis! Theomatics establishes that the woman in Revelation 12 is none other than Eve, who "became mother of all the living" (Gen. 3:20). In Genesis, God told Eve that her offspring or child was going to destroy Satan and crush the dragon's head (Gen. 3:15). In theomatics, the expressions "the man child," and "her child," both add up to 888, the numeric value for the name Jesus.

What is interesting is that the woman in Revelation is seen in heaven (how did Eve get up there?) However, reading the complete chapter of Rev. 12, all of this is tied into the original angelic rebellion that took place eons ago. All during the battle between the woman and the serpent, Revelation talks about the war going on in heaven and the stars (angels) falling to earth. *The two aspects are actually tied together.* Theomatics proves beyond any reasonable doubt that Eve represents all the angels of heaven who were cast down to earth. There are eternal and heavenly mysteries related to all of this—matters that no one has even thought of yet. When all of the pieces fall into place, it is evident how inextricably woven together Genesis and Revelation are.

It would take literally chapters to discuss this fully. (Lord willing, all of this will be discussed in my forthcoming book, *The Luciferian Rebellion*.) Every verse would have to be carefully examined and the logic of every argument evaluated and compared to *all* the verses in the Bible that are implicated. If the hypothesis is correct, everything must fit together perfectly; there can be no contradictions. Theomatics must always be in agreement with the clear statements of scripture.

The major fact I am seeking to point out here is that this chapter 12 of Revelation goes right back to the very beginning. It covers the entire span of this world's history. It is not limited to just the end times.

The Beast of Revelation 13

Without a doubt, the most famous chapter of Revelation is chapter 13. It concerns two beasts, one who rises out of the sea and another out of the earth. The second beast makes everyone bow down and worship an image of the first beast. People have universally tried to interpret the beast as being the supposed Antichrist who is yet to be revealed (chapter 18 of *Theomatics II* discusses this as well).

Here too, all goes back to Genesis, and is tied into Adam and Satan. Other passages such as Isaiah 14 and Ezekiel 28 are implicated. Isaiah 14 speaks of Lucifer, who fell from heaven. Ezekiel 28 talks about the anointed cherub who was in the Garden of Eden.

The original rebellion that took place in heaven (of which the garden of Eden story is only a model) is now implicated. The beast system is not something yet to occur in some sort of "end time late great planet earth scenario." It covers the time from the original satanic rebellion in heaven and the fall of man in the garden. The mark of the beast on the forehead or right hand is spiritually symbolic. It represents Satan's power over man's thoughts and actions and his being able to buy or sell in the world's spiritual economy. It apparently has nothing to do with people having a computerized mark in the hand or forehead (see chapter 19 of *Theomatics II*). This kind of event could happen, but that is not necessarily what Revelation 13 is talking about. It is a much bigger and broader picture than that.

There are other aspects of this world/beast system that can be understood only by reading the Book of Daniel. God also uses earthly kingdoms (such as Greece, Persia, Rome, etc.) to bring forth eternal truths as it relates to this world and its entire span of history.

All of this is extremely complex and convoluted. The depth of the symbolism can be overwhelming. We have not even scratched the surface of some of these areas. Right now, however, major building blocks are starting to fall into place.

Babylon the Great

In the latter chapters of Revelation appears the great harlot, symbolically Babylon the great city, who has a kingdom over the rulers of this world (Rev. 17:18). This woman is none other than the same woman, or Eve, who appears initially in Revelation 12. She rides on the back of a seven-headed dragon or beast, the same as in Revelation 12. *She is the great harlot because she committed spiritual fornication with Satan back in the garden of Eden.* All that transpires in this world stems from that.

Everything concerning the final conclusion of this present world system is typified by God's destruction of the great city Babylon. Actually, Babylon began in Genesis with the building of the city and tower of Babel. The word "Babel" is the same word as "Babylon" in Hebrew.

Some prophetic scholars have tried to take all of this literally by saying that the ancient city of Babylon (near present-day Bagdad, Iraq) is going to be rebuilt during the end times. That sort of interpretation is far-fetched. All of these chapters are spiritually symbolic. They relate to end time events only in the broadest manner. Once the spiritual symbolism is understood, we are able to fit the pieces into place to understand how the symbolic aspect relates to events happening right now in the real world.

All the Other Things Mentioned

There are many other things mentioned in Revelation that fit into this entire picture. Here are just a few examples. Revelation describes Jesus opening the seven seals of the scroll. As each seal is opened, certain things take place. We read of the four horsemen of the apocalypse, the cry of martyrs, cosmic disturbances. Seven trumpets are blown, seven vials are poured out.

All of this contains vast amounts of symbolism. Again, it relates to this earth more in a broad sense than to specific events during a supposed "end time scenario." The same is true for everything else mentioned in Revelation. One example is Revelation 11, which describes the "two witnesses." Positively no one, absolutely no one to date, has been able to figure out the meaning of that chapter. In reply, all of it is spiritually symbolic. Theomatics throws some amazing light on it, but there are aspects of it that have not yet been revealed to us—matters that no one has even thought of yet.

The Moon Turning to Blood

One of the things constantly foretold in Revelation, the Old Testament, and by Jesus in the gospels, is the sun being darkened, the moon turning to blood, and the stars falling from heaven. How absolutely ridiculous it is to try and take these things literally. (If the sun went out, how could life on this planet possibly survive? How could a literal star, or sun from another part of the galaxy, fall down to this earth without burning it up?)

In Revelation 12, the woman Eve, who appears in heaven, was clothed with the sun and she had the moon under her feet. Upon her head was a crown of twelve stars (Rev. 12:1). What could all of this possibly mean?

In Genesis, during the time of creation, God created a greater light (the sun) and a lesser light (the moon) that reflected the light from the sun. He put them into the firmament of heaven to give light upon the earth. This concerns not only physical celestial objects. It also contains vast realms of spiritual symbolism having to do with God's light and God's glory. Eve, who represents all the angels of heaven, was clothed with the sun (God the source of light), and she had the moon (God's reflected glory) put under her feet or her dominion.

All through the Bible many theomatic patterns surround women who have an issue of blood or hemorrhage. In other words, blood or life flows out much as when a woman has her monthly cycle. In all three gospels of Matthew, Mark, and Luke, the story is told of how Jesus healed the woman who had the issue of blood. She has wasted all of her resources on human doctors who can do nothing to help her. She is dead broke and dying. All of this has tremendous symbolic significance as it relates to Eve, the woman who fell from heaven after she lost her glory and protective male covering. Her sun or source of light has now gone out, and she is bleeding to death.

Now when the Bible says that the moon will be turned to blood, what does that mean? When we go to Revelation 12, where do we see the moon? It is under the feet of the woman. And if a woman is bleeding to death, where is the blood going to flow to? It is going to run down her legs to her feet. And if the moon is under her feet, what is going to happen to it? It is going to turn to blood! *Numerous theomatic patterns clearly indicate that the moon turning to blood and the woman having a flow of blood are the same thing.*

The Above Is One Tiny Example

This is just one example of literally thousands of things present in the Bible that are highly symbolic, and unless someone studies all the passages, and sees how God has embedded the meanings—and theomatics—throughout this huge network, the symbolism will never be seen or understood. So when Christians read a passage in the Bible about the moon turning to blood, they have no idea what the text is referring to. Is it some strange phenomena astronomically? Is it atomic war where the atmosphere is so polluted with fallout the moon turns red? What does it mean?

There are hundreds of things in the Bible that would be absurd if taken literally. A comparative analysis along with an in-depth study of theomatics, and the essential guidance of the Holy Spirit will give us insights into some of these areas that cannot be understood any other way. It is going to be a very slow and laborious job to get to the bottom of many of these things. The major difficulty is that so few Christians spend any time meditating and thinking on these deeper truths that are so close to the heart of God. We become bogged down in the cares of this life. As a result, vast numbers of precious Christian people are susceptible to the errors of the prophecy proponents, who themselves understand few if any of these things.

People Will Always Have Questions

This chapter would be incomplete without attempting to answer the major questions many Christians continue to have. What is going to happen in the days ahead?

Unfortunately, theomatics does not give us a crystal ball for viewing specific times and events. What it does tell us, however, is that God is in total control. It will give us much insight into the new heavens and new earth, and what God's ultimate objectives are for the plan of redemption. Those facts are present and can be understood clearly. We need to study the Bible and emphasize those basic things that God points out as important to Him. Nothing else really matters. A future world history is not God's purpose for the Bible.

I do not believe that it is God's will for every Christian to delve too deeply into some of these areas. There will be time enough in eternity to have all this explained to us. Right now we need to focus on living the daily Christian life and drawing closer to Him. If theomatics does nothing more than increase people's faith, all of this effort will have been well worth the cost.

God does give us absolute promises; He tells us that we are going to someday rule and reign with Him in heaven for all eternity. He gives us a blessed hope. But the Bible does not teach or anywhere imply that Jesus is going to someday return to this earth and set up a political kingdom. Jesus specifically stated, "My kingdom is not of this world" (John 18:36). "In my Father's house are many dwelling places: if it were not so, I would have told you. I go to prepare a place for you" (John 14:12).

Indeed, our Lord came to us, was born in a manger, died on the cross, and rose from the dead for one reason only. He did all that in order to make His Father our Father, and His God our God (John 20:17). That is the bottom line. God *wants to have us* as His prized possession, for we are His precious Bride. He is not interested in entertaining us. He wants to have a real, lasting relationship with us. He wants to share His deepest secrets with us, yet He is not about to do it on a superficial level. And sadly, just about everything being taught today in the Christian media about Bible prophecy and the end times is shallow and superficial.

So What Is Going to Happen?

Regardless of what anyone says, it is obvious, at least to me, that the world cannot go on much longer. At the rate man is destroying the environment, technology is exploding, and sin and wickedness are growing, I cannot see all of this lasting more than another fifty to hundred years, or even less. Jesus could actually "return" tonight. The seventh angel could blow his horn, and "time would be no more."

How is God going to end it all? There are a thousand possible ways. The Bible states that the heavens will melt with fervent heat and the earth will burn up. Is this to be symbolically understood, or is it physical? It could be both.

A Divine Prophetic Chronology

Bible prophecy scholars have searched and searched for some sort of Divine chronology or mathematical formula in the Bible—based upon all the dates and years mentioned—that will project out to the end of the world, i.e., from Adam up to the present. Countless scenarios have been worked out over the years, all of them different, all of them hoping to be exclusively right. On the Internet, there are numerous prophetic ministries doing this very thing.

Does such a scheme exist in Scripture? The answer is, Yes, there probably is one. But I don't believe anyone is going to discover it. God will have to reveal it, and that probably won't take place until after everything is said and done. Then we can all look back, and say, "Of course. Why didn't I see that?"

The Rapture Is for Sure

One of the most incredible theomatic patterns I have ever uncovered surrounds the rapture. Virtually every passage mentioning being caught up, taken up, rising from the earth, going up into the clouds, etc. is saturated with the number 107. (I showed a good part of this design in chapter 23 of *Theomatics II*, entitled "The Meaning of the Rapture.")

It definitely appears that there is going to be some sort of rapture. It may be a worldwide event, or it may be when each saint goes home privately to be with the Lord. Regardless, in being caught up we will forever be with the Lord. How, when, and where are not important. God knows the time and manner.

When you get on an airliner and fly from New York to Los Angeles, do you worry about whether the pilots are qualified to fly? Do you think they are capable of navigating the plane to its destination? Do you worry that maybe they forgot to put enough fuel in the tanks? Of course not. As Christians, we should have the same exact attitude. God is the pilot of eternity. He created everything to begin with and He has obviously thought through the future. He knows how to fly the plane. Let's just do our best, follow Him, and trust in His ability. Everything is going to work out in the end.

Conclusion

When Jesus came to earth two thousand years ago, everybody (including his own disciples), perceived that He was going to overthrow the Romans and then set up some sort of an earthly political kingdom. But His words were very clear. "My kingdom is not of this world." His emphasis always pointed towards the new heavens and new earth. *Jesus never once stated that He was going to return to this earth and rule and reign from Jerusalem.*

So the issue back then was that everybody was looking for the wrong thing. They were trying to take all the Old Testament passages about the coming of the Messiah literally. They were looking for a political kingdom.

Today, history is repeating itself. Christians are trying to force Christ down from heaven. We have failed to see the fact that God's real kingdom is eternal. It is heavenly. It has nothing to do with the political structure of this earth. Never has and never will.

Addendum: What about 1948?

There is one critical issue that I must address—because it will remain a nagging question in the minds of a few Christians after reading the above. What about Israel's becoming a nation in 1948?

Because so much has been said in the Christian media, many Christians will have a difficult time understanding why Israel exists, if the conclusions expressed in this chapter, are true. *Dispensationalists have used this one single event—irrespective of all the contradictions in Scripture—as "absolute proof" that their whole premise, and everything else they say about Bible prophecy, is correct.* They are using the newpaper to interpret the Bible.

My conclusion is that God is behind what happened in 1948, but not in the manner that many people think. Just because Israel became a nation "born in a day"—that does not prove that Revelation 20 describes a future restored Jewish Kingdom lasting for one thousand years. The passage in Revelation that discusses the millennium does not say a single thing about Israel of the Jews.

One key to understanding this perplexing issue is the fact that God has two wills: (1) His revealed will, and (2) His sovereign will. All of us are commanded and required to obey God's revealed will. People can violate God's revealed will, but no one can affect, delay, hinder, or thwart God's permissive or sovereign will. Confusion arises when people try to place into the realm of God's revealed will (a literal historic fulfilment), matters that are really hidden in God's sovereign will.

The reestablishment of a nation named Israel came about only because it was God's sovereign will. It may even be the fulfillment of certain spiritual things "prophesied" in the Bible. There may be certain natural and spiritual aspects to the event that run parallel and that God will fully reveal to us later on. Regardless, we know for sure that it is part of God's current program.

The founding of the nation of Argentina was in God's sovereign plan. But nowhere is that (or even the founding of America) mentioned in Bible prophecy. God is working out His purposes for all the nations and peoples of the earth. The events in the land of the Bible are no different.

One of the reasons God may have sovereignly allowed Israel to become a state is that the excitement surrounding the event has created tremendous awareness in the minds of many people that the Bible is relevant to our times. Millions of books on Bible prophecy would never have been written and read if this event had not taken place. *It was necessary in order to keep Christianity alive and dynamic.* If Christians misread the event (or road signs), that does not make God responsible for erroneous conclusions. Dispensationalists have taken the event and built a superstructure upon it, presuming that a whole host of Bible verses indicate a future world political kingdom. Those verses may not mean at all what some people think.

Theomatics II devotes four complete chapters to all of this, and discusses numerous issues, one of which is the fact that historical research strongly suggests that the majority of Jews living in Israel today are of gentile origin, and have no roots at all going back to Abraham—

the Ashkenazi Jews. The other group, the Sephardic Jews, evidently *are* distant descendants of Abraham.

The Ashkenazi Jews originally migrated from the Black Sea area, from the "land of the Khazars," or Khazaria, when an entire nation *converted itself* to Judaism around 740 A.D. From there they spread north into Russia and west into Eastern Europe. These Jews became the great Jewish populations in Poland and Eastern Europe that were destroyed in Hitler's concentration camps. The Ashkenazi Jews are the ones that promoted the Zionist movement and the reestablishment of a homeland for Jewish people. The history surrounding this conversion and migration is thoroughly documented from numerous sources (see *Theomatics II*, pp. 427-429).

Over the centuries, since Bible times, the Jews have become so disseminated and diluted, that as the *Encyclopedia Britannica* states, "there is no Jewish race." One of the most difficult anthropological questions is "How to define what constitutes a jew?" All of these issues are extremely problematic for dispensationalists who are trying to take everything in the Bible literally.

As Christians we should support the nation of Israel and the Jewish people. This is a human rights issue. Also, we should also show kindness to the Palestinian people. Everything should be done to bring peace and prosperity to that part of the world.

14   The Last
Chapter
of This Book

Some Closing Thoughts

As I am about to conclude this book, I would like to gather some of my most intimate thoughts relative to this discovery and share them with you.

The amount of data that has been presented between these covers is obviously a tiny fraction of that which exists. Like an artist who comes suddenly upon an exciting new subject, this presentation could at best be described as a *sketch*—a single snapshot.

Our vessel has now landed upon the shores of a newly discovered world. Like wide-eyed explorers seeking adventure, we come ashore anxious to begin the quest.

Now that we know for certain that God has indeed structured His entire word with a coded numerical system, where do we go from here? What are the future plans? What is supposed to happen next? In *Theomatics II*, pp. 263-272, I discuss the potential for future academic research.

Circa 1900

There are two ways of looking at this entire theomatics issue: man's point of view and God's point of view. As humans our natural tendency will be to pick up the ball and run with it—get right into a full blown investigation. Yet we must realize that none of this was our own creation, it does not even belong to us. It is the Creator of all things, who is ultimately going to determine how far man may explore this system.

God could have easily revealed this truth and released it to the world a hundred years ago. For the Creator of universe to have done so would have been as easy as releasing a feather in the wind. The fact that this has not taken place is evidence that it was not in the Father's plan for it to happen. Are we to believe that God is now frustrated, anxious, beside Himself, running out of time, desperate? Hardly.

Personally, *I am the one* champing at the bit. There is a spiritually starving world out there that desperately needs this. The situation is urgent! People need objective proof and substance—to see God's power manifested and revealed, picked up and felt. The fields are ripe and ready for harvest—the fruit is going to die on the vine. How can I sit still in my little *hacienda*, when there are beggars outside the door with their hands out and I am sitting on top of all this nourishment! The dam is ready to burst!

These are the sorts of emotions I wrestle with each and every day. It is not an easy task, being the keeper of the flame. So many emotions tearing at me. As I turn and look again at the theomatics database, seeing more inherent patterns unfold themselves, tears stream down my face. "What am I supposed to do with all of this?"

God's Ways Are Not Our Ways

Right now the Bible code issue is creating a firestorm of controversy and confusion. People are making all sorts of egregious claims; others mock and call the whole thing ridiculous nonsense. The man who wrote *The Bible Code* does not even believe there is a God. Christians are warning other Christians to stay away from it. Books trying to debunk the whole thing are being published. It is turning into a circus atmosphere. If theomatics were to burst into the limelight, and this was not God's will, the same type of confusion would perhaps occur. The Lord—so far—has kept that from happening.

God does not measure success by human standards. In God's economy, bigger is not always better. Jesus referred to His own sheep as being a "little flock" (Luke 12:32). God does most of His work unnoticed, like a duck gliding on water. Above the water, the duck looks calm and relaxed. Underneath, out of sight and away from view, its little feet are paddling like crazy. When I am able to push my own thoughts to the side of the road, it is only then that I can clearly see where God's hand has been, every step of the way.

God's Security System

What is exceedingly perplexing is how so few people have any interest in looking further into this subject. Why is it that the one thing that holds virtually all the answers to everything is almost completely ignored—even to those who are adamantly seeking knowledge? Nobody seems to have any interest in researching theomatics. This has always perplexed and frustrated me.

It is as though someone prepared the most sumptuous feast and banquet table imaginable, loaded it with every delicacy and tasty treat. People simply walk up, stare at the food with their hands in their pockets, and walk away. They have no appetite. Why?

In speaking to His disciples Jesus stated the following

> Unto you it is given to know the mysteries of the kingdom of God: but to others in parables; that seeing they might not see, and hearing they might not understand (Luke 8:10).

> At that time Jesus answered and said, I thank thee, O Father, Lord of heaven and earth, because thou hast hid these things from the wise and prudent, and hast revealed them unto babes (Mat. 11:25).

In *Theomatics II*, I made the following profound statement.

> In a certain sense, God in His sovereignty has allowed this subject to become obnoxious and of little interest to present-day theologians and evangelical scholars. He has allowed it to become a taboo subject among the theological establishment [and academia], because as long as all the scholars feel that way, no one is going to take the time to even investigate the subject. That is "God's security system" at work.

The Luciferian Rebellion

Seeking knowledge outside the boundaries, limitations, methods, and timing that God has established for us is why Lucifer and all the angels rebelled in heaven and were cast down to earth. That is why each one of us is born a sinner and that is why hell (whether symbolical or literal) exists. It was prepared for the devil and his angels (Mat. 25:41). This will be the topic of my next book, *The Luciferian Rebellion*. Over the past seven or eight years, 75 percent of all my time in theomatics research has involved the unfolding of patterns related to the original rebellion of Lucifer—the fall of Adam, the mysteries of the garden of Eden, and why this world exists—why billions of people have been born, lived, and died. Theomatics is opening up the big picture concerning everything!

Why is all of this happening? Few evangelical scholars have any comprehension of the degree and the extent to which the whole angelic, human, and demonic realms, are all intertwined. They know that the Bible talks about those things, but they do not understand the depth to which all of it goes. The reason they don't fully comprehend these mysteries is because they are embedded behind such deep symbolism. There are hundreds of verses present in the Bible that few people have ever looked at seriously or even considered. We don't perceive that something here connects to something over there. Theomatics is opening up a whole new world of understanding, relating to the entire angelic/human realm and why God created the present "6,000-year" environment we are living in.

Entering Heaven's Gate

Delving into the eternal mysteries of God is a serious matter. Because God has now revealed theomatics, our comprehension of the Almighty has the potential to reach a whole new plateau or level of understanding. From this point onward, the tools are in our hands to climb the ladder that Jacob could only dream about.

> And he lighted upon a certain place, and tarried there all night, because the sun was set; and he took of the stones of that place, and placed them for his pillows, and lay down in that place to sleep. And he dreamed, and behold a ladder set up on the earth, and the top of it reached to heaven: and behold the angels of God ascending and descending on it. And, behold, the LORD stood above it, and said, I am the LORD God of Abraham thy father, and the God of Isaac: the land whereon thou liest, to thee will I give it, and to thy seed. And Jacob awaked out of his sleep, and he said, Surely the LORD is in this place; and I knew it not. And he was afraid, and said, How dreadful is this place! this is none other but the house of God, FOR THIS IS HEAVEN'S GATE (Gen. 28:11-19).

By Way of the Cross

With theomatics, we are treading on extremely holy and fearful ground. The Bible tells us that heaven's gate is a dreadful place. *Attempting to enter it on one's own terms, or in a less than serious manner, will bring about the stench of death.* The seeking of knowledge, apart from God's approved plan and method, is a door that will lead straight down, not up. The serpent told our first parents in the garden that if they would partake of the forbidden fruit, they would "become like God, knowers"—self-sufficient determiners of right and wrong. The pronouncement for disobeying God's command, was a death sentence. "For in the day that thou eatest thereof thou shalt surely die."

The only way through heaven's gate is by way of the cross. Only by sacrificing our own will, our own selfish way of seeing and understanding things, and accepting the death of God's Son on calvary, embracing God's way in full repentance, and making Jesus the Lord of our lives will we have any hope of salvation. There just isn't any other way.

Here is the Important Thing

In spite of the wonderfulness—the breathtaking truths this new light of day will bring us, those things in and of themselves are not what theomatics is all about. Theomatics is not about knowledge. It is not just about facts and figures. It is not about loading our brains with the "heavy revelations" of Divine information. It is not about understanding the deep eternal mysteries behind the creation of the universe, the realm of angels, and all sorts of spiritual dimensions. Understanding those things will eventually come with the territory. But the major purpose behind God's showing us this amazing aspect of His glory is entirely different.

A person who does not understand what I am about to say next will miss everything. *The following statement is the most important item in this entire book.* Nothing counts, nothing matters, but the following.

Knowing God as Father

People have asked me over the years what is the single most important thing is I have learned from this investigation. What stands out the most in my mind? What has theomatics taught me? Where has it touched me the deepest?

The one overpowering feeling that I get, as I find more and more of these patterns and see the phenomenal truths that come out from all of them, the feeling that positively overwhelms me at times is one simple thing. I feel a tremendous love emanating from the Heavenly Father.

My Son, the reason I placed all of this in the Bible, is because of my love for you. I want to reveal myself to you. I want to share my innermost secrets with you. I want to show you the manner in which I think. I want to make you a part of me. I have now made a way for you to come into my holy presence—a level of relationship that I never could have when I created the angels. The middle wall of partition separating us, the distrust, has been broken down (Eph. 2:14,15). We can be friends at last, with complete trust and confidence in one another. Won't you please come into the secret chambers of my palace so I can share my secrets with you. I want to show you my plans for the future, and make you a part of it. I don't want to be just your God; I want to be your friend as well. And I want you to be my friend. I want to show you why, from the very beginning, I created you, how much you mean to me. When I made you, I broke off a part of myself, and that piece of me became you (Heb. 12:9). When you left your first love, my heart was broken. But I don't hate you for it, I never have. In fact, I gave my very life for you, so that we could start everything over again. We can build a new life together, one that this time will last forever. I have been saving all of these most intimate things, treasuring them in my heart—things that I never could share with the angels (1 Pet. 1:12). That's why they rebelled. They thought they could get all this knowledge on their own. So they ate of the fruit that I knew—based upon all my eternal wisdom—could only bring about death. But the rebellion is now over with. You are welcomed back home. I had to give my very life to redeem you. No, it wasn't easy, but I did it because of the joy that was set before me (Heb. 12:2). We are now one. I have forgiven all your sins from the past. They are gone forever. Now we start to think alike. You are my precious bride for all eternity. Our marriage will never end in divorce. All that is mine is now yours. I will now clothe you with the best robes and put shoes on your feet and a ring on your finger. It's time to kill the fatted calf and rejoice. Come inherit the kingdom prepared for you from the foundation of the world.

God HIMSELF Surpasses All Knowledge

If I could be in the position of making one point of emphasis to everyone who reads this book, it would be the following.

Information is not what theomatics is all about. God is not primarily interested in giving us information and knowledge. What God really wants to do, is give us HIMSELF. He wants to have an intimate love relationship with us. He not only wants us to know Him as Father, but most importantly, He wants to be our friend. After that relationship has been established, then and only then, does God want to give us His wealth of knowledge. Knowledge without relationship will do us no good, and can only bring about death.

> Jesus saith unto her, Touch me not; for I am not yet ascended to my Father: but go to my brethren, and say unto them, I ascend unto my Father, and your Father; and to my God, and your God. (John 20:17)

In that one statement to Mary Magdalene—a woman out of whom He had cast seven demons—Jesus right after His resurrection gave to us the entire picture. He came to make His Father our Father, and His God our God.

> To him that overcometh will I grant to sit with me in my throne, even as I also overcame, and am set down with my Father in his throne. (Rev 3:21)

This is the Reason Why

All of the above is perhaps the major reason why God has not released this discovery to the world on a major scale. Even as theomatics is positively true, mankind really wouldn't know what to do with it, because people never will understand what theomatics is all about until they enter into an intimate relationship with the Creator and are properly bonded with Him. God is simply not going to cast His pearls on the ground. To have a right relationship with God is to know what it means to fear Him. "The fear of the LORD is the beginning of knowledge" (Pro. 1:7). Fear is not a scaredy kind of fear or terror, but an awesome respect and comprehension of who God really is.

We Must be Born Again

In John 3, a great and learned man by the name of Nicodemus came to Jesus under the cover of darkness. He was very well educated, a ruler of the Jews. He had a burning desire to know and understand the things that Jesus taught, but he just couldn't "get it." The Lord told Him that no matter how much knowledge He had, if He was ever going to understand the things of God, He would have to be reborn. He would have to be born "from above," of God's spirit, with a new birth that was heavenly in origin.

As fallen humanity, we are capable of creating space shuttles and Pentium computer chips. But we are babes in diapers when it comes to the eternal things of God. We have massive technological capability, a Library of Congress full of knowledge and information. But when it comes right down to it, without God's life, without His Spirit living within us, we are really nothing more than wandering stars, stumbling around in a high tech wilderness—having no knowledge of what lies beyond the grave, severed from the Creator.

There Is a New Day Coming

But there is a new day coming. And we are all invited to become a part of it. The Father's arms are open wide, waiting to embrace us. God has done everything within His power to let us know that the door is standing wide open, and He wants us to come inside. He does not want to hide His secrets from us, He wants to share all of them (Mat. 10:26). With theomatics, He has given us a means to do just that.

To Him be the glory for ever and ever. Amen.

Appendix

What About ELS And the Bible Code?

This is a book about theomatics. It is not about ELS or the Bible code phenomenon. Because of the massive interest surrounding this subject, people want to know what my opinion is relative to this issue. So for whatever it might be worth, I submit the following.

Look to the Internet

If you have more than a passing interest in this subject, there is enough information on the World Wide Web to keep you busy for weeks. There are literally hundreds of web sites and newsgroup postings, discussing every aspect of the supposed phenomenon. Most of the discussion is shallow hearsay, but there are a few serious sites. I thought of including a number of URL addresses in this book, but since the Internet changes so often, in five years everything might be totally out of date. Your best approach is to run a search on Altavista, Hot Bot, or some other search engine. Try key words "ELS," "Equidistant Letter Sequences," "Torah codes," "codes in the Torah," "the Bible code," etc.

Note: The Hebrew word Torah, means "the law." The Torah comprises the first five books of the Old Testament, written by Moses. It is also referred to as the Pentateuch or The Law of Moses. Virtually all ELS evidence that has been discovered so far has come from these first five books of the Old Testament—Genesis, Exodus, Leviticus, Numbers, and Deuteronomy.

This appendix is a general overview accompanied by my tentative conclusions. I do not have the time or the required interest to adequately pursue ELS. I only want to be a spectator, not part of the story. In order to submit a valid, objective evaluation, a person would have to devote a major portion of his life to the investigative pursuit—literally hundreds of hours. Other people are currently doing just that. Right now I have my hands full with theomatics. As the basketball legend Michael Jordan would probably say, "Don't try to be a big-league baseball player when your God-given talent lies somewhere else."

Eliyahu Rips

In 1958 a Rabbi named Weissmandel observed an unusual phenomenon in the original Hebrew text of the book of Genesis. Upon close examination he found patterns of coded words and phrases buried "beneath" the surface of the book. Because he was unable to pursue this discovery due to lack of computer technology, the study died with him. Some students at Hebrew University examined Weissmandel's research in 1988 and incorporated computers in the search for these "Torah Codes." Of late, the major player, is an Israeli mathematician by the name of Eliyahu Ripps of Hebrew University, a world-renowed mathematician who formed the original research team along with Doron Witztum and Yoav Rosenberg.

A Brief Description

The investigative research uses an Equidistant Letter Sequence (ELS) analysis method. The technique is relatively straightforward. The Hebrew text is stripped of all of its spaces and entered into the computer as one long string of characters. For example, the entire Book of Genesis becomes a continuous string of 78,064 characters or letters.

If a hidden word in Hebrew such as "Torah" is being looked for in a particular verse, once the first (Hebrew) letter for Torah is found, the computer searches forward through the text to locate the second letter. When the second letter is located, the distance (in letters) is noted. Let's say the distance between the first and second letters is fifty. The computer then continues through the text at forty-nine letter intervals, and *only* that interval, and records the letters at those positions to see if they form coherent words or phrases. Of course you have to first know what word you are looking for and ask the computer to look for its first letter to initiate the search.

As the researchers continued their investigation, they began discovering all sorts of words embedded in the text. Most startling were numerous words—transliterated into Hebrew—that pertained to many well-known historical events and famous people through the centuries—long after Genesis was written.

For example, the researchers took *The Encyclopedia of Great Men of Israel* and searched for pairs of meaningful entries in proximity to each other. The entries that they searched for were the names of individuals along with their dates of birth or death as listed in the encyclopedia. The dates were specified by the Hebrew day and month. A list was drawn up of all thirty-four men mentioned in the encyclopedia whose date of birth or death was given and whose lives were significant enough. Later, a second list was prepared; it consisted of thirty-two additional men.

The entire process was repeated many times, and the researchers found many matches. When they compared the name/date matches, they found that they were closer together than one would expect on the basis of chance. The results were significant: ($p = 0.000016$), i.e., 1 chance in 62,500.

The findings were submitted to *Statistical Science* magazine. This is a peer-reviewed journal that requires that every proposed article be scanned by a number of experts in the field before it is accepted for publication.[1] Because of the incredible nature of the discoveries, the review process took six years to complete. Robert Kass, the editor of *Statistical Science,* wrote:

> Our referees were baffled: their prior beliefs made them think the Book of Genesis could not possibly contain meaningful references to modern-day individuals, yet when the authors carried out additional analyses and checks the effect persisted. The paper is thus offered to *Statistical Science* readers as a challenging puzzle.

Harold Gans, a former cryptologist (or code breaker) at the U.S. Defense Department and Pentagon, replicated the work of the Jerusalem team. He was able to corroborate their results. He further expanded the original study by finding the names of important Jewish individuals and their cities of birth and death. His "p" value was even more significant.

Michael Drosnin and The Bible Code

Michael Drosnin was an investigative reporter, formerly with the *Washington Post* and *Wall Street Journal.* He began an investigation into this story and later became part of the story itself, performing his own research and analysis and working in cooperation with the Israeli investigators at Hebrew University.

Various techniques were used in the analysis. The long string of characters was transformed into large blocks or squares that resemble a crossword puzzle. Once the grid is laid out, it is easy to see where all of the embedded words and skips occur, going in different directions.

The book *The Bible Code* begins by discussing the assassination of Israeli prime minister Yitzhak Rabin. Drosnin claimed to have uncovered information about the assassination one year before it occurred and tried personally to warn Mr. Rabin. He had previously found embedded in the codes the assassinations of Lincoln, Gandhi, and John F. Kennedy. References to the Gulf War, the collision of a comet with the planet Jupiter, the Oklahoma City bombing, Richard Nixon's resignation, World War II, the Holocaust, and the fall of Communism were also decoded. The book predicts a cataclysmic earthquake in Los Angeles in 2010 and a nuclear war in Israel before 2001 (taken from the religious tolerance web page).

At last count, *The Bible Code*[2] has sold over half a million copies and topped the best-seller lists. It is written in an easy-to-read format.

Jeffrey Satinover—Cracking the Bible Code

Just recently, I purchased another book on this subject. Jeffrey Satinover, who is a medical doctor and an MIT and Harvard graduate, has put together a 350-page volume.[3] It is extremely well-written and thoroughly documents the findings from a scientific perspective. *Cracking the Bible Code* appears to be a book of substance. It is my impression that the book is superior to Drosnin's. Unlike Drosnin, Dr. Satinover attributes the whole phenomenon to "God," which of course is the only possible conclusion, if all of it is true.

Other Efforts

Another research effort has been carried out by Yacov Rambsel, a Christian Messianic Jew from San Antonio, Texas, in his book *YESHUA*.[4] The approach Rambsel has taken is not to look for current world events but to find ELS references in the Old Testament to Jesus, Messiah, and all the various attributes of God. He has worked closely with Grant Jeffrey, who has written the best seller *The Signature of God*,[5] which has brought ELS to the forefront of the premillenial/dispensational evangelical community. Most individuals involved in prophecy ministries are enthusiastic proponents of the ELS discoveries.

Jeffrey describes how the word "Eden" is encoded sixteen times within the short Gen. 2:4-10 passage dealing with the garden of Eden. The odds against sixteen "Edens" occurring by chance in such a short passage is claimed to be 1 in 10,000. Also in Genesis 2, scientists have discovered twenty-five different Hebrew names for trees. The odds against this happening is 100,000 to 1.[6]

There are many other freelancers investigating this and seeking results. However, it will probably be the first efforts that get the lion's share of the publicity.

Not Everyone Is Jumping Up and Down

Reactions to the Bible code discoveries have been both enthusiastic and cool. Numerous scholars (who still believe in ELS and the codes), have been highly critical of both Drosnin's method and conclusions. Both Rips and Witztum have been quite vocal. Witzum states,

> I was the first one to investigate the possibility of divining the future through these codes. Following logical and empirical tests, I found incontrovertible evidence proving its impossible to predict the future with the hidden codes.

And Eliyahu Rips declares,

> The only conclusion that can be drawn from the scientific research regarding the Torah Codes is that they exist and that they are not a mere coincidence.

Numerous others have tried to debunk the findings, particularly Brendan McKay of Australia National University, who has made a career out of trying to debunk all sorts of "egregious" claims.

For example, on one of his web pages, McKay takes a page from *Moby Dick* (obviously not of Divine inspiration) and, laying out a grid and following the same method as Drosnin, found the following words embedded in various skip intervals.

> PRINCESS DIANA
> ROYAL
> DODI
> HENRI PAUL
> MORTAL IN THESE JAWS OF DEATH

NOTE: I have repeatedly challenged Brendan McKay to investigate theomatics, but as of this date, he has refused to do so. He has stated twice: "Send me a letter from an academic statistician stating that theomatics is worthy of investigation. Such person must hold a tenured teaching or research position in a statistics department of a university and must have published at least five papers in statistics or probability theory in peer-reviewed scientific journals."

At the time this book was headed for press, there were some serious rumors circulating on the internet that a critical flaw had been discovered from the famous Rabbis experiment that appeared in *Statistical Science,* the flaw evidently admitted by the individuals who performed the original experiment.

A large number of scholars and scientists are currently working on the codes to either establish their credibility or put the subject to bed—once and for all. There is one web site listing the names of 45 prominent mathematicians and scientists who have all signed their names to the following statement:

> There is a common belief in the general community to the effect that many mathematicians, statisticians, and other scientists consider the [ELS] claims to be credible. This belief is incorrect. On the contrary, the almost unanimous opinion of those in the scientific world who have studied the question is that the theory is without foundation. The signatories to this letter have themselves examined the evidence and found it entirely unconvincing. (http://math.caltech.edu/code/petition.html)

One of the criticisms is that many of the individuals involved in the research are Jewish academics of high standing—either orthodox in their beliefs or sympathetic to Jewish causes. Other proponents are from the evangelical pop culture. Therefore, the proponents must be biased and have a secret religious agenda. *They want the discovery to be true and will do everything possible to make sure that it is.* This may or may not be a valid criticism.

The Evangelical Backlash

In December 1997, *Charisma and Christian Life* magazine carried an article on the Bible code. It was intended to be a firm warning to all Christians to stay completely away from the subject. The headline read:

CHRISTIANS REJECT BIBLE CODE THEORY
Evangelical theologians have dismissed the idea
that the Old Testament contains a Secret Code

The article quoted many well-known evangelical theologians collectively saying that the whole thing was a bunch of rubbish and that "Evangelicals ought not to be so gullible as to buy into this." They equated it with fortune-telling and the occult.

In the following month's issue, the letters-received page printed a half-dozen letters from outraged Christian readers lambasting the magazine for being so biased.

Another reason for the rejection is that most of the research is being done by secular mathematicians. As I stated earlier, Michael Drosnin claims to not even believe in God but instead believes that some sort of "ancient knowledge" has enabled the Bible to be encoded. That fact, to some degree, warrants caution.

The Most Disturbing Factor

The most disturbing fact is, What if the Bible code really is true? What if God really did do it? Maybe He did? How do we know? If so, the evangelical community is rejecting—outright—something that God may have divinely and supernaturally implanted, *simply because it does not fit into their theological system(s) and method(s) of interpreting the Bible. It is not the traditional grammatical-historical approach.*

NOTE: A major review appeared in *Christianity Today* lambasting the original *Theomatics*. The magazine's verdict was that Christians should not take this subject seriously, the article implying that there never has been and never will be any validity to the idea of hidden codes in the Bible.

Sadly, this attitude is the prevailing evangelical consensus toward any and all research into biblical codes. It is an extremely biased demeanor that is not the least bit conducive to the advancement of objective knowledge.

The only way to discover whether ELS is true is to test and retest the data mathematically. Also, there will need to be major breakthroughs in the operative principles of the ELS system. There is an old saying in science, "Extraordinary claims require extraordinary proof." That is certainly true here. Again, this is not a theological issue; it is only an issue of existence or nonexistence.

Here Is My Conclusion

My conclusion is guarded. Only recently, after reading up on the subject and consulting with others, have I come to the conclusion that

ELS may perhaps be true. At first, I rejected the theory. Why in the world would God embed the names of modern-day Jewish rabbis or Timothy McVeigh in the Old Testament? I must admit that even still the whole idea seems incredible. The Yacov Rambsel approach of finding the names and attributes of God and other truths seems far more consistent with the type of thing God might do.

> NOTE: Recently on the Internet I found a major web site that provides extensive mathematical evidence that many of Yacov Rambsel's findings are simply the product of random chance. There are enough skip intervals present, to explain his results. If Rambsel's findings are not statistically significant, then "God" supposedly embedding current-day events seems even less likely.

Yet it appears (according to some experts) that groups of modern-day words are being discovered in close proximity, defying explanation. In fact, the investigators are claiming that just about every significant event in history is embedded somewhere in the codes. They have also worked on the hypothesis that the entire grid system will eventually go three-dimensional and the amount of data and hidden codes could almost be infinite. Each person, the time of his or her birth and death, the events in his or her life, acceptance or rejection of Christ could all be in there. Some people even suggest that when God completely pulls the wraps off, the very Bible itself will be the book of life mentioned in Revelation 20:12. Every deed done by every person will be embedded in the coded system.

In all honesty, I am not yet ready to swallow this whole idea. But it seems, just like theomatics, if the phenomenon is really in there and present, where will it end? If God can create one galaxy, he can just as easily create a hundred billion galaxies.

Another interesting idea is that God is not limited by time. It is entirely possible that God could have gone forward in time, recorded all the events of history, and then gone back in time and encoded it in the Torah that was handed to Moses.

Please understand that I do not wish to get carried away with all this. But I have seen enough miracles in theomatics as to doubt nothing. Let's all keep an open mind. If ELS is not true, someone will eventually expose it and it will crumble, or just die out and disappear. If God is the author behind it, He will continue to nourish it at the pace He deems best. More facts will come to light.

There Are Problems

Certain aspects of ELS are highly suspect. The computer is capable of finding just about any possible word(s) with some sort of skip sequence. The only real evidence, according to the investigators, is the fact that so many words seem to be bunched together in close proximity. According to the proponents, the statistical results cannot be duplicated randomly or in other Hebrew works of literature.

The other problem is the various ways modern-day words might be spelled in Hebrew. There would be far more word matches in an ancient Hebrew text than in an English text. Since Hebrew is a consonantal language, it is quite flexible in that manner. This approach of using modern nonbiblical words is extremely problematic and suspect.

I have only heard of one major statistical study, and that is the one that appeared in *Statistical Science*. How many other extensive controlled tests have been performed? Some of the statistic probabilities do not appear to be tremendously significant. They are much, much higher with theomatics. If the world-renowned statisticians who are investigating ELS would examine theomatics, their computers would melt down.

What about Theomatics?

Recently I have been corresponding with a top executive with Chrysler in Detroit who is very interested in pursuing his own research. One of the questions that fascinates him is, What connection is there between ELS and theomatics?

I have spent a lot of thought on this question, and in all honesty, I don't yet see any connection. It is one of the factors that has made me doubt the validity of ELS. How could both systems operate concurrently and still work? God would have to be an incredible juggler, to say the least. The bases for both systems are radically different.

I have received numerous e-mails from people who want to experiment with the New Testament in order to find ELS. That is not even remotely possible. The New Testament text is so jumbled with variant readings as to render ELS null (see appendix D, *Theomatics II*). The letter-skipping requires huge stretches of text that are absolutely flawless. However, the textual variants do not affect theomatics to any significant degree, because theomatics does not generally consider phrases more than 4 to 5 words in length.

Also, it appears that the researchers are having trouble finding ELS in much of the Old Testament. Everything seems to work much better in the Torah, the first five books. The book of Isaiah is also said to contain some phenomenon.

Another Major Observation

Theomatics was discovered twenty years ago. Some who may be thoroughly overwhelmed by the evidence, may ask, "Why has the ELS phenomenon received so much attention and publicity in the media and theomatics, basically ignored? This is a fairly easy question to answer. There are two reasons.

First, the ELS discoveries created a lot of excitement long before Michael Drosnin's book. Numerous scholars all over the world were involved in the investigation. For the past decade word has been slowly leaking out about the research, and hundreds of small articles have been written in newspapers and publications all over the world. There was a groundswell of excitement already in place. Theomatics, on the other hand, has been a one-man show. I am somewhat isolated and work by myself. It's not that the subject is not true; others are simply not involved in the effort—particularly those of academic standing and means. If that were to change, it would make a huge difference.

The other, very significant reason, is that theomatics confronts people with unpleasant issues, such as the fact that man is a sinner and needs to repent. Sinful man does not want to think about those sorts of things. *You cannot understand the eternal things of God until a right relationship is established with the Creator. Repentance and faith must preclude knowledge.*

Today, it is not politically correct to tell people that they are sinners, that they need to repent and submit to God's will. Therefore, the realm of God's Spirit and the things that are heavenly, spiritual, and eternal is a dimension of reality that very few people will understand—only those whose consciences have been exercised (Heb. 5:14). The implications of theomatics, by nature, are not the type of thing most people are generally thinking about or truly interested in. Most individuals look at everything in a temporal, earthly manner. ELS can appeal to our mystical and occultic fallen nature—to know and understand (and eventually control) the future. One major reason Drosnin's book took off is that fact. That is also why Hal Lindsey has sold millions of books. God is strictly against that approach. People are much more inclined to put their hands into the cookie jar if it has been placed off limits. Today, sin sells; righteousness does not.

A new book by an evangelical publisher, *Decoding the Bible Code*, attempts to show that the entire ELS system is a form of spiritual deception.[7] This is a distinct possibility. If so, then the supposed scientific data supporting ELS would be either a fraud or some sort of self-induced delusion the proponents have fallen into.

The Publicity Has Helped

All in all, the publicity surrounding ELS and the Torah codes has been extremely helpful for theomatics. *People are being softened up to the possibility that, "Hey, maybe God did do something like this."* People everywhere are starting to think about codes in the Bible. Even if the wheels eventually come off the ELS wagon, God has no doubt had a purpose in it. I don't know how far the wave will carry theomatics, but I certainly won't complain.

If ELS is eventually proven to be true and universally established, I will be surprised. If it is eventually debunked, I will not be disappointed.

Reference Notes

Chapter 2: *A High-tech Wilderness*

1. *The Sunday Oregonian,* Dec 1997, Portland, Oregon

Chapter 3: *The Original Code in the Bible*

1. *Charisma and Christian Life,* December 1997, quote by Michael Brown.
2. Ibid, quote by Messianic rabbi Daniel Juster
3. John MacArthur, Jr., *Charismatic Chaos,* (Zondervan, Grand Rapids, Michigan, 1990) pp. 88-92.

4. **Notes on Sources for Hebrew and Greek Codes**

   Most any edition of *Webster's Dictionary,* under category "Special Signs and Symbols."

   E.W. Bullinger, *Number in Scripture* (Kregel Publications, Grand Rapids, Mich., 1894), pp. 48,49.

   John J. Davis, *Biblical Numerology* (Baker Book House, Grand Rapids, Mich., 1968), pp. 39,43.

   Manahem Mansoor, *Biblical Hebrew* (Baker Book House, Grand Rapids, Mich., 1980), p. 13.

   Bligh Bond & Lea, *Gematria* (Thompson Publishers Ltd., Willingborough, Northhamptonshire, 1977), p. 6.

   Georges Ifrah, *One to Zero* (Viking Penguin, Inc., New York, 1985), pp. 254, 261.

   James Harrison, *The Pattern & the Prophecy* (Isaiah Publications, Peterborough, Ontario, Canada, 1985), pp. 49, 56.

   Any of the works of Ivan Panin.

5. Bruce Metzger, The Text of the New Testament (Oxford University Press, New York, 1968), p. 38.

Chapter 9: *Understanding the Implications*

1. Kevin J. Conner, *Interpreting the Symbols and Types* (Bible Temple Publications, Portland, Oregon, 1980).

242

Chapter 11: Theomatics and the Scientific Method

1. *World Book Encyclopedia*
2. Ibid.
3. Del Washburn, *Theomatics and the Scientific Method* (Institute for Theomatics Research, Portland, Oregon, 1989).
4. John Weldon, *Decoding the Bible Code* (Harvest House, Eugene, Oregon, 1998).

Chapter 12: The Clustering Phenomenon

1. *Bible Science Newsletter*, Walter Lang, editor (2911 E. 42nd Street, Minneapolis, Minn.), October 1980.

Chapter 13: The Great Bible Prophecy Debacle

1. Jack Deere, *Surprised by the Power of the Spirit* (Zondervan, Grand Rapids, Mich., 1993) pp. 46, 47.

Appendix: What About ELS and the Bible Code?

1. Doron Witztum, Eliyahu Rips and Yoav Rosenberg, Equidistant Letter Sequences in the Book of Genesis, *Statistical Science*, Volume 9, Number 3, August 1994.
2. Michael Drosnin, *The Bible Code* (Simon & Schuster, New York, N.Y., 1997).
3. Jeffrey Satinover, *Cracking the Bible Code* (William Morrow & Co., N.Y., 1997).
4. Yacov Rambsel, *Yeshua* (Frontier Research, Toronto, Ontario, Canada, 1996).
5. Grant R. Jeffrey, *The Signature of God* (Frontier Research, Toronto, Ontario, Canada, 1986), pp. 207, 208.
6. Ibid
7. John Weldon, *Decoding the Bible Code* (Harvest House, Eugene, Oregon, 1998).

About the Author

Del Washburn was born in Colombia, South America, to evangelical Christian missionaries. For fifteen years he worked in the field of church design and architecture. He is currently a real estate and land developer, having developed several of the largest retirement communities in the State of Oregon as well as a number of residential subdivisions. In addition to his business activities, Washburn runs the Institute for Theomatics Research. He resides in Portland.